He Rents,
She Rents

D0862231

He Rents, She Rents

The Ultimate Guide to the Best Women's Films and Guy Movies

RICHARD ROEPER & Laurie Viera

ST. MARTIN'S GRIFFIN
NEW YORK

HE RENTS, SHE RENTS. Copyright © 1999 by Richard Roeper and Laurie Viera. All rights reserved. Printed in the United States of America. No part of this book may be used or reproduced in any manner whatsoever without written permission except in the case of brief quotations embodied in critical articles or reviews. For information, address St. Martin's Press, 175 Fifth Avenue, New York, N.Y. 10010.

Design by Maureen Troy

All photos courtesy of Archive Photos.

Library of Congress Cataloging-in-Publication Data

Roeper, Richard.
    He rents, she rents : the ultimate guide to the best women's films and guy movies / Richard Roeper and Laurie Viera. — 1st ed.
    p. cm.
  ISBN 0-312-19897-3
    1. Motion pictures—Catalogs. 2. Video recordings—Catalogs. 3. Motion pictures for women. 4. Motion pictures for men. I. Viera, Laurie. II. Title.
  PN1998 .R565 1999
  016.79143'75—dc21

                                         98-51990
                                           CIP

First St. Martin's Griffin Edition: April 1999

10 9 8 7 6 5 4 3 2 1

Contents for *He Rents*

Contents for *She Rents*

Acknowledgments for
He Rents

Richard Roeper would like to acknowledge the following people for their support and understanding as he worked on this book:

My coauthor, Laurie Viera, who always managed to laugh at my utter guyness as we talked about movies; our terrific and always author-friendly agent, Sheree Bykofsky, and her skilled associate Janet Rosen; our movie-loving editors, Dana Albarella and Heather Jackson; my family, especially my parents, for instilling in me a love for the movies; my friend Paige, the best moviegoing partner a guy could hope for; the many editors I've had at the *Chicago Sun-Times* who have encouraged my appreciation for films, notably Laura Emerick, who assigned me interviews with the likes of Sean Connery, and Lon Grahnke, who gave me my first movie review, *Friday the 13th, Part VI*; Neil Steinberg, Leslie Baldacci, Bill Adee, Joyce Winnecke, Phil Rosenthal, Rob Feder, Bill Zwecker, Nigel Wade, Larry Green, Jenniffer Weigel, Sherri Gilman, Bebe Lerner, Anita Huslin, Tobi Williams; "Big Mike" and "Teen" and all the other guys from the neighborhood who agree with me that *Goodfellas* is quite possibly the finest film ever made; Robert Mitchum, for showing us the way; Bruce Willis, for not letting the *Die Hard* series die; and every actress who understands that nudity is almost always "integral to the part."

Finally, special thanks to Carla, who always understood when I said I had to work yet again—even when that work consisted of watching *The Magnificent Seven* or *Caddyshack* just one more time.

Acknowledgments for
She Rents

Laurie Viera would like to acknowledge the following people for their unfailing support and inspiration in the writing
of this book:

My coauthor, Rich Roeper, who dreamed up the idea for *He
Rents, She Rents*, and who is one of the funniest people I know;
my goddess agent, Sheree Bykofsky, and her trusty associate
Janet Rosen; Dana Albarella and Heather Jackson, our editors
at St. Martin's Press; Thomas Rigler, my very own four-star
heartthrob and the only man I know who would sit through
Sense and Sensibility twice; Mary Hagen, who offered wisdom
and insightful feedback, and who came up with the concept of
Guilty Pleasures; Melitta Fitzer, who loves Jane Austen and
Jackie Chan with equal passion; my friend and teacher Aure-
lia Haslboeck-Kerr, because resistance to her unconditional
love is futile; Larry "Kathy" Amoros for comic inspiration;
Christina Baglivi-Tinglof, Esther Boynton, Lori Gerson,
Angie Golden, Laura Graham, Bridget Hedison, Christie
Lemmon Lear, Hope Moskowitz, Gabrielle Raumberger, Beth
Shube, Louisa Waldner, and Shalini Waran for their enthusi-
astic endorsements of their favorite films; Jean Wells for a
valuable piece of advice; Video Journeys for having all the
films I want to rent; and my family: Sara Levine, Cary Puma,
and Felice Levine.

He Rents,
She Rents

Introduction

FADE IN

INT. THE BOOK

Laurie Viera and *Richard Roeper*, the authors of the book, are sitting side by side in Laurie's living room.

Richard: Welcome to the Introduction to *He Rents, She Rents*—

Laurie: Wait a minute, why do you get to talk first?

Richard: Because the book is called *He Rents, She Rents*, and I'm the "he" and you're the "she," and the "he" comes first.

Laurie: Yeah, but we agreed that if you came first in the title, I'd get to speak first in the Introduction, remember?

Richard: Fine, ladies first.

Laurie: I've always hated the subtextual condescension of that phrase. Anyway, this is a book about some of the greatest Gal Movies of all time, like *84 Charing Cross Road* and *Pride and Prejudice* and *All About Eve* and *Green Card* and don't forget the wonderful *Auntie Mame*.

Richard: I've seen none of those movies. I bet they talk a lot in those movies. I bet nothing ever explodes in any of those movies. Now, if there was a movie called *Auntie MAIM*, and it was about some crazy old aunt with a butcher knife who slices her nieces and nephews to pieces, that I might watch!

Laurie: You're sick, you know that?

Richard: Thank you very much. Now for those guys out there who are freaking out after reading about some of Laurie's favorite movies, don't you worry, this book also pays tribute to *Scarface* and *Caddyshack* and *Goodfellas* and *Red River* and *Goldfinger* and nearly fifty other classic Guy Movies.

Laurie: Yeah, movies with Neanderthals like Arnold Schwarzenegger walking around killing everyone in sight, flexing their muscles while the special effects people do all the work, ooh that takes a lot of acting ability. Now, if you're looking for an action hero who can act, check out *Gloria* or *La Femme Nikita*.

Richard: Now don't be talking about my Arnold. He's one of the great actors of our generation, and it's only a matter of time before the Academy recognizes that and gives him a Lifetime Achievement Award.

Laurie: That's pathetic. If you want to read about movies where things go boom every five minutes and the men act with their muscles and the women are always taking their shirts off for no reason, read Richard's half of the book. But be forewarned: You might learn more about men than you want to know. If you want to read about intelligent, finely crafted films that will resonate in your heart and mind long after the final credits have played, with a few guilty pleasures thrown in for good measure, then you must read my half of the book. Whether I'm discussing screen legends like Bette Davis or talented young actresses like Winona Ryder—

Richard: You know, that Winona Ryder would be quite a babe if she'd get a little sun and let the hair grow out. She's never done nude, has she? If Winona did nude, I'd even consider sitting through one of her movies.

Laurie: That's pretty much all you care about, isn't it?

Richard: Well, it's just one of the key factors. You've got your car chases, your fistfights, your gun battles, your explosions, your male bonding, your memorable one-liners, your great drinking scenes, and yeah, your female nudity factor. The more of those elements I find in a film, the more likely I am to recommend it.

Laurie: Silly me. When I'm watching a film I look for grand passions, scintillating dialogue, women who do more than just serve as window dressing, men who do more than just grunt in monosyllabic utterances, fabulous clothes . . . and yeah, a nicely formed, scantily clad male bod is always a welcome bonus.

Richard: So you rate your films on each of those factors, and I'll rate mine for the really important things. Hey, have you ever seen *Fast Times at Ridgemont High*? Man that's a classic. I've got that on my list so you can't use it, all right?

Laurie: Gee, what a disappointment. I was really hoping to give praise to a movie where a high school girl teaches her friend all about the art of fellatio with a carrot.

Richard: So you have seen the movie! Isn't that a great scene? I'll never understand why Phoebe Cates didn't get nominated for her role as Linda Barrett in *Fast Times*. Instead they're always handing out statues to that snooty Meryl Streep and all her accents. She's such a showoff.

Laurie: I think I should get an award just for putting up with this. Why don't we just explain how we came up with the idea for this book.

Richard: It's simple, really. Walk into a video store and watch a man who has wandered into the Foreign section, where they have all those movies made by, um, foreigners. He'll squint at the artsy-fartsy black-and-white photos on the boxes, he'll go slack-jawed at the multisyllabic names of the unfamiliar stars—and when he realizes where he's at, he will dash out of there as quickly as if he'd found himself in the Pregnant Mom Workout section. Guys don't dig foreign movies.

Laurie: Now watch a woman react when her date suggests they see the new Jean-Claude Van Damme flick together. She'll shudder at the thought of sitting in a theater where the testosterone level gets so high it must just leak into her Diet Coke. Then she'll smile condescendingly at her man and explain that if she wants to contemplate a world filled with double-digit body counts, she can make better use of her time watching a PBS special on gang violence instead of going to the movies. And wouldn't he rather cuddle up with her on the sofa and spend a cozy evening watching *Sense and Sensibility*? After all, she's only seen it twice, and didn't he admit he hadn't had a chance to see it yet?

Richard: Everybody knows that men and women have different tastes in movies. Amazingly, though, nobody has written a book about this phenomenon—until now.

Laurie: Gal Movie: *Little Women*.

Richard: Guy Movie: *The Deer Hunter*.

Laurie: You're doing it right now, aren't you, friendly reader? Mentally compiling your own list of Guy and/or Gal Movies?

Richard: Leonard Maltin wishes he had come up with this idea! Then again, he probably wishes he was taller and funnier, too.

Laurie: Sure, there are some movies that transcend the differences between the sexes. There's *Schindler's List,* for example, and, and, there's . . .

Richard: Well. There's *Schindler's List.*

Laurie: The truth is, nearly every type of movie—even the big hits—appeals much more to one gender than the other.

Richard: Hence, *He Rents, She Rents.*

Laurie: "Hence"? Did you say "hence"? There may be hope for you yet. I believe it was Anthony Hopkins in *Remains of the Day* who said—

Richard: Anthony Hopkins? When he's not eating people I have no use for that guy. Why is he always playing some polite butler or some country gentleman—

Laurie: Women of the world, flip to my section of the book before it's too late.

Richard: Just give me the clicker, all right? You don't even know how to work it right.

Laurie: You're the one who broke it the last time you came over. Now the only two channels I get are ESPN and the Playboy Channel . . .

DISSOLVE TO:
THE REST OF THE BOOK

About Last Night . . .

Rated R, 116 min., 1986
Director: Edward Zwick
Screenplay: Tim Kazurinsky and Denise DeClue
Cast: Rob Lowe, Demi Moore, James Belushi, Elizabeth Perkins
Drinking: ****
Male bonding: ****
Memorable dialogue: ***
Nudity: ***

Rob Lowe is not a guy's guy. He's too goddamn pretty, for one thing. Also, he runs and throws and drinks like a girl. The scenes in *About Last Night . . .* in which Lowe has to play softball or run to Wrigley Field to catch a Cubs game or even down a shot of tequila are painful to watch, because you know he's never done any of these things in his real life. (Well, perhaps he's downed a shot of tequila as a prelude to videotaped sex with teenage cheerleaders.)

Most of the women on the professional tennis tour are manlier than Rob Lowe.

Nevertheless, *About Last Night . . .* is a four-star, singles bar, Guy Movie. Yeah, I know it's a love story, but it's a love story filled with softball games and one-night stands and bars with names like Mother's and graphic nude scenes with Demi Moore before her body was inflated like a tire on an Indy 500 car.

About Last Night . . . was adapted from a cheerfully coarse play from the 1970s by David Mamet that was originally titled *Sexual Perversity in Chicago.* Lowe plays Danny, a somewhat lecherous but sweet-natured salesman who has dreams of opening a diner some day. His best friend is Bernie Litko, a sausage-chomping, beer-swilling, butt-biting pervert with the map of Chicago on his face. Bernie is played with great gusto by James Belushi, in the role of his lifetime. John would have been proud.

Danny and Bernie spend their days hawking restaurant supplies and their nights playing softball in Grant Park and then getting drunk and chasing babes. Their counterparts are the angelic, beautiful Debbie (Moore), and the hard-faced, man-hating Joan, played with such a hard edge by Elizabeth Perkins that you get the feeling this kindergarten teacher is one bunny-boil away from Glenn Close territory. Joan has sex with men but she's obviously got a major latent thing for Debbie, who's too hung up on Danny to notice.

Classic moment: While Joan bitches at Debbie for spending the night with Danny and not calling, a hairy bear of a man stumbles out of Joan's bedroom and asks what's for breakfast.

"Egg McMuffin, corner of Belmont and Clark," snaps Joan. You go, girl.

Not long after hooking up for a one-night stand, Danny and Debbie make the mistake of moving in together, much to the dismay of their less attractive, much meaner friends. They have some great slow-motion sex to the music of "Livin' Inside My Heart" by Bob Seger, but soon Danny begins to feel trapped by the fact that Debbie is basically perfect and he's basically a guy, which means he'd rather be drinking with his buddy Bernie and picking up some bimbo than spending his time eating salads and fixing up the apartment and making the bed with Debbie. They break up on New Year's Eve, but soon Danny is acting like a typical stupid ex-boyfriend, calling Debbie at work, following her into bars, standing in the rain, and whining that he didn't know how good he had it with her.

Of course, he comes to this realization only after he's boinked four or five chickies.

Guys like *About Last Night . . .* because it allows them to live the fantasy that they can meet a great girl, screw up the relationship, fool around a few more times, and still have the opportunity to get back together with the girl of their dreams, without having to take an AIDS test or even giving up softball.

After Hours

Rated R, 96 min., 1985
Director: Martin Scorsese
Screenplay: Joseph Minion
Starring: Griffin Dunne, Rosanna Arquette, Linda Fiorentino, Teri Garr, John Heard, Catherine O'Hara
Drinking: ★★★
Memorable dialogue: ★★★
Nudity: ★★★

Directed by the great Martin Scorsese, who must have been smoking from the Nostradamus bowl when he made this thing in 1985, *After Hours* was so far ahead of its time that it scared people away from the theaters. That's too bad, because you missed such mind-boggling pleasures as Linda Fiorentino's breasts in their prime, Rosanna Arquette doing a monologue about a *Wizard of Oz*–obsessed sex partner who always cried out "Surrender Dorothy!" at the moment of truth, Catherine O'Hara as a Mr. Softee driver, and Cheech & Chong as a couple of art-loving thieves. Good thing we have video and cable!

After Hours stars Griffin Dunne, the American Dudley Moore, as a smarmy computer programmer named Paul Hackett. One night the pretentious little twit is in a coffee shop, reading *Tropic of Cancer*, when he makes the moves on the buck-toothed but juicy Marcy (Rosanna Arquette). Bored and restless, Paul rings up Marcy that same night, and she invites him over. Thus the journey through the looking glass begins.

Marcy shares a loft with the kinky Kiki (Linda Fiorentino), a papier-mâché artist known for her bagel-and-cream-cheese paperweights. She's wearing a black bra and working on a frightening sculpture when Paul greets her.

"You have a great body," he says.

"Yes," she replies, deadpan. "Not a lot of scars."

A moment later, Kiki doffs her top, for no reason. You almost expect Dunne, who was also the producer of this film, to turn to the camera and wink at us.

From this high moment in Paul's evening, things go to hell. He's already lost the lone twenty-dollar bill he had in his wallet, and he has a fight with Marcy after she gives him some really lousy pot. ("This isn't Colombian!" he spews. "I don't even think it's *pot*.") Rain-soaked, miserable, and unable to afford the cost of a subway token to get home, Paul stumbles into an all-hours bar where a waitress named Julie (Teri Garr) is dressed like Goldie Hawn circa *Laugh-In* and the bartender (John Heard, nearly a decade away from playing the dad in *Home Alone*) has a quietly menacing demeanor. Paul has a brief rendezvous with Julie in her apartment across the street from the bar, but all he really wants to do is use her phone, while she's trying to seduce him by playing songs such as "Last Train to Clarksville" and "Chelsea Morning." Seeking escape, Paul tells Julie he'll call her, honest he will, but he really has to get going. Can he have her number?

"Five-four-four-three-three," says Julie.

"Not enough numbers, but okay," Paul mutters under his breath.

Paul arrives back at the bar just in time to watch the bartender get a phone call telling him his girlfriend has committed suicide.

"Marcy!" the bartender wails, smacking his hand against the cash register. "Marcy Marcy Marcy!"

Paul goes a whiter shade of pale. That's right, the bartender's girlfriend is Marcy, last seen getting yelled at by Paul for giving him lousy pot. This is but one of the many plot twists that give *After Hours* a sort of noir *Seinfeld* feel, a couple of years before *Seinfeld* came to be. Seemingly unrelated story lines converge to propel Paul deeper and deeper into the tunnel of a New York night. *After Hours* is a hidden treasure of a Guy Movie because it confirms what every man knows, deep down: When you do your thinking below the belt, it can land you in a heap of trouble.

At Close Range

Rated R, 115 min., 1986
Director: James Foley
Screenplay: Nicholas Kazan
Starring: Christopher Walken, Sean Penn, Christopher Penn, Mary Stuart Masterson
Drinking: ***
Gunplay: ****
Male bonding: ***
Memorable dialogue: **
Nudity: **

Nobody wears eye makeup like Christopher Walken. When this guy applies eye makeup to his strange and wonderfully chilling visage, it's as if Satan himself is wielding the brush. In the right role, Walken makes Charles Manson look about as scary as a Cirque de Soleil tumbler.

Based on a true story, *At Close Range* is a creepy, beautiful crime thriller containing the darkest and best performance of Walken's legendary career as a screen psycho. He plays Brad Whitewood, Sr., a career thief and killer who is like a famous ghost among the working poor of rural Pennsylvania. Even when he's off doing long stretches of time, Brad Senior is the kind of dominating presence who lives on in the stories told by the high school toughs and the barroom lowlifes.

Fresh—more like rotten—from prison, Brad Senior shows up one day at the rundown shack of a house where his ex-wife lives with her mother and two sons, Brad Junior and Tommy (whose paternal heritage is undetermined). Golden hair all puffy, eyes sunk deep into his skull, Brad Senior tosses a wad of cash at his wide-eyed son, played by a pumped-up, pigeon-toed Sean Penn. (Penn's younger brother, Chris, is half brother Tommy.)

Despite stern warnings from his mother and grandma, Brad Junior starts hanging out with his dad's band of cutthroat thieves, gradually gaining the trust of everyone except Brad Senior's girlfriend (Candy Clarke, virtually unrecognizable from her role as the blond chatterbox in *American Graffiti.*) After proving himself by stealing tractors and trucks in the dead of night with the help of Tommy and his friends (including the always-spooky Crispin Glover), little Brad is taken under his father's bent wing and given a position of responsibility within the gang. Brad Junior is smart enough to realize his dad is pure evil, but he's also mesmerized by the old man's dark charisma, and he's naturally drawn to the life of crime. Like father, like son.

We know it's all going to go bad. We know blood will spill, and relatively innocent people will die. But like Brad Junior, we're hooked on Brad Senior. We can't take our eyes off this weird, mumbling guy who pulls out a gleaming gun and shows it to his boys over lunch as casually as if he's displaying a fishing reel. Even when he's uttering innocuous lines such as "You want some Corn Flakes?" Walken will chill your spine.

For Brad Junior, the romance of hanging with his father dies when he watches one of Brad Senior's henchmen casually drown a suspected squealer in the river. Bathed in eerie lighting, Walken fixes a dead-eyed gaze on his son and puts his finger to his lips, silently telling the boy to keep this to himself—or else.

That's it for Brad Junior. He and his tomboy girlfriend, Terry (Mary Stuart Masterson), make plans to get out of town, but it all falls to hell when the feds get involved and Brad Senior fears little Brad and his teenage buddies will rat him out. What follows is a stunning medley of violence culminating in a tense confrontation between father and son, with one of them apparently bleeding to death and the other wondering if his face is going to get blown off.

At Close Range is a blue-chip effort, from the direction by James Foley and the outstanding screenplay by Nicholas Kazan to the universally stellar performances and a haunting score including "Live to Tell" by Madonna, which plays over the closing credits. When the movie's over, you'll probably want to double-bolt your door and hide under the covers. Just hope that when you dream you don't see Christopher Walken's face staring at you from a dark corner of your bedroom.

Barfly

Rated R, 110 min., 1987
Director: Barbet Schroeder
Screenplay: Charles Bukowski
Starring: Mickey Rourke, Faye Dunaway, Alice Krige, Frank Stallone
Drinking: ****
Fights: ****
Memorable dialogue: ****

There's no justice in a world where Nicolas Cage wins the Academy Award for playing a poetic drunk in *Leaving Las Vegas*, while Mickey Rourke was barely noticed for playing a poetic drunk in *Barfly*, which was released ten years earlier and is much the superior drunk poet movie. Watch *Barfly* and you'll realize Cage was merely doing a Method-lite impersonation of Rourke. In *Vegas*, Cage wears puffy shirts and he falls down a lot, but he still has the thirty-two-inch waist and the broad shoulders even though all he does is guzzle booze and pass out. And, no matter how much trouble he causes, Elisabeth Shue, the pie-faced angel from the *Karate Kid*, moons over him as if he were a misbehaving German shepherd. Yeah right, *that* happens a lot.

Contrast that with the gritty realism of *Barfly*, with the oily, hunched-over, pot-bellied, belching, farting Rourke truly soaking himself in the role of sometimes-writer, always-drinker Henry (the alter ego of screenwriter Charles Bukowski). His mouth dripping chocolate-colored blood from his latest barroom brawl, reaching over the bar to steal a drink like a two-year-old making a grab for candy, raiding his neighbor's refrigerator for food and booze, Henry is a big fat loser and he knows it and he doesn't care if you know it. Just give him another drink, all right? That's all he cares about in this world. He lives to drink, and drinks to live.

Because this is a Hollywood movie, the loathsome, smelly Henry does get to hook up with a rather great-looking alcoholic named Wanda (Faye Dunaway), whose *Vogue* cheekbones shine right through the stringy hair and the smudge on her face. "A distressed goddess," is the way Henry describes her, in his strange, beat-poet cadence.

But unlike Shue's character in *Leaving Las Vegas*, Wanda doesn't just stand by her man as he falls to the floor. She's an irresponsible drunk herself, so when Henry's hated nemesis, Eddie the bartender (Sylvester Stallone's brother Frank, surprisingly effective), offers her a bottle, she not only takes the booze, she takes Eddie for the night, too.

Alcoholic missteps aside, Wanda truly cares for Henry, but she has a rival for his affections: Tully (Alice Krige), a wealthy editor who has bought some of Henry's writings, but has to hire a private detective to track him down just so he can be paid. The slumming Tully is at least as infatuated with Henry's grimy lifestyle as she is with his writings, and after she takes him to her mansion and they (of course) get drunk, they end up in bed. Tully envisions some sort of star-crossed romance, but all Henry wants to do is return to his regular seat at the Golden Horn bar so he can flash the cash from this writing success and buy a round for the house.

"To all my friends!" he bellows, as the motley bunch applaud their hero Henry. Even Eddie gets a tip, as Henry tells him, "Pour yourself a drink, go buy yourself some bubble gum!"

Tully shows up at the bar in one last attempt to win over Henry, but Wanda goes after her with a mighty growl, and a great, hair-pulling catfight ensues. If you thought Dunaway was a force as Joan Crawford, wait until you see her rolling around the floor of a dingy bar, fingernails flashing at a princess who's trying to steal her man.

Guys will love *Barfly* because no matter how drunk and stupid we get, we'll never sink as low as Mickey Rourke does in this movie.

Big Bad Mama

Rated R, 83 min., 1974
Director: Steve Carver
Screenplay: William Norton and Frances Doel
Starring: Angie Dickinson, William Shatner, Tom Skerritt, Susan Sennett, Robbie Lee
Car chases: ★★★
Gunplay: ★★★
Nudity: ★★★★

"Men, Money and Moonshine: When It Comes to Vice, Mama Knows Best!"

So reads the copy on the "digitally remastered" home video version of *Big Bad Mama*, a lascivious and low-rent version of *Bonnie and Clyde* from producer Roger Corman, the master of exploitation films. I don't know if *Big Bad Mama* deserves such reverential treatment, but it is a great selection if you're in the mood to see car crashes and a naked Angie Dickinson at the top of her game.

The fantabulous Ms. Dickinson made this movie just before she had a mainstream comeback playing Pepper Anderson on *Police Woman*. Here she's on the wrong side of the law as Wilma McClatchie, a gun-totin', randy widow who takes her two ripe teenage daughters (Susan Sennett and Robbie Lee) on a robbing spree through backwoods America in the Roaring Twenties. As always, Dickinson's acting is as wooden as a Louisville Slugger, but she looks great.

Like most Corman films, *Big Bad Mama* is cheap, but sexy and funny. The action is set in the 1920s but the characters all sport 1970s haircuts,

Telltale Signs You're Watching a Gal Movie

When clicking around the dial or inserting a random tape into the VCR, there are some easy warning signs that will always indicate you've stumbled upon the dreaded Gal Movie.

- If the opening credits are in the form of handwritten wedding invitations, you're watching a Gal Movie.
- If smiling cowboys are dancing with women who are tossing their hoop skirts to and fro, you're watching a Gal Movie.
- If there's a song on the soundtrack called "Love Theme from [Whatever the Movie's Title Is]," you're watching a Gal Movie.
- If the movie begins with a lush shot of the dewy countryside, or a scene of horse-drawn carriages clomping down a brick street, with the caption, "England, 1875," you're watching a Gal Movie.
- If anyone is in a wheelchair, you're watching a Gal Movie.
- If there's a scene in which a woman is trying on hats and dresses while a pop song plays on the soundtrack—Gal Movie.
- If the men are wearing powdered wigs, it's a Gal Movie.
- Subtitles? No matter what they're saying, the real message is, "You're watching a Gal Movie."
- If a woman is brushing her hair and crying while looking in the mirror, you're watching a Gal Movie.
- If one of the following actors is in the cast, chances are it's a Gal Movie. If two appear, it's almost certainly a Gal Movie. If three or more show up, run for your life.

June Allyson	Ingrid Bergman
Julie Andrews	Helena Bonham Carter
Fred Astaire and Ginger Rogers	Jill Clayburgh
Jean-Pierre Aumont	Montgomery Clift
Lucille Ball	Glenn Close
Anne Bancroft	Joan Crawford

Bette Davis	Liza Minnelli
Geena Davis	Maureen O'Hara
Doris Day	Laurence Olivier
Daniel Day-Lewis	Maureen O'Sullivan (like a guy can
Gerard Depardieu	tell the difference between the two
Richard Dreyfuss	Maureens)
Sally Field	Geraldine Page
Judy Garland	Gwyneth Paltrow
Richard Gere	Brad Pitt
Whoopi Goldberg	Lynn Redgrave
Cary Grant	Vanessa Redgrave
Hugh Grant	Debbie Reynolds
Joel Grey	Diana Ross
Julie Harris	Meg Ryan
Rex Harrison	Winona Ryder
Goldie Hawn	Susan Sarandon
Helen Hayes	Barbara Stanwyck
Audrey Hepburn	Meryl Streep
Katharine Hepburn	Barbra Streisand
Glenda Jackson	Patrick Swayze
Diane Keaton	Jessica Tandy
Gene Kelly	Elizabeth Taylor
Deborah Kerr	Emma Thompson
Christine Lahti	Lily Tomlin
Jessica Lange	Kate Winslet
Carole Lombard	Alfre Woodard
Shirley MacLaine	Any cutesy kid, from Shirley Temple to
Marsha Mason	Jonathan Lipnicki
Bette Midler	

and there apparently wasn't enough room in the budget for background extras. What we do get is a bunch of car chases on dirt roads while sassy fiddle music plays on the soundtrack as Ma McClatchie quotes John D. Rockefeller in an effort to explain to her daughters why it's okay for them to rob banks and shoot G-men for a living. It doesn't make any sense, but the giggling girls sure do look pretty as they squirm around in their skimpy outfits, practically jumping out of their skin with hormonal curiosity.

While pulling a heist at a racetrack, the gals hook up with a sweet-talkin' dandy of a con man, portrayed by William Shatner if you can believe it. This was during a dark time in Shatner's career, after the cancellation of *Star Trek* but before Captain Kirk became a movie franchise for him, so he was obviously taking work anywhere he could get it. Not that this is a bad gig; after all, he has a steamy love scene with Angie in which they're both naked and the camera boldly goes where no one has gone before, nearly showing us way too much of Shatner's own starship *Enterprise*. Mercifully, the scene is poorly lit.

Also sharing Angie's bed is a young Tom Skerritt, who, when he's tossed aside in favor of Shatner, ends up in a threesome with the giggling daughters. If Skerritt was paid $100 for making this movie, it was too much.

If that's not enough gratuitous nudity for you, there's also a naked cameo by Sally Kirkland before she got those ridiculous implants, and a kidnapping plot involving a spoiled brat played by Joan Prather, best known as the oldest boy's wife on *Eight Is Enough*. Like every other female in the movie, Prather has to take off her clothes. It must have been a Corman rule.

I'm not going to kid you. *Big Bad Mama* isn't a great film. It's not even a very good film. But jeez, it's only eighty-three minutes long, and if you fast-forward to the sex and shootout scenes, you can have the whole *Big Bad Mama* experience in about the time it would take to watch a rerun of *3rd Rock from the Sun*.

The New Horizons release of *Big Bad Mama* includes the bonus of "Leonard Maltin's exclusive interview with Roger Corman." Don't worry, they both have their clothes on.

The Big Picture

Rated PG-13, 95 min., 1989
Director: Christopher Guest
Screenplay: Christopher Guest and Michael McKean
Starring: Kevin Bacon, Michael McKean, Martin Short, Jennifer Jason Leigh, Teri Hatcher, J. T. Walsh
Male bonding: ***
Memorable dialogue: ****

This movie is one of the key elements in that stupid Six Degrees of Kevin Bacon game because the eclectic cast listed above is augmented by cameos from Fran Drescher, Elliott Gould, Roddy McDowall, Richard Belzer, John Cleese, and Eddie Albert. If you can't find a Bacon connection to other stars through any of these people, then stop playing the game right now. But look, stop playing the game right now anyway. It's pointless and you're wasting your time.

Not so if you rent *The Big Picture*! This is a knowing, scathing, hilarious yet affectionate send-up of the movie business, brought to you by director Christopher Guest, one of the architects of *This Is Spinal Tap*. The ever-boyish Bacon is Nick Chapman, a talented young director who wins a student film award and is overwhelmed when Hollywood begins courting him. (His chief suitor is J. T. Walsh, a producer whose cavernous office includes a fireplace operated by remote control.) When the offers come pouring in, Nick decides he needs an agent, so he lunches with the bewigged and wigged-out Neil Sussman (Martin Short).

Here's Neil's pitch to Nick: "If you decide to sign with me, you're going to get more than an agent. You're going to get three people. You're going to get an agent, a mother, a father, a shoulder to cry on, someone who knows this biz inside and out."

By my count, that's four people and a shoulder, but that's Hollywood for you.

As soon as Nick gets a deal, he turns into a jerk, abandoning his best friend, his girlfriend, and his principles for the lure of easy riches and Hollywood glamour, as personified by the incredibly beautiful (and incredibly big-haired) Gretchen, an actress who practically wraps her thighs around Nick's head the moment she learns he's a director with a deal. Gretchen is played by the braless Teri Hatcher, who utters one of the most devastatingly simple rejections in the history of movies, moments after she finds out Nick's deal has gone sour due to a shake-up at the executive level of his studio.

"Do you think we could, um, I don't know, see a movie or something later?" Nick asks, as he pathetically clings to the belief that someone like Gretchen would still be interested in him even though he's no longer useful to her career.

She squints at him as if he's an alien and says, "Uh, no. I think I might be doing something."

Ouch!

As soon as Nick's deal disintegrates, his life follows suit. He can't even find work on C movies like *Abe and the Babe*, the "true" story of the friendship between Abe Lincoln (who was shot in 1865) and Babe Ruth (who was born two decades later). Just to make ends meet, he's working for a messenger service when he bumps into the insane Lydia (Jennifer

Jason Leigh), a former classmate of his who dresses like Minnie Mouse and shares a loft with a band called Pez People.

"Nick, you dick!" Lydia says when she spots him on the street.

Nick agrees to direct a video for the Pez People, and suddenly he's in demand again—but this time around, he's going to do it right. Maybe.

Ultimately, *The Big Picture* is a nice little Guy Movie because it's funny as hell, but also because all guys can relate to young Nick Chapman, who wants to be a straight shooter but would abandon everything he believes in just for the chance to hang out with a braless Teri Hatcher.

Blood Simple

Rated R, 96 min., 1985
Director: Joel Coen
Screenplay: Joel and Ethan Coen
Starring: Frances McDormand, John Getz, Dan Hedaya, M. Emmet Walsh
Fights: ****
Gunplay: ***
Memorable dialogue: ****

Forget about Frances McDormand's Academy Award–winning role in *Fargo* as the doughnut-shaped sheriff who spouts "You betcha" and is married to a dork who paints pictures of ducks. I much prefer her as the slinky, adulterous, pistol-packing Abby in *Blood Simple*, the first and maybe the best movie from those wacky brothers Coen.

They oughta call themselves the brothers Grim, given their predilection for exploring the dark and violent side of human nature. This is a realistically violent thriller—intelligent and complex, but not too complex for its own good. But the Texas accents are almost as difficult to interpret as all that Minnesota-talk in *Fargo*, so pay attention, dammit.

Blood Simple begins with a sordid love triangle involving Abby, her scuzzy husband, Marty (Dan Hedaya, he of the serial killer eyes and the Nixonian five o'clock shadow), and a lanky, laconic bartender named Ray, played by John Getz, who went on to play the guy who gets all chewed up by Jeff Goldblum at the end of *The Fly*. After a fat, sweaty private detective in a canary-yellow leisure suit and a big stupid cowboy hat confirms the affair, Marty offers him $10,000 to kill the both of them.

The fat sweaty private detective is played by M. Emmet Walsh, one of the great character actors of all time, and perhaps the only man in America named M. Emmet. (Try saying "M. Emmet" three times real fast. It's nearly impossible, isn't it?) When Marty calls the PI a snake, M. Emmet just laughs and says, "Give me a call if you want to cut off my head. I can always crawl around without it."

Not surprisingly, the private detective decides to double-cross old Marty—a plan that creates all sorts of bloody complications that lead a number of characters to their demise. (*Blood Simple* refers to the simple—as in stupid—reactions the characters have to the spilling of blood.) Even though Ray and Abby love each other, there's an inherent lack of trust in their Motel 6 of a relationship, and it's a fatal flaw for one of them.

I don't want to spoil any of the neat twists and turns of the plot here; suffice to say the Coen brothers are such masters of original storytelling that they can set up a gruesome climax in which Abby thinks she's fighting for her life against an opponent who's already been buried alive.

Blood Simple contains at least four jump-out-of-your-seat moments of true terror—and it's not the usual stuff like cats landing on someone's shoulder in the dark, or hands reaching out and grabbing somebody's ankles. Nah, this is fresh stuff. In fact, the use of sound and light is innovative and fresh throughout the movie as the Coen brothers make a bold, bloody, brilliant debut.

A nice bonus from the Coens is their trademark penchant for mixing in some sick humor with the violence. There are a number of great twisted and funny moments in *Blood Simple*, including M. Emmet's hilarious story about a man who had both hands in casts and thus had to ask his wife to take a "true test of love" involving, well, you figure it out. And if you listen closely, you'll hear the voice of an uncredited Holly Hunter (soon to star in the Coens' *Raising Arizona*) as a jilted babe bitching away on a main character's answering machine. When it happens, you can blurt out, "Say, isn't that Holly Hunter?" which will make you seem smarter than everyone in the room, much like the Coen brothers are smarter than almost everyone else in the big room that is Hollywood.

Bullitt

Not Rated, 113 min., 1968
Director: Peter Yates
Screenplay: Alan R. Trustman and Harry Kleiner, based on the novel *Mute Witness* by Robert L. Pike
Starring: Steve McQueen, Robert Vaughn, Jacqueline Bisset, Robert Duvall
Car chases: ★★★★
Gunplay: ★★★
Memorable dialogue: ★★★

In some ways, the 1968 suspense thriller *Bullitt* seems more outdated than a cop movie from the 1940s. It's not just the far-out soundtrack music, or the men with their bad sideburns and the women in their loud print miniskirts; it's the way the story itself is dictated by the technology (or lack thereof) of that era. There must be a half-dozen scenes where somebody has to pull over to make a phone call, because of course they didn't have cellular phones way back then. And a pivotal moment in the film involves a bunch of cops standing around a newfangled Telecopier machine that can transport photos like magic from one city to another, Ooooooooooooh.

Nevertheless, *Bullitt* holds up as a first-class Guy Movie precisely because it is thirty years old, and thus can be honored as one of the first of the modern, antihero cop films featuring a lone wolf detective who spends as much time battling corruption and compromise within his own department as he does duking it out with the bad guys. Before there was Dirty Harry Callahan, before there was Martin Riggs of *Lethal Weapon* fame, before there was *Beverly Hills Cop* Axel Foley, there was Frank Bullitt, the San Francisco copper who trusts his instincts a whole lot more than the directives he receives from his captain or the district attorney. And who better to play Bullitt than Steve McQueen, who specialized in playing sarcastic misfits who were often their own worst enemies? In movies such as *The Cincinnati Kid, The Hunter,* and *Baby, the Rain Must Fall,* McQueen was always on the outskirts of conventional society and not particularly interested in working his way to the inside. That's also the way he plays it in *Bullitt,* at one point stealing a corpse and holding it hostage until he can figure out who's on his side and who's trying to set him up.

The rather tricky plot of *Bullitt* begins with our man McQueen assigned to protect a government witness who is going to testify against "the Organization" in a sensational case that could fuel the political ambitions of a ruthlessly ambitious prosecutor, Walter Chalmers (Robert Vaughn). Bullitt refers to it as nothing more than a "baby-sitting detail," but the assignment turns deadly when the witness and Bullitt's partner are ambushed by a couple of mob hit men. Not that this necessarily means the witness is dead; he's just missing in action, and only Bullitt knows his true whereabouts. The cat-and-mouse game with the mob reaches its climax with one of the most memorable car chases in movie history, as McQueen in his souped-up Mustang tails a black Barracuda through the hilly streets of San Francisco. Cameras were mounted in the backseats of the cars, providing us with a roller-coaster point of view—at the time, a revolutionary technique. Even today, this ten-minute, dialogue-free chase scene ranks as one of the best ever.

Also on hand for this classy thriller are Jacqueline Bisset, showing a lot of leg as Bullitt's girlfriend as she robotically spouts such movie-girlfriend clichés as "Everything you do is a part of me," and Robert Duvall as a cab driver who helps Bullitt unlock part of the mystery. But it's McQueen, Mr. Turtleneck-with-a-Gun, who carries the movie. His entire career is summed up in a confrontation with Vaughn, who tells him, "Frank, we must all compromise."

"Bullshit!" barks McQueen. "Get the hell out of here, now."

Butch Cassidy and the Sundance Kid

Rated PG, 112 min., 1969
Director: George Roy Hill
Screenplay: William Goldman
Starring: Paul Newman, Robert Redford, Katharine Ross
Fights: ★★★★
Gunplay: ★★★★
Male bonding: ★★★★
Memorable dialogue: ★★★★

THE SCENE: Butch Cassidy and the Sundance Kid have managed to escape from an American posse, but now they're cornered by what appears to be half the Bolivian army. The situation is hopelessly fatal.

> SUNDANCE
> I never want to hear another of your great ideas, all right?
> BUTCH
> All right.
> SUNDANCE
> Good.
> BUTCH
> Australia. I figured you secretly wanted to know, so I told you—Australia.
> SUNDANCE
> That's your great idea?
> BUTCH
> The latest in a long line.

By now the buddy movie is such a cliché, I'd rather endure an Emma Thompson film festival than watch another flick starring two mismatched wisecrackers who trade barbs while fending off a hail of gunfire from dozens of sharpshooters. (For the record, the movie that killed the genre was *Tango and Cash,* a movie so bad Sylvester Stallone and Kurt Russell should have been kicked out of the acting profession for allowing it to happen.) In 1969, though, the concept was exhilarating—as were the two great actors who brought William Goldman's nearly perfect script to life.

You think Brad Pitt and Keanu Reeves are cool? Ha. Take a look at Newman and Redford in their prime if you want to see bona fide, ten-foot-tall *movie stars* in their prime. As Butch and Sundance, these guys are handsome, macho, vulnerable, and funny—the ultimate underdogs.

(However, in a nod to the ladies, Redford kept his late-sixties sideburns and blow-dried hair intact.) Sure, they're a couple of thieving no-goods, but they don't mean any harm, they just want to gather as much cash as possible while staying a thousand paces ahead of the relentless posse tracking them through most of the story.

"Who are those guys?" Butch and Sundance ask, again and again. Ultimately they learn the posse is comprised of the toughest lawmen in the country, an all-star collection of sheriffs and bounty hunters hired to capture the famous bandits, dead or alive. Time and again, it appears as if our boys have run out of options—but they always seem to find a way to elude their pursuers, even if it means jumping from a cliff to almost certain death while hollering, "Oh ssshiiiiiiiiiiiiiiiiiiiiiiiiiiiiittttttt!"

I have to admit I'm not a big fan of the whimsical interlude in the middle of the film, where Butch and Sundance fawn all over Katharine Ross—who acts with such a lack of emotion I think she was already preparing for that Stepford wives movie—while the insufferable "Raindrops Keep Fallin' on My Head" plays on the soundtrack. Those scenes play like something out of a Gal Movie, but you can fast-forward past them and cut to the chase, literally speaking. Anyway, that brief misstep is obliterated by any number of great scenes, from the opening poker confrontation to the poignant moment, late in the film, when Butch and Sundance happen into a movie theater and see a wildly inaccurate silent reel purporting to tell their story.

"This isn't how it was, it wasn't like that!" Butch cries out, but the audience is too busy cheering the onscreen posse to notice him.

Most real guys have one true buddy who sticks with them through it all: school, marriage, divorce, career changes, good times, and tragedies. Such buddies may never put it into words, but almost always, one of them thinks of himself as Butch, and the other knows he is the Sundance Kid.

Caddyshack

Rated R, 99 min., 1980
Director: Harold Ramis
Screenplay: Harold Ramis, Brian Doyle-Murray, Douglas Kenney
Starring: Chevy Chase, Bill Murray, Rodney Dangerfield, Ted Knight,
    Michael O'Keefe
Drinking: ★★★
Explosions: ★★★
Male bonding: ★★★★
Memorable dialogue: ★★★★
Nudity: ★★★

Since 1980, every guy who has ever picked up a golf club for a couple of practice swings has been heard to intone something like this: "He's a Cinderella boy . . . former greenskeeper, about to become Masters champion. . . . It looks like a mirac—it's in the hole! It's in the hole!"

Women who witness these spectacles shake their heads and think, Assholes. They don't realize we're paying tribute to a classic comedy by doing our best imitations of the immortal Carl Spackler, one of Bill Murray's most unforgettable big-screen characters. Murray had only a couple of scenes in *Caddyshack,* but he has made a lasting impression on guys everywhere with his grimy portrayal of the hapless, horny assistant greenskeeper who, when he's not lusting after the ladies on the course, has developed his own hybrid of golf turf, a combination of Kentucky bluegrass and Northern California pot.

"The amazing thing about this stuff is, you can play thirty-six holes on it in the afternoon, take it home, and just get stoned to the bejesus bells that night," Carl tells club pro Ty Webb, played by Chevy Chase back when Chase was skinny and funny.

Caddyshack is another product of the sick and fertile minds developed in the comedy lab of the *National Lampoon.* Chase, Murray, director Harold Ramis, and cowriters Brian Doyle-Murray (who also plays the head of the caddyshack) and Douglas Kenney are alums of the legendary comedy troupe. They band together here for a raunchy, tasteless, and relentlessly hilarious film about the caddies and players who hang out at the exclusive Bushwood Country Club, cofounded by the uptight Judge Smails (the late Ted Knight, overacting so furiously his face is beet red throughout the film).

Michael O'Keefe is Danny Noonan, a good-hearted but rather aimless veteran of the caddyshack who knows his days of toting bags for rich doctors are numbered. Either he's going to win a coveted college scholarship or he's going to spend the rest of his life toiling at his dad's lumberyard. Danny has a pretty Irish girlfriend, but like everyone else at Bushwood he falls in lust with the judge's naughty niece, Lacey Underalls (Cyndy Morgan, also seen in *Tron* and then never seen again). Lacey, whose hobbies include "skinny-skiing and going to bullfights on acid," seduces Ty and Danny before the judge sends her away.

But a nympho niece isn't the only problem plaguing Judge Smails. He also has to contend with obnoxious, nouveau riche developer Al Czervik, who has invaded the country club like a polyester-clad fungus, spreading bad taste, big tips, and loud jokes everywhere. If Rodney Dangerfield doesn't steal the film as Czervik, he at least burrows it from time to time as he spouts one-liners directly lifted from his stand-up routine.

"Hey baby," Czervik says, casting a lascivious eye toward the judge's wife, "you must have been something before electricity."

The feud between the judge and Czervik escalates until they face off in a big-stakes match in which Danny has to take over for the "injured" judge. Will Danny throw the match so he can get the scholarship, or will he be true to himself and play for his honor?

Ah, who cares. *Caddyshack* isn't about some caddy coming of age, it's about laughing your ass off at a completely ridiculous comic book of a movie. I know men—educated men, mind you—who have seen this movie fifteen or twenty times. I admire them for that.

Clerks

Rated R, 92 min., 1994
Director: Kevin Smith
Screenplay: Kevin Smith
Starring: Brian O'Halloran, Jeff Anderson, Marilyn Ghigliotti, Lisa Spoonhauer
Male bonding: ★★★★
Memorable dialogue: ★★★★

Starring a bunch of nobodies and shot almost entirely on a street corner in New Jersey, *Clerks* is about as low budget as a movie can get without being a home video. But unlike most film festival–critical darling underdogs—*The Brothers McMullen* with that self-important, greasy-haired Edward Burns and his stiff of a girlfriend comes to mind—*Clerks* truly is a unique and groundbreaking piece of work. Plus it's funny as hell.

True, this is another one of those "independent" films made by a twentysomething guy who stole money from his grandmother's purse or something to finance the thing. And yes, it's shot in black and white, but don't be afraid—there are no scenes with guys playing chess against Death or anything like that. In fact, the black-and-white thing actually works here because *life* in Jersey is in black and white, especially if you're like Dante, a lowly clerk in a Quick Stop convenience store, or his buddy Randal, who works across the street in a crappy video store.

Dante's troubles begin when he's called in to work on his day off, thus blowing his big plans to sleep in and then play an afternoon game of street hockey. They're compounded when his girlfriend Veronica nonchalantly mentions she "snowballed" the loser who just walked out of the store. (To snowball someone is to—ah, forget it, if I even try to describe this disgusting sexual maneuver, this entire book will be shrinkwrapped and placed behind the counter.) When Dante presses Veronica about her sexual history, she says she slept with only three guys—but she's performed oral sex on three *dozen*. Dante flips out; Veronica storms off.

"Hey, try not to suck any dick on the way through the parking lot!" Dante yells at her, much to the amusement of the ubiquitous Jay and Silent Bob, a couple of drugged-out goofballs who hang around outside the store out all day.

(By the way, the theme of the boyfriend dealing with his girlfriend's wild past is also explored in Smith's third film, *Chasing Amy*, which is almost a sequel of sorts to *Clerks* in that many of the fringe characters reappear. You don't have to see one film to appreciate the other, but it enhances the experience. Just make sure you stay away from Smith's second effort, *Mallrats*, the worst movie in the history of movies.)

While sorting out his feelings for Veronica and addressing some unresolved business with an ex-girlfriend who's about to get married, Dante must also deal with a medley of weird customers, including a nutball guidance counselor obsessed with creating a carton of perfectly formed eggs, and a doofus who gets his arm caught in a tube of Pringles potato chips. These episodes are interspersed with philosophical discussions with Randal, whose hobby is screening videos with titles such as *Chicks with Dicks*. The highlight is Randal's verbal dissertation contending that when the second, uncompleted Death Star was destroyed at the end of *Return of the Jedi*, a lot of "innocent construction workers" lost their lives. The slacker's got a point.

As for the mysterious Silent Bob (played by Smith), he speaks only a few lines—but like Yoda, Silent Bob spouts wisdom worth heeding. Because of these insights, Dante realizes it's okay to care for Veronica, even though she's gone down on thirty-six other guys.

So there, a love story *can* be a Guy Movie.

Con Air

Rated R, 110 min., 1997
Director: Simon West
Screenplay: Scott Rosenberg
Starring: Nicolas Cage, John Cusack, John Malkovich, Ving Rhames, Steve Buscemi, Rachel Ticotin
Car chases: ★★★★
Explosions: ★★★★
Fights: ★★★★
Gunplay: ★★★★
Male bonding: ★★★
Memorable dialogue: ★★★

Take a little bit of *Silence of the Lambs*, sprinkle in some *Passenger 57*, add a dash of *The Rock*, stir in some elements of *Die Hard 2* and *The Shawshank Redemption*, and you've got *Con Air*, a Guy Movie that knows it's a Guy Movie and revels in this knowledge. This is an absolutely ludicrous but beautifully executed action thriller that'll pin you to your seat and hold your interest right through the weird closing credit sequence, which features a montage of smiling psychopathic killers.

Con Air plays like a big budget movie version of one of those shockingly violent video games your kid brother likes to play, in which you rack up points based on the number of "kills" you score. A beefed-up Nicolas Cage stars as Cameron Poe, a country-talking prisoner who is returning home to his wife and daughter after spending eight long years in the joint for beating up some guys who had picked on him outside a tavern. In one of those "Don't do it!" moves that are made only by heroes at the beginning of action movies, he hitches a ride on a C-123K troop transport plane that is loaded with insane, hard-core killers, including the evil genius Cyrus the Virus (John Malkovich) and the loathsome Johnny 23, so named because he's been convicted for rape twenty-three times.

"It would have been Johnny six hundred if they knew the whole story!" brags Johnny 23 as he leers at a female security guard (Rachel Ticotin) on the plane.

Also on board is Steve Buscemi as Garland Greene, an infamous serial killer who has killed more than thirty children. *Con Air* is such a sick twist of a movie that we actually find Greene to be one of the more sympathetic and humorous characters in the film. (After the inmates hijack the plane, they celebrate by dancing to "Sweet Home Alabama," and only Greene notes the irony of dancing on an airplane to a song by a band that was effectively decimated when several of its members were killed in a plane crash.)

Cameron wants no part of the hijacking—after all, he's already been paroled—but he finds himself caught in the crossfire as the inmates do battle with cops and soldiers and federal agents. His only hope is John Cusack (obviously slumming here so he can pick up a big paycheck to fuel his quirky career), as a U.S. marshal who believes Cameron might be a secret good guy and not part of the cutthroat band of killers aboard the plane.

The plot stalls on the runway but the action careens all over the place as Malkovich and his boys try to stay one step ahead of the agents who are trying to blow the transport plane out of the sky. It's hilarious to watch all these critically acclaimed actors jumping around and punching each other and crashing cars into airplanes, just like Seagal and Van Damme and Chan. You can tell they had a lot of fun spending the $80 million or so it took to make a movie that includes a scene where a plane seems to crash-land on the Vegas strip, ripping away the guitar on the Hard Rock Casino sign.

Nicolas Cage has now starred in two movies where he fell out of the sky and landed on the Strip—the other being *Honeymoon in Las Vegas*. No doubt this is a record that will stand a long, long time.

Con Air: The Sequel

by Laurie Viera

Like any blockbuster action flick, it makes sense for *Con Air* to have a sequel. I have my own ideas about how this sequel should open, but I doubt if the studio would approve.

Here's how I see it.

The time: Twenty years later. The little girl who played Nicholas Cage's daughter is a grown woman.

The situation: The woman has been unable to form any sort of meaningful relationship with a man.

The setting: Her therapist's office.

The action: Under regressive hypnosis, the young woman remembers a traumatic event that has screwed up the rest of her life. That event was her very first meeting with her father, which was the end of *Con Air*. The woman remembers how she spent the first years of her childhood dreaming of the dad who would one day come home from jail and rejoin the family. Then, finally, came the answer to her childish prayers. Daddy was coming home! And on her birthday! But what did she get? She got to stand in the middle of the Vegas Strip, surrounded by carnage, dead bodies, and wreckage from an explosion. The man who emerged from this Armageddon and introduced himself as dear old Dad was covered in filth, wearing torn clothes, and had long, greasy hair. Quaking with fear, that little girl clung to her mother's legs, while the grime-streaked giant thrust a torn, smelly, dirt-encrusted stuffed bunny into her hands. She was then forced to go home with both filthy beasts and to sleep with one of them under her pillow.

The Deer Hunter

Rated R, 183 min., 1978
Director: Michael Cimino
Screenplay: Deric Washburn and Michael Cimino
Starring: Robert De Niro, Christopher Walken, John Savage, Meryl Streep
Drinking: ★★★★
Explosions: ★★★
Gunplay: ★★★★
Male bonding: ★★★★
Memorable dialogue: ★★★★

The Deer Hunter is about three men who go off to Vietnam, with life-shattering results. But it's not a war movie, it's a male-friendship movie. A *great* male-friendship movie. These guys spend nearly all their time in one another's company, whether they're working in the steel mills of Pennsylvania, getting blasted at the local tavern, hunting deer, or fighting for their country on the other side of the planet in a war they don't understand. Oh sure, they love women, but mostly as a hobby. They feel most alive when in the company of other men. Check out the joy on their faces as they shoot pool, guzzle beers, and sing along with "Can't Take My Eyes off of You" on the jukebox. They're in Guy Heaven.

Notice how the really tough men in the movies—and in life—aren't afraid to touch each other affectionately. The mobsters in *The Godfather* and *Goodfellas*, the jocks in *North Dallas Forty*, the steel workers in *The Deer Hunter*, are constantly hugging, throwing their arms around one another, even saying "I love you," as Bobby De Niro says to Christopher Walken at a key moment in this film. But there's no homoerotic undertone to this physicality; these men are simply secure enough in their manhood to celebrate their friendships. They're like ancient warriors.

The Deer Hunter is bookended by a wedding and a funeral. The wedding celebration, doubling as a good-bye party for the three young men who will soon be leaving for Vietnam, takes up nearly a third of this epic film and is the best wedding in movie history, better even than the nuptials in *The Godfather*. It is the heart of the movie. Set in an American Legion hall, the wedding segment hits all the right notes in capturing moments familiar to anyone who's been to a blue-collar reception—the ethnic dancing and singing, the heavy drinking, the fights between couples, the temporary acknowledgments of forbidden mutual attractions, the general deterioration of the evening until everyone is wrinkled, frazzled and flushed. You almost get a hangover just watching the proceedings.

Not that you can blame Michael, Nick, and Steven for getting hammered. After all, they're about to trade in their lunch buckets for K rations. The Vietnam War might have been controversial in other parts of the country, but it would never occur to Michael (De Niro), Nick (Walken), and Steven (John Savage) to avoid service; in fact, they've enlisted in the army and they hope to go where the action is the heaviest. But before they leave for Vietnam, there's time for one more deer hunt, during which the metaphysical Michael bags a buck with one shot.

"One shot. That's all that matters," Michael says.

His words take on an eerie resonance in Vietnam, when he and his buddies are taken captive by the North Vietnamese and forced to play Russian roulette for the gambling amusement of their captors. Eventually the three escape, but only the great Michael seems to survive with his whole self intact. Still, even Michael has a tough time when he returns to Pennsylvania as the conquering hero. How do you go back to bowling when you've been a Green Beret?

"I feel a lot of distance," Michael tells Linda (Meryl Streep), who used to be with Nick but obviously loves Michael. "I feel far away."

By this time the war in Vietnam is staggering to a chaotic close, but the violence isn't over. We'll say no more than this: If you think guys don't cry at the movies, you haven't seen the ending of *The Deer Hunter* with a real guy.

Die Hard

Rated R, 114 min., 1988
Director: John McTiernan
Screenplay: Jeb Stuart and Steven de Souza, based on the novel by Roderick Thorp
Starring: Bruce Willis, Alan Rickman, Bonnie Bedelia, Reginald Ve Johnson
Car chases: ★★★
Explosions: ★★★★
Fights: ★★★★
Gunplay: ★★★★
Male bonding: ★★★★
Memorable dialogue: ★★★★

Bruce Willis is a great actor.

It's quite possible that sentence has never appeared in print before, but real guys know it's the truth. Consider Willis as John McClane in *Die Hard*. He's a cynical and weary cop from New York who finds himself in a furious cage match in a Los Angeles skyscraper, going up against a team of terrorists who are armed with "missiles, automatic weapons, [and] enough plastic explosives to orbit Arnold Schwarzenegger," as McClane puts it.

And that's just it. If Schwarzenegger or Stallone had starred in *Die Hard*, it would have been just another ridiculous action movie, with the musclebound hero knocking around the bad guys as if they were some of the lesser Stooges. Willis, though, is regular guy–sized, and he has the ability to seem vulnerable and human in his movies, whether it's in great films such as *Pulp Fiction* or crap like *The Last Boy Scout*. Like Robert Mitchum or Humphrey Bogart, Bruce Willis is not pretty-boy handsome or theatrically impressive; he's just solid and good and believable.

I'll take Bruce Willis over that guy from *Shine* any day of the week.

In *Die Hard*, New York cop John McClane shows up at Nakatomi Plaza to spend Christmas with his estranged wife, Holly, who as director of corporate affairs has retaken her maiden name. Moments after McClane's arrival, the company's Christmas party is besieged by the erudite but cold-blooded Hans Gruber and his henchmen, who execute Nakatomi's CEO and announce they're taking everyone hostage until their demands are met. Gruber's so cool and sophisticated he's seen flipping through his Filofax even as his boys spray the air with gunfire. Only when he's truly riled does he resort to spouting German obscenities like some commandant from *Hogan's Heroes*.

Gruber is there for $600 million in cash and bonds, but he pretends to be an international terrorist as he demands the release of, among others, "The five imprisoned leaders of Liberty du Quebec, [and in] Sri Lanka, the nine members of the Asian Dawn." (When one of his own men looks at him quizzically, Gruber shrugs and says, "I read about them in *Time* magazine.") While scores of L.A. cops and FBI agents bumble around outside the plaza, McClane starts picking off Gruber's men one at a time, all the while engaging in spunky debate with the West German insaniac via walkie-talkie. Gruber mocks McClane's cowboy attitude, to which McClane responds, "Yippee, ki-yay, motherfucker."

Alan Rickman is so good as Hans, he should have won the Academy Award for Best Supporting Actor. Of course, he wasn't even nominated because the industry never recognizes action movies or comedies. That's because the industry is stupid.

While you're enjoying the performances of Willis and Rickman, and the great explosions and gunfights, look for a couple of minor but glaring goofs in continuity. Halfway through the movie, McClane's white T-shirt becomes dark—not from bloodstains; it just becomes a different color. And the cop who befriends McClane from the outside has a bleeding head wound that miraculously disappears, as if the cop is a cyborg or something.

No big deal. *Die Hard* is the first and best of all those movies pitting a lone hero in a closed environment against a mad terrorist. It was the film that made Bruce Willis a movie star, and for that all guys are grateful.

Diner

Rated R, 110 min., 1982
Director: Barry Levinson
Screenplay: Barry Levinson
Starring: Kevin Bacon, Mickey Rourke, Daniel Stern, Timothy Daly, Steve Guttenberg, Paul Reiser, Ellen Barkin
Car chases: **
Fights: **
Male bonding: ****
Memorable dialogue: ****

By the time most women reach their early twenties, they're ready for real life. Careers, mature relationships, their own apartments, separating the whites from the colors in the laundry basket, all that jazz.

Not guys. When guys are in their early twenties, they're still clinging desperately to the teen pleasures they've come to love. Responsibilities be damned! They want to spend their time chasing chicks, drinking too much beer, playing practical jokes, dropping in on Mom so she can do their laundry and make lunch for them—and most important of all, hanging out with their buddies until dawn as they argue about important things like music, football, and the hilarious stuff that happened in third grade.

Diner understands this perfectly, and that's why guys love it so much. The movie is basically a series of episodes illustrating the vast chasm between young men and young women in Baltimore, circa 1958. Eddie, Boogie, Shrevie, Fenwick, Billy, and Modell are a bunch of overgrown adolescents who spend nearly all their postmidnight hours hanging out at the local diner, shooting the shit with the casual humor of longtime friends who can talk about anything with one another.

"We've got a history," is the way Eddie puts it.

Nearly every one of the guys is facing a crisis of some kind. (Only Paul Reiser's Modell seems worry free, giving him time to comment from the sidelines on everyone else's trouble.) Womanizing Boogie (Mickey Rourke) has lost a big bet and is in deep with the local bookies. Fenwick the prankster (Kevin Bacon) is starting to drink before noon. Shrevie (Daniel Stern) is married to the crookedly lovely Beth (Ellen Barkin), but she might as well be from another planet as far as he's concerned. Billy (Timothy Daly) is in love with a woman who thinks of him as more of a friend, even though she's pregnant with his child. Eddie (Steve Guttenberg) is ready to call off his impending nuptials if his fiancée can't pass his sports-trivia quiz.

These miniplots are really just excuses for one great scene after another of the guys wrestling with looming adulthood. Here's Shrevie, standing outside the diner with Eddie late one night, attempting to explain the strange new world of married life.

"You know the big part of the problem? When we were dating, we spent most of our time talking about sex. Why couldn't I do it? Where could we do it? Were her parents going to be out so we could do it. Talking about being alone for a weekend. A whole night. You know. Everything was about getting sex or planning our wedding. Then when you're married . . . it's crazy. You can have it whenever you want. You wake up. She's there. You come home from work. She's there. So, all the sex-planning talk is over. And the wedding-planning talk. We can sit up here and bullshit the night away, but I can't have a five-minute conversation with Beth. But I'm not putting the blame on her. We've just got nothing to talk about."

Oh, man. Women might be disgusted by that monologue, but guys know exactly what Shrevie is talking about—even if they won't admit it. *Diner* is absolutely loaded with moments like that, whether the boys are arguing about who's going to finish a roast beef sandwich, or Boogie's chances of getting Carol Heathrow ("She's death!") to touch his member on their first date. The young cast of future stars is uniformly terrific, and director Barry Levinson's screenplay is like a handbook of Guy Talk. If you're a woman and you want to understand the secrets of men, watch this movie. In some ways, things really haven't changed very much since 1958.

Dumb and Dumber

Rated PG-13, 106 min., 1994
Director: Peter Farrelly
Screenplay: Peter Farrelly, Bennett Yellin, Bobby Farrelly
Starring: Jim Carrey, Jeff Daniels, Lauren Holly, Karen Duffy, Cam Neely
Fights: ****
Male bonding: ***
Memorable dialogue: ***
Nudity: **

Nothing in this world matters more to Jim Carrey than making us laugh. For proof of this, consider a fantasy sequence in *Dumb and Dumber* involving Carrey's idiotic Lloyd embracing the exquisite Lauren Holly, who is wearing a frilly little miniskirt (sigh). Even though Holly was the object of Carrey's affections in both the movie and real life at the time, Carrey doesn't hesitate to leer at the camera and then slowly hike up Holly's skirt, revealing her entire naked right buttock. What an ass! Carrey, I mean. Yet you have to laugh at his unbound determination to extract a chuckle at any expense.

(For those of you keeping score at home, this moment occurs at the 36-minute, 51-second mark of the movie. I offer this statistic only in the name of accurate research, not for any cheap titillation.)

Jim Carrey is the Jerry Lewis of our times, and either he makes you laugh or he doesn't. If he doesn't, you're probably a woman. I could have selected *The Mask* or one of the fine *Ace Ventura* movies for inclusion here, but *Dumb and Dumber* gets the nod because of a top supporting cast including Holly in the Priscilla Presley–*Naked Gun* babe-foil role; the underrated Jeff Daniels as Lloyd's buddy Harry; ex-VJ Karen Duffy, aka Duff, as a kidnapper with great lips; and hockey great Cam Neely as Sea Bass, a backwater bully who is somehow outsmarted by the astoundingly stupid Lloyd and Harry.

I've seen this movie four times, which means I've used up 424 minutes of my life laughing out loud at poop jokes and adolescent pranks—424 precious minutes that could have been spent volunteering in a soup kitchen or teaching a child to read. Thank God I made the right choice! Now, if you were offended by that little anecdote, don't watch this movie, because you'll really be put off by the scenes of a blind boy getting ripped off when he buys a dead parrot with a taped-on head ("I just thought he was really quiet!" the boy later moans), and the inadvertent assassination of a rare snow owl.

As I said, Carrey is shameless—and hilarious.

The plot, such as it is, has Lloyd and Harry driving from Providence, Rhode Island, to Aspen so they can return a lost briefcase to the beautiful, if slightly dim, Mary Swanson (Holly).

"[It's a place] where the beer flows like wine," Lloyd says of Aspen, reassuring the dubious Harry, who has expressed his reservations about going to California, where he apparently thinks Aspen is located.

These boys have lots of trouble with geography. Lost in Nebraska but thinking they're in Colorado, Lloyd surveys the endless flatland and moans, "John Denver was full of shit!"

Finally Lloyd and Harry do make it to Colorado, where they stumble into a ton of money and live it up for a few days while competing for Mary's affections. The slapstick fight scene between Daniels and Holly proves that a Jim Carrey movie can be fall-down funny even when Carrey is offscreen. It's also one of the many scenes in which the actors can barely keep a straight face—a tendency that used to be annoying in those crappy old Burt Reynolds movies but is actually sort of endearing here. Though the movie is called *Dumb and Dumber* and most of the jokes are aimed squarely below the belt, the actors are obviously talented and intelligent performers who recognize how difficult it is to make a truly hilarious movie. If you ask me, *Dumb and Dumber* should have been called *Funny and Funnier*, and I'm Leonard Maltin for *Entertainment Tonight*.*

Embrace of the Vampire

Not Rated, 93 min., 1995
Director: Anne Goursaud
Screenplay by: Halle Eaton, Nicole Coady, Rick Bitzelberger
Starring: Alyssa Milano, Martin Kemp, Charlotte Lewis, Rachel True, Jennifer Tilly
Drinking: ★★★
Explosions: ★★
Memorable dialogue: ★★
Nudity: ★★★★

As the fabulously talented actress Alyssa Milano matured into a fetching young woman on *Who's the Boss?*, young men across the country thought to themselves, Wouldn't it be cool if Alyssa one day starred in a vampire exploitation flick where she kept taking off her clothes and making out with someone like that babe from *The Golden Child?*

All right, so nobody thought of that exact fantasy—but it's a good one, isn't it? Amazingly enough, such a movie was actually made in 1995, and had it been given the proper advertising and distribution deal, I'm quite certain it could have grossed a $100 million on the horny male teen repeat business alone.

---

*Sorry, that last comment didn't really mean anything. It was just that for one brief shining moment, I wanted to know what it would feel like to be Leonard Maltin. And let me just tell you, I wasn't the least bit disappointed.

Embrace of the Vampire is one of those high-camp erotic thrillers that show up on Cinemax and The Movie Channel after midnight. The superstars of this type of movie include former *Playboy* Playmate of the Year Shannon Tweed; eternally preppy-looking Andrew Stevens; former *Charlie's Angel* Tanya Roberts; oft-troubled ex-golden boy Jan-Michael Vincent; and the balloon-breasted Amazons, Julie Strain and Lisa Boyle. It wasn't easy for me to pass over *Inner Sanctum 3* or *I Like to Play Games* as the representative selection from this unfairly overlooked genre, but there was no way I could keep *Embrace of the Vampire* off the list. Not when Alyssa Milano takes her clothes off five times in a ninety-minute film.

The plot, as if anyone cares, is about some tortured vampire guy from the past who keeps popping into the dreams of virginal college freshman Charlotte (Milano), who spends most of her waking hours fending off the advances of her horny boyfriend, Chris. She's so innocent she tells the boyfriend to turn around when she changes clothes—but of course the camera doesn't turn around, it stays focused on the naked Alyssa Milano. Eventually the vampire man starts pestering Charlotte in the daytime as well, spouting Shakespearean dialogue into her ear while she tries to pay attention in class. It's especially embarrassing for Charlotte when she talks back to the vampire man, because she's the only one who can see him.

All this weirdness causes a split between Charlotte and Chris, who seeks comfort in the arms of the always-busty Jennifer Tilly. I'm pretty sure Tilly is also a vampire—she has scary tattoos on her chest and she talks in Shakespearean clichés, too—but that doesn't really matter because Charlotte is now hanging out with a slutty lesbian photographer, played by Charlotte Lewis from *The Golden Child*. (It must have been confusing on the set, with one actress playing a character named Charlotte and the other having the name of Charlotte. "Now Charlotte, I want you to stand over there. No, not Charlotte, *Charlotte*.") Not since Susan Sarandon rolled around with Catherine Deneuve in *The Hunger* has there been such a sexy lesbian-vampire-makeout scene in the movies.

But wait, there's more. In one of Charlotte's dreams, she has a four-way with the lesbian slut photographer, the horny boyfriend, *and* the pretentious vampire man. Talk about great acting!

As any gal would tell you, *Embrace of the Vampire*, is, of course, trash. And as any guy would reply, "Yeah—and your point would be?"

Farewell, My Lovely

Rated R, 95 min., 1975
Director: Dick Richards
Screenplay: David Zelag Goodman, based on the novel by Raymond Chandler
Starring: Robert Mitchum, Charlotte Rampling, John Ireland, Sylvia Miles, Harry Dean Stanton, Jack O'Halloran, Sylvester Stallone
Fights: ****
Gunplay: ***
Memorable dialogue: ***
Nudity: **

Robert Mitchum is dead, but he's still about the third-toughest guy in Hollywood. He's almost a different species when you compare him to rail-thin stud boys such as Brad Pitt, William "Don't Call Me Billy" Baldwin,

and that Leonardo DiCaprio, who's skinnier than Kate Moss on a rice cake diet. Mitchum was a *man*, not some long-lashed cutie pie with gel in his hair and dark eyeliner. The gravel-voiced legend was in his fifties when he played Philip Marlowe in *Farewell, My Lovely,* and he looks his age and then some—but that's perfect for the role of a world-weary private eye who considers it a personal triumph if he gets through the day without getting shot at or beaten up.

This movie is what they call a film noir, a fancy term for "a movie with chicks who cheat on their husbands with tough guys who drink whiskey during the daytime while a saxophone wails on the soundtrack." We join Marlowe as he's on the trail of an underage girl who is spending too much time in dance halls, in the company of shady characters.

"[She was] an honor student, majoring in men," says Marlowe. "She got all As, but none of 'em on her report card."

After returning the ungrateful young floozy to her parents, Marlowe hooks up with an ex-con named Moose Malloy, who hires him to find the mysterious Velma, whom he hasn't heard from in seven years. "She's cute as lace pants, my Velma," Moose tells him.

From that moment on the plot gets more complicated than what you'd find in the average Guy Movie. Dead bodies turn up everywhere, and Marlowe becomes the prime suspect in the series of murders. (As is usually the case in cool detective movies, everyone on the force resents the private eye, with the exception of one decent cop who believes in him.) Mitchum's deadpan voice-over takes us through the twists and turns of the story, and the narration is filled with gems such as, "I was having some Chinese food when a dark shadow fell over my Chop Suey," and "I've got a hat, a coat, and a gun, that's it."

The hat may be even more integral to Mitchum than the gun. Nobody wears a hat like Mitchum. When Brad Pitt wears a hat in a movie, he looks like a ten-year-old boy trying on daddy's chapeau.

Charlotte Rampling plays a character who is the femme fatale, a fancy term for "the good-looking chick who has sex with the leading man ten minutes after she meets him." She's wickedly attractive and not at all shy about what she wants; as Marlowe puts it, "She was giving me the kind of look I could feel in my hip pocket."

Also livening up the action is a very young Sylvester Stallone as a low-level bad guy who's in love with a hooker who works for a big fat mean madam—an unholy triangle that leads to much bloodshed. Marlowe also has an encounter with the big fat mean madam, who slaps him but good—and gets decked in return.

Farewell, My Lovely has a nifty plot with a semi-surprise of an ending, but that's not nearly as important as the richly textured masculinity of Robert Mitchum, who is to Guy Movies what Joe DiMaggio is to baseball—an all-time great who made it look easy.

Fast Times at Ridgemont High

Rated R, 92 min., 1982
Director: Amy Heckerling
Screenplay: Cameron Crowe, based on his book
Starring: Judge Reinhold, Phoebe Cates, Jennifer Jason Leigh, Brian
 Backer, Ray Walston, Sean Penn, Eric Stoltz, Forest Whitaker
Car chases: ***
Male bonding: **
Memorable dialogue: ****
Nudity: ****

Even if this wasn't one of the most hilarious movies of the 1980s, it would be on this list solely because of the scene where Judge Reinhold goes into the bathroom and fantasizes about Phoebe Cates emerging from the swimming pool in slow motion to the sounds of "Moving in Stereo" by the Cars, and she unsnaps the top of her red bikini and suddenly she really is moving in stereo if you know what I mean, and big stupid Judge Reinhold in his big stupid pirate restaurant outfit gets to kiss a topless Phoebe Cates.

Judge Reinhold—the luckiest man on the face of the Earth.

There's also the scene where Jennifer Jason Leigh has premature teenage sex in the changing room next to the pool while Jackson Browne sings "Somebody's Baby." That's pretty good, too. Jennifer Jason Leigh is so cute and so naked.

Oh, but there's so much more to *Fast Times*. Loosely based on Cameron

Crowe's account of the year he went undercover as a student at Claremont High in San Diego, this is a breezy, sexy, joyous video time capsule of a teen comedy that perfectly captures the relatively carefree days of the early 1980s, before AIDS and Reaganomics and the success of Michael Jackson ruined everything. Although the two unknown guys who played the lead horny male teens were forgettably bland, *Fast Times* was fueled by a peppy soundtrack from the Go-Go's, Tom Petty, and Jimmy Buffet, among others, and some of the best character leads of any film of its time, from Sean Penn's toasted surfer Spicoli to Ray Walston's dead-perfect portrayal of the legendary Mr. Hand.

At one point Mr. Hand's history class is interrupted when Spicoli orders a large double cheese from Mr. Pizza Guy.

"Am I hallucinating here?" says Mr. Hand. "Just what in the hell do you think you're doing?"

"Learning about Cuba, having some food," deadpans Spicoli.

Ms. Cates turns in a fine performance as Linda Barrett, counseling sweet little Stacey on the ways of the world, including a graphic practice fellatio session on a carrot stick. And when Stacey mopes because she hasn't heard from stereo salesman Ron Johnson, who deflowered her at "the Point," Linda puts it in perspective: "Stacey, what does it matter? He's a stereo salesman, what'd you want to do, marry him? Have kids with him? Have this guy come home, fifty years old and bald, he'd have that little Pacific Stereo sign on?"

Fast Times is to movie careers what Notre Dame is to the NFL—a veritable launchpad. In addition to the aforementioned Cates, Reinhold, Penn, et al., look for these familiar faces:

*Nicolas Cage, then known as Nicolas Coppola, walks by for three seconds in the parking lot of Ridgemont High. In the credits he's listed as "Brad's Bud."

*Forest Whitaker is the hulking football star whose car gets trashed.

*Eric Stoltz and Anthony Edwards play Spicoli's stoner buddies.

Nancy Wilson of Heart also makes a cameo, as the beautiful blonde in the car who laughs at Reinhold in his pirate outfit. The reason she's in the movie is she's married to Cameron Crowe, who went on to direct *Say Anything*, which is kind of a Gal Movie because it has that scene with John Cusack holding up the boom box that's playing "In Your Eyes" while Ione Skye pretends to ignore him from her bedroom. Ione Skye is the daughter of Donovan, who had a big hit with "Atlantis." Hail Atlantis!

The Top Ten Naked-Babe Moments in Movie History

With the exception of a few cheesy black-and-white films from the 1950s and 1960s starring pasty blondes with heaving bosoms, actresses really didn't start taking off their clothes in films until the 1970s.

This is why we refer to that period as the Golden Age of Cinema.

There are only a few actresses working today who haven't taken off their clothes for their art. Even the most pristine stars have done it. Go ahead, try to name an actress who hasn't done nude.

Meryl Streep, you say? Nope. She bared a breast in *Silkwood.*

Gwyneth Paltrow? Yeah she's classy and all, but she's also topless in *Flesh and Bone* and in *Shakespeare in Love,* which of course is a film I didn't see because it has the word "Shakespeare" in the title.

What about America's sweetheart, Meg Ryan? Well, she was quite topless in *The Doors.*

Michelle Pfeiffer? She was in the buff when she walked across the hallway, much to Jeff Goldblum's surprise, in *Into the Night.*

Of the hundreds of naked-actress scenes filmed in the last couple of decades, here are ten of the greatest:

10. Susan Sarandon makes out with Catherine Deneuve in *The Hunger.*

9. JoBeth Williams gets naked in the school hallway in *Teachers.* (Not that there's any great need to see JoBeth Williams naked, but there's something to be said for a grown woman who makes a point by shedding her clothes in a high school hallway.)

8. Phoebe Cates takes the world's longest shower in *Paradise.*

7. Sharon Stone uncrosses her legs in *Basic Instinct.*

6. Mia Sara, best known as Sloan Peterson in *Ferris Bueller's Day Off,* goes skinny-dipping in *Blue Night, Black Moon.*

5. Teri Hatcher takes off her shirt in *The Cool Surface,* much to the delight of *Terminator 2* bad guy Robert Patrick.

4. Emma Thompson realizes Hugh Grant is not married and in fact loves her, in *Sense and Sensibility.* Ah, just kidding! Emma Thompson's best moment as an actress comes in *The Tall Guy,* when she has naked sex on the piano with Jeff Goldblum. Tell you what, I'll include that as one my selections, just to prove I can appreciate fine acting.

3. Elizabeth Berkley, previously known for her role in the high school series *Saved by the Bell,* lap dances in *Showgirls.*

2. Rosanna Arquette in, like, ten different movies.

1. Phoebe Cates emerges from the swimming pool in *Fast Times at Ridgemont High.*

Ferris Bueller's Day Off

Rated PG-13, 103 min., 1986
Director: John Hughes
Screenplay: John Hughes
Starring: Matthew Broderick, Mia Sara, Jeffrey Jones, Alan Ruck, Jennifer Grey
Car chases: ★★★
Male bonding: ★★★★
Memorable dialogue: ★★★★

The world according to Ferris Bueller: "Life moves pretty fast. You don't stop and look around once in a while, you might miss it."

Ferris (Matthew Broderick, who looks exactly the same now as he did in 1986) addresses the audience as he says this. He often talks to us as the movie goes along, inviting us along for the ride on this near-perfect comedy from the 1980s Philosopher King of Teen Comedy, Mr. John Hughes (*clap-clap-clap-clap*).

For the ninth time in his senior year of high school, Ferris is ditching class so he can spend a glorious spring day in Chicago with his preternaturally glum best friend, Cameron (Alan Ruck), and his astonishingly pretty girlfriend, Sloan (Mia Sara). Ferris is a self-centered, arrogant little shit who's nearly as smart as he thinks he is, and he's got the entire high school in the palm of his hand—much to the dismay of the uptight "Edward R. Rooney, dean of students," who is willing to do anything to prove Ferris isn't really seriously ill, as everyone seems to believe. He's just pulling another fast one.

Here's Jeffrey Jones as the cliché-spouting Dean Rooney, lecturing Ferris's sweet but easily duped mom: "Wake up and smell the coffee, Mrs. Bueller, it's a fool's paradise, he is just leading you down the primrose path."

Is it any wonder Ferris can stay a step ahead of a doofus like that?

Of much bigger concern to Ferris is his jealous little sister, Jeannie, played by Jennifer Grey before she had the nose job. Jeannie's efforts to bust Ferris backfire and land her at the police station, where she encounters none other than Charlie Sheen in a cameo as a drugged-out loser. (What acting!)

"You wear too much eye makeup," Sheen says. "My sister wears too much eye makeup. People thinks she's a whore."

Meanwhile, Ferris and Co. are enjoying a tour guide's view of Chicago, taking in a few innings of a Cubs game, enjoying the view from the Sears

Tower, joining a children's field trip at the Art Institute, even scamming their way into a fine lunch at the snooty Chez Luis when Ferris masquerades as "Abe Froman, the sausage king of Chicago."* At nearly every turn they *almost* get busted, but they always manage to escape and move on to the next adventure. Before the day is over, Ferris will find himself atop a parade float, lip-synching to "Twist and Shout" as thousands dance and sing along.

Although there's an underlying serious motive behind all the fun, *Ferris* isn't nearly as angst-ridden as most of Hughes's other teen classics. It's a romp. The adults are like characters in a Charlie Brown cartoon—you almost expect to hear "Mwahm-mwahm-mwahm" when they talk—and the scams Ferris pulls would never work in the real world, but we're too busy laughing to care. There's a little bit of Ferris Bueller in every guy—even though 99 percent of us will never get within a hundred yards of someone as good-looking as Mia Sara.

The Godfather (Epic Version)

Rated R, 386 min., 1981 (based on the films released in 1972 and 1974)
Director: Francis Ford Coppola
Screenplay: Francis Ford Coppola and Mario Puzo, based on the novel by Puzo
Starring: Al Pacino, Robert De Niro, Marlon Brando, James Caan, Robert Duvall, Diane Keaton, John Cazale, Talia Shire
Drinking: **
Gunplay: ****
Male bonding: ****
Memorable dialogue: ****
Nudity: **

Clemenza is in the basement of his home with young Michael Corleone, schooling him on the nuances of how to behave after you've whacked a rival mob boss and a corrupt police captain who's busted your jaw.

"They're going to be staring at your face, Mike," he says. "So walk out of the place real fast, but you don't run. Don't look nobody directly in the eye, but you don't look away either. Ah, they're going to be scared shitless of you, so don't worry about nuthin'."

---

*Historical footnote: During the height of the Ken Starr hearings, a *New York Times* reporter asked Kathleen Willey's twenty-five-year-old son what he did for a living. The young man's Bueller-inspired reply: "I'm the sausage king of Chicago."

As Michael points the emptied gun at an unseen target, the meatball-shaped Clemenza awkwardly tries to tell Michael how much he cares for him.

"You know, Mike, we was all proud of you, being a hero and all. Your father too."

Michael squeezes the trigger, his eyes cold and dead and determined. He's not a war hero anymore. He's stepping into the dark side of the business.

I was on the sofa late one night, clicking around the dial, when I happened upon that scene from *The Godfather*. Even though I own *The Godfather* parts I and II on videotape—as well as the Epic Version, which contains extra scenes in a compilation put together by Coppola himself—I stopped clicking.

You have to understand, *The Godfather* is literally the godfather of Guy Movies. If you were to ask a hundred guys to pick just one movie they'd have to watch once a month for the rest of their lives, at least seventy would pick *The Godfather*. (The rest would probably go with an XXX film such as *Tool of the Nile* or *Cape Rear*.)

Guys know this movie inside out. Every scene. Hyman Roth sharing his birthday cake with his fellow crooks as they talk about slicing up profits in Cuba. Hollywood mogul Jack Woltz waking up to find a horse's head in his bed. Sonny doing that macabre dance of death in the causeway, his body riddled with one hundred bullets. The Senate hearings probing the finances of Michael Corleone and his family. The gruesome demise of Luca Brasi. Don Corleone picking out fruit in the moments before he is gunned down, his weakest son unable to do anything about it. Moe Green getting it right in the eye!

So there I was on the sofa, clicker by my side, getting all tensed up as I watched Michael frantically search the bathroom of the Italian restaurant for the gun that had been planted there, then watching with antici-

---

*Note: *The Godfather III* isn't included here because it's a mediocre shadow of the original two—not a horrible movie but kinda stupid. Pacino has that butch crew cut, and you have to contend with that poor untrained Sofia Coppola (filling in for Winona Ryder, who was too pale and tired to take on the role she'd been signed to do), as the love interest of Andy Garcia in his crinkly black leather jacket. Also hanging around is the always silly George Hamilton, who is there only because they were too cheap to pay Duvall an extra couple of million. Having George Hamilton fill in for Robert Duvall would be like having David Hasselhoff play Mad Max's long-lost brother in a sequel to *Beyond Thunderdome*. That's just plain *wrong*.

pation as he walked quickly into the restaurant, sat back down at his table, and *pop-pop!* Sterling Hayden gurgles for breath, his napkin still tucked under his chin as the blood comes bubbling up.

What a great death scene. Nobody gurgles like Sterling Hayden. I was hooked once again. I knew I'd watch *The Godfather* till the credits rolled.

Citizen Kane is routinely voted the greatest American film of all time. That's because those sissy critics don't have the balls to vote for *The Godfather.*

If I ever find a woman who feels the same way about *The Godfather* as my male friends do, I'm going to marry her.

Goldfinger

Rated PG, 117 min., 1964
Director: Guy Hamilton
Screenplay: Richard Maibaum and Paul Dehn
Starring: Sean Connery, Gert Frobe, Honor Blackman, Bernard Lee
Drinking: ****
Fights: ***
Gunplay: ***
Memorable dialogue: ***

His name was finger. Goldfinger.

He was the Babe Ruth of modern movie bad guys. Thirty years before our multiplex screens were crawling with the urbane Eurotrash villains of the *Die Hard* and *Lethal Weapon* series and the hammy caricatures of the *Batman* movies, the German actor Gert Frobe practically created the prototype with his icy portrayal of a loopy genius who wants to rule the world through a Byzantine scheme so ridiculous and evil that it . . . just . . . might . . . work!

If not for a fellow named Bond, that is.

There's no way you can't include a James Bond movie in a list of the greatest guy flicks of all time—and there's no way it can be anything but a Sean Connery Bond movie. What, you thought I was going to pay tribute to George freakin' Lazenby, or that pencil-necked guy from *Remington Steele?* I don't think so.

Released in 1964, *Goldfinger* is as much of a period piece as any Dickensian flick. Guzzling his famous "shaken, not stirred" martinis and grabbing any babe who gets within arm's reach (in just the first fifteen minutes of the movie, Bond beds three Barbie-looking young things),

James Bond is like a trim Kennedy, so politically incorrect only a humorless prude would be offended by him. Even before the classic opening credit sequence featuring the brassy title tune by Shirley Bassey ("Missssssssssssssster Goldfinger, he's the man, the man with the Midas touch!"), Bond finds himself in the embrace of a wet naked gal who feels the sharp edge of his gun and complains, "Why do you always have to wear that thing?"

"I have a slight inferiority complex," replies James with his patented raised eyebrow, in the first of a dozen double entendres that must have seemed awfully racy in 1964. (Bond also reveals himself to be a man unwilling to accept the cultural heroes of the younger generation when he complains to another conquest that drinking Dom Pérignon at a temperature over 38 degrees is "as unacceptable as listening to the Beatles without earmuffs." Oh, James.)

Bond's indiscretion with Goldfinger's girlfriend ends badly, with the Korean icebox Odd Job knocking Bond cold with a blow to the neck. The girlfriend killed in spectacular fashion when she is spray-painted gold from head to toe, causing her skin to suffocate. Bond's supervisor, the ever-detached M, threatens to pull Bond off the job and replace him with the unseen Agent 008 if Bond can't get it together, but 007 promises he'll keep his emotions to himself and find out what Goldfinger's Operation Grand Slam is all about. Turns out Goldfinger wants to break into Ft. Knox—not to steal the gold, but to blast it with a nuclear bomb so it's rendered radioactive for exactly fifty-eight years, thus increasing the value of Goldfinger's own gold "tenfold, at least." Bond congratulates Goldfinger on the plan, but of course he's going to do everything in his power to thwart the chuckling madman. Along the way, Bond meets Goldfinger's "personal pilot," the incredibly named Pussy Galore. ("I must be dreaming," Bond says when she tells him her name.)

The part of Pussy is played by the splendid Honor Blackman, one of the many sterling beauties who made a big splash as a Bond Girl but did little of note after that. Then again, what did Gert Frobe or the guy who played Odd Job ever do?

That's all right, though, because they contributed enough to the history of cinema with their appearances in this, the best Bond movie of them all. Of course, as good as the villains and supporting babes are, *Goldfinger* belongs to Sean Connery, who was born to be Bond. Every schlub who's ever approached a bartender or donned a tuxedo has, at least for a moment, pretended he's Bond, James Bond. Only Connery can actually pull it off, but for the rest of us, it's nice to have the role model.

Goodfellas

Rated R, 146 min., 1990
Director: Martin Scorsese
Screenplay: Nicholas Pileggi and Martin Scorsese, based on Pileggi's book
  WiseGuy
Starring: Ray Liotta, Robert De Niro, Joe Pesci, Lorraine Bracco, Paul
  Sorvino
Drinking: ****
Fights: ****
Gunplay: ***
Male bonding: ****
Memorable dialogue: ****

    Goodfellas is about the guys in the trenches who work for the upper
echelon mob types we saw in *The Godfather.* A mix of Irish, Jewish, and
Italian heritage, these midlevel crooks know they'll never get officially
"made" by the outfit because their lineage isn't 100 percent linked to the
old country.

    "Real greaseball stuff," is the way Henry Hill sums it up. Henry (Ray Li-
otta) is a likable, efficient career criminal who has dropped out of school
at an early age to pursue "the life" under the wing of local mob captain
Paul Cicero (Paul Sorvino). He looks up to wiseguys like Jimmy Conway
(Robert De Niro), a thief and killer who loves to spread tips around when
he's celebrating at the end of another long and violent day. "The bartender
got a hundred just for keeping the ice cubes cold," Henry says.

    Director Martin Scorsese is the undisputed king of Guy Movies, from

Mean Streets and *Taxi Driver* to *Raging Bull* and *Casino*. There simply isn't room for all of Scorsese's work in this book—although it'd be fine by me if we just plowed into the Gal Movie section with reviews of a half-dozen of his flicks—but we must pay tribute to *Goodfellas*, a charter entrant in the Guy Movie Hall of Fame.

How great is Scorsese? Put it this way—would you even *want* to see a movie starring Ray Liotta, Lorraine Bracco, and Joe Pesci if anyone else were directing them? Please. But in *Goodfellas* they're all outstanding, as of course are De Niro and Sorvino. As real-life mobster-turned-rat Henry Hill, Liotta looks like a sweaty raccoon as he plunges deep into cocaine addiction and desperation, knowing that if the cops don't get him, one of his fellow mobsters will.

Not that he ever expected it to turn out that way. In the early years, Henry, Jimmy, and Tommy DeVito (Pesci) ruled their neighborhood through sheer intimidation. "We were like movie stars with muscle, we had it all," Henry says. This is best illustrated through the famous, unbroken shot of Henry and Karen entering the Copacabana through the kitchen, winding their way to the front of the club where a table has been created just for them.

"What do you do?" Karen asks, looking at Henry with a mixture of fear and awe.

"I'm in construction," Henry replies.

Soon we have scenes of birthday parties and barbecues, interspersed with hits and hijackings. The goodfellas go about their business like any other working stiffs—only their business includes turning quite a few people into stiffs, often because of Tommy's legendary temper. When guys recite their favorite lines from *Goodfellas*, they usually recall Tommy's mock anger at Henry—"Like I'm a clown, I amuse you, I make you laugh? I'm here to fucking amuse you?"—but I prefer the scene in which the boys visit Tommy's mother (played by Scorsese's mom) in the middle of the night to borrow a carving knife, while the barely breathing Billy Batts is in the trunk of their car.

"Why don't you get yourself a nice girl?" says Tommy's mother.

"I get a nice one almost every night, Mom," replies Tommy. He also explains he needs to borrow the knife to cut away the hoof of a deer caught in the grill of his car. "Otherwise, it's a sin, you know, to leave it there."

Authentic in every touch, shockingly violent at times, *Goodfellas* is also filled with more genuine laughs than most comedies. It's so damn good I completely forgive Scorsese for making *The Age of Innocence*, which I'm sure he did just to impress some chick anyway.

The Great Escape

Not rated, 168 min., 1963
Director: John Sturges
Screenplay: James Clavell and W. R. Burnett, based on the book by Paul
   Brickhill
Starring: Steve McQueen, James Garner, Richard Attenborough, Charles
   Bronson, James Coburn, Donald Pleasance
Drinking: **
Gunplay: ***
Male bonding: ****
Memorable dialogue: ****

The Great Escape is the movie version of an all-boys tree house with a
big sign hanging at the entrance: No Girls Allowed. This classic World
War II adventure movie has a running time of nearly three hours, but
there's not a woman in sight, not even as window dressing. It's pure
testosterone from start to finish.

Director John Sturges, who also helmed *The Magnificent Seven*, understands the utter guyness of this movie. The action is set in a German
prison camp and the villains are Nazis and Third Reich officers, but that's
no reason for them to speak German! German-accented English is good
enough. That way the viewer can put his feet up without worrying about
his toes obscuring any subtitles.

The Great Escape, based on a true story, stars Richard Attenborough as
the leader of a multinational band of prisoners holed up in a supposedly
escape-proof prison camp.

"It is the sworn duty of all officers to escape," he says to the understanding commandant of the camp, and sure enough, a number of the
boys try to sneak out on the very first day. James Coburn, sporting an unbelievably bad Australian accent, tries to hitch a ride on a truck loaded
with trees, while Steve McQueen tests the limits of the barbed wire
fence—an act that lands him in "the cooler," where he chips away the
time by bouncing a ball off the concrete wall and into his American baseball glove.

"Give up your hopeless attempts to escape!" says the commandant,
who seems more forgiving than a real German officer might have been at
the height of global warfare.

These weak little attempts are really nothing more than diversions, as
the boys work on an elaborate master plan designed to spring more than
two hundred men at once. Each of our heroes has a particular skill, and is
nicknamed accordingly. James Garner, for example, is the Scrounger be-

cause he can get you just about any kind of machine part you want, while Donald Pleasance is the Forger, so named for his ability to fabricate documents. The men come up with an ingenious plan for digging a 350-foot tunnel that should take them at least fifty feet into the woods surrounding the camp. (Whether it's *The Shawshank Redemption* or *The Great Escape*, the bad guys never consider posting a few guards just *outside* the walls. Might save them a lot of headaches.) But even if they make it out of the camp, it's unlikely they'll ever flee Germany without getting recaptured or shot on sight. Nevertheless, they will try to escape, because they are men, they are soldiers, they are action stars in a big Hollywood movie!

You get so worked up watching *The Great Escape* you want to go back and fight World War II all over again. The Americans, Brits, Aussies, and Scots are such spirited freedom-loving rogues, while the Germans are such cold bastards. When Steve McQueen is riding his motorcycle through the German countryside while dozens of Nazis give chase, you root so hard for him you can't stay on the sofa. Go, Steve, go! Get out of there and come back to America, so you can meet Ali McGraw and lots of other excellent American babes!

With all the crappy remakes oozing out of Hollywood every year, I'm surprised no studio has attempted to retry *The Great Escape* with the likes of Stallone, Ford, Seagal, and Van Damme. (It might be too costly to even attempt such a multistar epic.) Maybe it's better that they don't try, because it would be difficult if not impossible to match the original.

Heat

Rated R, 179 min., 1995
Director: Michael Mann
Screenplay: Michael Mann
Starring: Al Pacino, Robert De Niro, Val Kilmer, Tom Sizemore, Ashley Judd, Amy Brenneman, Natalie Portman, Jon Voight, Mykelti Williamson, Dennis Haysbert
Car chases: ★★★★
Drinking: ★★★
Explosions: ★★★★
Gunplay: ★★★★
Memorable dialogue: ★★★★

If you can't be Sammy Sosa when you grow up, the next best thing would be to star in a movie like *Heat*. Filmed in cool tones of blues and blacks and silvers, pulsating with a macho soundtrack, this is the ultimate cops-and-robbers flick, filled with great dialogue, amazing action sequences, and multiple opportunities for the lead actors to fire realistic guns, toss around much larger stuntmen, and hop into bed with great women such as Amy Brenneman and Ashley Judd.

Robert De Niro is Neil McCauley, the leader of a sophisticated ring of thieves that includes Val Kilmer as a ponytailed sharpshooter with a screwed-up personal life and Tom Sizemore as one bad barrel-chested S.O.B. On the other side of the law we have Al Pacino as Vincent Hanna, a veteran cop who is about to lose his third wife because he spends all his time tracking the bad guys. Coming home late one night to his pissed-off spouse, Vincent wearily says, "I got three dead bodies off Venice Boulevard, Justine, I'm sorry if the goddamn chicken got overcooked."

Pacino is over the edge throughout the movie, screaming with such intensity ("Gimme all you got! *Gimme all you got!*") that the veins in his forehead look like they'll explode. They probably had a production assistant standing by with a bottle of Extra Strength Tylenol for Mr. Pacino after every scene. In contrast, De Niro is quiet and civilized most of the time, but when he snaps, he really snaps. Double-crossed by a slimy business executive, he calls the exec at work and says in a chilling tone, "What am I doing? I am talking to an empty telephone, because there is a dead man on the other end of this fucking line."

There will be a lot of dead men splayed about before *Heat* reaches its conclusion, but this isn't just a quality thriller with nifty kills, it's a literate piece of work about good vs. evil and all that shit. De Niro and Pacino dominate this film in alternating scenes, but they don't appear together onscreen until ninety minutes into the action. In a tense, riveting scene, Vincent tries to talk Neil out of pulling any more heists.

"I do what I do best," says Neil. "I take scores."

"So you never wanted a regular-type life?" asks Vincent.

"What the fuck is that, barbecues and ballgames?" replies Neil.

The truth is, neither one of these men could do anything else. In a perverse sort of way, they need each other.

There are a number of scenes in *Heat* that'll stay burned in your memory long after the movie is over, but the outstanding highlight is the twelve-minute robbery and shootout. Containing a minimum of dialogue, the action starts with a bank holdup and spreads out over several blocks of Los Angeles in broad daylight. I've seen it a half-dozen times and I still can't figure out how they choreographed the thing. It feels like a documentary filmed with about ten cameras.

De Niro and Pacino carry this nearly three-hour epic, but they have plenty of help from a huge and hugely talented cast. You go about twelve-deep in the credits and you're still finding names of actors who have starred in major movies.

Heat did pretty well at the box office but it should have been a much bigger hit. We give the movie its just due here as a charter entrant in the Guy Movie Hall of Fame.

What Becomes an Action Hero Most?

by Laurie Viera

Ever wonder why your typical action hero can't seem to hold onto a woman? It doesn't matter whether it's Sly, Jean-Claude, Bruce, or Ah-nold. As long as they adhere to the following rules, they're sure to make most women run to the nearest exit.

- *Poor grooming.* This ranges from blood- and debris-stained clothing to unwashed bodies. A shave is simply out of the question. The stressful pace of keeping up a steady body count precludes such niceties.
- *Poor or nonexistent ability to maintain a meaningful relationship.* This varies from Nicolas Cage's enforced separations from his *Con Air* bride, first through military service, then through incarceration—something he could have avoided in the first few minutes of the film if he'd only had enough brains to get in the car and drive away—to Bruce Willis's record-breaking estrangement from wife Bonnie Bedelia in the *Die Hard* franchise. In the last installment, someone finally told him to pick up the phone and call her. Big duh!
- *Poor vocabulary.* These guys are just too busy oiling their guns and becoming demolitions experts to catch up on their reading.
- *Poor foreign relations.* When the good guys are Americans, their terrorist foes almost always speak English as a second language. And thus these leading men do much to nurture good old American xenophobia, a word they probably wouldn't understand anyway.

Henry: Portrait of a Serial Killer

Not Rated, 90 min., 1986
Director: John McNaughton
Screenplay: Richard Fire and John McNaughton
Starring: Michael Rooker, Tracy Arnold, Tom Towles
Drinking: ***
Fights: ****
Memorable dialogue: ***
Nudity: **

So you want to watch a movie about a serial killer? *Friday the 13th* and all the sequels are cartoons. *A Nightmare on Elm Street* is for wimps. *Halloween* is pretty cool but it's about as realistic as your chances of scoring with Jamie Lee Curtis. *Scream* is sly fun, but it's never to be taken seriously. If you've got the guts to absorb an unrelenting, shockingly realistic film about a beast who kills as often as most human beings brush their teeth, rent *Henry: Portrait of a Serial Killer.* Just don't plan on sleeping much that night.

Filmed by John McNaughton (who went on to make *Mad Dog and Glory* and *Sex, Drugs, Rock & Roll*) on the streets of Chicago in 1986, *Henry* lingered in ratings limbo for three years before the MPAA bluenoses finally threw up their hands and said, "We give up." They were freaked out by *Henry* because it has the look and feel of a documentary, rather than some stylized bloodfest influenced by MTV. From the opening image of a naked corpse lying in a field to the stunning final shot of Henry disposing of his last victim, there's never a moment when the action feels contrived or glamorized. It's almost as if the camera just happens to be there to capture the everyday doings of a man who lives to kill.

In a story loosely based on the confessions of real-life serial killer Henry Lucas, Henry (Michael Rooker) is an ex-con living in a rundown apartment with Ottis (Tom Towles), a perverted buddy from prison, and Ottis's teenage sister Becky (Tracy Arnold), who has returned to Chicago to escape a bad marriage, a daughter she can't take care of, and a "career" as a topless dancer. The unholy trio spend their days working at odd jobs, and their nights sitting around a fold-up table in the kitchen, eating lousy dinners and quaffing cans of Old Style beer. When Becky learns that Henry was in prison for killing his mother because mom used to make Henry wear a dress and watch her have sex with a variety of men, Becky is intrigued; suddenly Henry seems like a tortured figure of mystery and passion. Besides, her only other romantic possibility seems to be brother Ottis, who makes a move on every man, woman, and boy he happens upon.

The twisted romance between Becky and Henry doesn't have much time to develop because Henry would rather concentrate on his hobby, which is killing people, seemingly at random and without provocation. At first we see only the bloodied corpses he has left in his wake, as the soundtrack swells with the horrific noises made by the victims in their final moments. When Ottis joins Henry on his killing spree, we're witness to the acts themselves—brutal episodes of senseless destruction, including a sick sequence where Henry and Ottis videotape themselves wiping out a husband, wife, and their teenage son.

There are a few moments of levity, as when a cashier says to Henry, "How about those Bears?" and Henry gives him the evil eye and says, "Fuck the Bears." But then again, you don't expect a lot of laughs from a movie called *Henry: Portrait of a Serial Killer*.

High Plains Drifter

Rated R, 105 min., 1973
Director: Clint Eastwood
Screenplay: Ernest Tidyman
Starring: Clint Eastwood, Verna Bloom
Drinking: ****
Fights: ***
Gunplay: ****
Male bonding: ***
Memorable dialogue: ***

Ask someone to name a spaghetti Western, and *The Good, the Bad and the Ugly* is usually the title that'll come to mind. But that movie sucks. It's nearly three hours long, and it has that annoying music—not to mention really bad dubbing and some lousy acting. *High Plains Drifter*, once again starring Eastwood as the Man with No Name, is much the superior film, more macho and chilling than any of the earlier efforts. It's a horror Western, is what it is.

The action begins when "The Stranger," as director Eastwood refers to himself in the credits, rides into the mining town of Lago, his sombrero tilted over his face as he disregards the gawking citizenry. He enters a dark saloon populated with unsavory characters, who stare at him as if he's Clint Eastwood or something.

The Stranger's order: "Beer. And a bottle." All he wants to do is drink his suds and whiskey in peace, maybe grab a warm bath, and be on his way. Yeah right. He's not even halfway through the beer when one of the

local toughs regards him with disdain and says, "Flea-bitten range bums don't usually stop in Lago."

Uh-oh.

The local tough and a couple of his honchos attempt to ambush the Stranger in a barber shop, but they're blown to bloody bits by the stoic gunman, who seems more upset about his shave being interrupted than the three corpses he's left in his wake. Spurs a-janglin', he walks away, leaving the townsfolk to clean up his mess, but he doesn't take more than a few steps before a brassy blonde knocks into him and picks a fight, telling him he has "the manners of a goat."

Uh-oh.

The Stranger takes her by the arm and tosses her into the hay of a nearby barn, and forces himself on her—though she seems to get into it after a couple of minutes.

So the guy's been in town for what, fifteen minutes, and he's already killed three men and forced himself on one semireluctant woman. Talk about an entrance!

Guys know we can't act like the Stranger in the real world; we'd be locked up, and rightly so. Still, he appeals to the hidden, unshaven, cigar-chomping, gun-slinging beast in all of us. The antihero, if you will.

High Plains Drifter aims to be more than another shoot-'em-up, as things get hazy and mysterious after the Stranger's big bang of an introduction. Turns out the town of Lago has a deep, dark secret—and the Stranger is the key to unlocking that horrible memory.

First, though, he enjoys his reign as the king of the town. He grabs all the free whiskey, cigars, guns, leather products, and women he wants, and he instructs the townsfolk to participate in some bizarre rituals in preparation for an anticipated showdown with some evil killers who have just been released from prison. The Stranger even helps himself to the local hotel owner's wife, who despises him—until they go to bed. By the next morning she's humming away contentedly, combing her hair and gazing at him with dreamy eyes as she tells him, "Mister, whatever you say is fine with me."

The Man with No Name really does have a name in *High Plains*

Drifter—a fact revealed after the final gun battle, when Clint rides out of town and literally disappears into the haze so he could go back to playing Dirty Harry Callahan, a guy who didn't make the list of our top fifty Guy Movies only because he's really just the Stranger with a clean shave, a bigger handgun, and a car. He even kept the cowboy boots.

How to Murder Your Wife

Unrated, 118 min., 1964
Director: Richard Quine
Screenplay: George Axelrod
Starring: Jack Lemmon, Virna Lisi, Terry-Thomas, Eddie Mayehoff, Claire Trevor
Drinking: ****
Gunplay: **
Male bonding: ****
Memorable dialogue: ****

No one would have the guts to remake this movie in the 1990s, and it's just as well because the original is near perfect in every way. Jack Lemmon, less twitchy and more lecherous than usual, is Stanley Ford, a dashing thirty-seven-year-old bachelor who is the author of the wildly popular comic strip *Bash Brannigan: Secret Agent*, which appears in 463 newspapers nationwide. We learn about Stanley's world from Terry-Thomas, who addresses the camera directly as he introduces himself as "Charles, Mr. Ford's man," and leads us on a tour of Stanley's posh and very manly Manhattan town house.

"Notice the complete absence of the so-called woman's touch," says Charles as he gathers the high heels left behind by Stanley's latest conquest. "In fact, [this is] the sort of place you could have had, if only you'd had the sense *not* to get married."

Indeed, Stanley does seem to have it made, especially in contrast to his best friend and attorney, played by Eddie Mayehoff as a stuttering, muttering nincompoop married to the kind of woman who walks around with one of those yip-yip dogs, carrying it like a purse. While other mopes are schlepping off to work each morning and running home to the wife every night, Stan divides his time between sipping perfectly chilled martinis and running around town acting out *Bash Brannigan's* adventures, whether it's making out with a belly dancer or engaging in a mock shootout at the docks. As Stanley puts it, "I'd never ask Bash to do anything I hadn't already done myself."

How to Murder Your Wife retains this cheerfully sexist tone through much of the film. When Stan attends a bachelor party for "good old Toby," the Neal Heff score turns funereal and the men all stand around as if in shock.

"Good evening, Judge Blackstone," Stanley says to an old friend. "I'm afraid this is a somewhat mournful occasion."

"Not at all, my boy," the judge replies. "Been married thirty-eight years myself and I don't regret one day of it. [Pause.] The one day of it I don't regret was August 2, 1936. She was off visiting her ailing mother at the time."

I love that joke!

Only when good old Toby shows up and announces the wedding is off does the bachelor party kick into gear, as the men start singing "Happy Days Are Here Again" and a beautiful blonde (the Italian treasure Virna Lisi) pops out of a cake.

The next morning, Stanley wakes up with the blonde in his bed—and a wedding ring on his finger. It's a nightmare! Soon his butler has left him in disgust, his bachelor pad has been turned into a purple, frilly disaster, and his comic strip has been transformed from *Bash Brannigan: Secret Agent* to *The Brannigans*, featuring "America's Favorite Hen-Pecked Boob!" Stanley puts on twenty pounds and falls into a deep funk—a funk that is lifted only on those numerous occasions when his gorgeous wife ravages him.

When Bash Brannigan rebels by murdering his wife in the comic strip, Stanley's real wife disappears—and he's put on trial because, after all, Bash wouldn't do anything Stanley himself wouldn't do. The resultant trial scene is ridiculous but hilarious.

In the *1996 Video Movie Guide*, the authors say the "premise and attitudes" of *How to Murder Your Wife* are "unbelievably sexist."

What more of a recommendation can you ask for?

In the Company of Men

Rated R, 93 min., 1996
Director: Neil LaBute
Screenplay: Neil LaBute
Starring: Aaron Eckhart, Matt Malloy, Stacy Edwards
Drinking: ★★★★
Male bonding: ★★★★
Memorable dialogue: ★★★★

Message to the women of the world: It's only a movie. So take a deep breath and relax.

Chad and Howard, the lead characters of *In the Company of Men*, are not murderers, nor are they rapists or child molesters. They do not strike women with their fists. They are not criminals of any kind; as far as we know, they don't even own guns.

Nevertheless, women have a special kind of loathing for Chad and Howard, beyond anything they'd feel for, say, a serial killer in the movies. Why? Because Chad and Howard are (gasp!) *manipulative*. And if there's one thing women hate, it's guys who are manipulative.

In the Company of Men is the rare movie that takes no prisoners and makes no compromises. You keep expecting Chad and Howard to reach some sort of enlightenment regarding their cavalier disdain for women, but it never happens. Dogs they are when the movie opens, and dogs they remain till the bitter end.

This is one of the few films that takes us inside the modern corporate workplace and shows us the macho jockeying that takes place among young men (and women) on the rise. Chad (Aaron Eckhart) and Howard (Matt Malloy) are hotshot consultants who have been given a six-week assignment at a nameless company in a nameless town. They're major players in the office and on the dating field, constantly competing with each other and with every other guy out there to be the best, conscience be damned.

Lately, though, they've been having a rough time with women. We're talking dump city. Aaron is bitter, and Chad's in the mood for some gender revenge. So one night after a few too many cocktails, Chad comes up with a plan: They'll both go after a suitable wallflower in the office and romance her silly with flowers and dinners and gifts and sweet talk—and then they'll both dump her, "to restore a little dignity to our lives," as Chad puts it.

Enter Christine (Stacy Edwards), a new receptionist at the office where Chad and Aaron will be working for the next month and a half. Not only is she pretty and sweet, she's deaf. In other words, the perfect target for these two cads. Within days, she's dating Chad and Aaron, without realizing they even know each other.

But here's the thing. Even after she finds out Chad and Aaron are buddies, Stacy continues to "deceive" the boys. So while they're scheming to break her heart, she's scheming to keep both relationships going. It's interesting that the women who so despise *In the Company of Men* conveniently ignore Stacy's two-timing dishonesty.

This is not to say she gets what she deserves. Nobody deserves what Chad and Aaron do to Stacy. However, for the few women who have the guts to stick around for the multiple-surprise ending, *In the Company of Men* does provide some measure of satisfaction, at least when it comes to Aaron. As for Chad, he's stronger and more arrogant than ever at the end of the film—a smirking, charismatic, sociopathic hunk. One can only hope he surfaces again in some sort of sequel. In his own way he's as mesmerizing as Hannibal Lecter.

Thoughts on *In the Company of Men*

by Laurie Viera

I thought a lot about seeing *In the Company of Men*. After all, several of my more erudite friends and acquaintances said it was a must. "Thought-provoking," said some. "Shocking," said others. But when I actually pictured myself paying for the privilege of watching a woman play lame-duck victim to two guys who got their dating tips from Dr. Mengele, I decided to pass. I mean, there are so many other ways to indulge one's masochistic fancies. Take self-mutilation, for example. Or, if the kitchen knives are too dull, there's always Howard Stern. Personally, I think the guys who dreamed up *In the Company of Men* should be locked up in a small room with a giant TV screen that plays endless loops of every Merchant Ivory and Jane Austen film adaptation ever made at top volume for all eternity. Now that's thought-provoking.

Judgment Night

Rated R, 109 min., 1993
Director: Stephen Hopkins
Screenplay: Lewis Colick
Starring: Emilio Estevez, Denis Leary, Cuba Gooding Jr., Stephen Dorff, Jeremy Piven
Car chases: ***
Explosions: ***
Fights: ****
Gunplay: ***
Male bonding: ****
Memorable dialogue: ***

It's not easy putting an Emilio Estevez vehicle on a list of top Guy Movies. He's the spoiled Beverly Hills brat who played the insufferable Kirby in *St. Elmo's Fire,* for crying out loud. (Rest assured, I draw the line at *St. Elmo's* costar Andrew McCarthy, that spindly little jerk whose entire repertoire consists of holding his cigarette in a mannered fashion and poking his eyes until they open wide, indicating surprise or grief or God knows what. The only way Andrew McCarthy could be in a Guy Movie would be if he took a role in a film where someone like Sigourney Weaver beat the crap out of him.) I'll make an exception here because Estevez's smirky-boy persona suits him perfectly for his role in *Judgment Night* as Francis Howard "Frank" Wyatt, a Chicago North Shore yuppie-in-training who finds himself in a world of trouble after he leaves his pissed-off wife and his three-month-old baby in their cozy-comfy home for a night out with the boys. Also along for the ride are his best friend, Mike (Cuba Gooding Jr.), his little brother (Stephen Dorff), and their smarmy buddy Ray, played with oozy glee by Jeremy Piven.

Ray has talked a salesman into letting him use a fully stocked luxury RV for the night, so as the boys battle traffic on the expressway on their way to a boxing match, they're boozing it up and playing with all the toys on board. Things take a turn for the ugly after Ray leaves the expressway and gets lost in the no-man's land of Chicago's West Side ("I bet there's some tremendous real estate bargains here," mutters Ray), where the yupsters witness a murder and find themselves on the run from a savage band of drug-dealing killers led by the sociopath Fallon, played by Denis Leary in an extension of his leather-jacketed stage persona.

Fallon is a piece of work. At one point, he guns down a bum who is wearing Mike's letterman jacket from Purdue, but when he finds out he's been duped he exclaims, "Shit, a hobo from Purdue. I hate Purdue. When was the last time they won anything, anyway?" Then, after gaining possession of Frank's wallet, he reads the address out loud: "1922 Deadwood Drive. That's a fucking riot, Deadwood Drive!"

In fact, Fallon is so much fun that you almost start rooting for him to eliminate Francis and friends. How can you not laugh when he grabs the public address system in a market where the boys have been hiding and announces, "Attention, we have a special in our frozen foods department tonight—dead meat, plucked juicy and fresh from our North Shore farm. Shop til you drop, right, Frank?"

Fallon is so nuts he doesn't hesitate to enter the dank hallways of a housing project, where most Irish guys would last about fifteen seconds, and where Frank and his friends might be hiding. "People of the housing projects!" he announces. "Give them up and this will *not* be the worst night of your lives!"

I guess you have to root for Frank because he does have the fantastic-looking wife and the adorable baby waiting at home for him, but it's a tough call. Fallon is much funnier. In a better world, Denis Leary would have been nominated for Best Supporting Actor for his performance here, but he'll have to settle for the prestigious honor of elevating a well-made but fairly standard thriller into the stratosphere of Guy Moviedom.

King of New York

Rated R, 106 min., 1990
Director: Abel Ferrara
Screenplay: Nicholas St. John
Starring: Christopher Walken, Laurence Fishburne, David Caruso, Wesley Snipes, Janet Julian, Steve Buscemi, Theresa Randle
Drinking: ★★★★
Fights: ★★★
Gunplay: ★★★★
Male bonding: ★★★
Memorable dialogue: ★★★
Nudity: ★★★★

The 1990s gave rise to a new breed of highly entertaining if morally dubious exploitation films about urban gang warfare, each of them containing certain key elements:
- Show-motion shoot-outs
- Outrageous street dialogue ("Homey, I'm gonna bust a cap on this mofo!")

- Rap music blasting on the soundtrack
- Naked, coke-sniffing babes shimmering in the background
- Large acting by guys dressed in black and waving big silver guns

Among the best of the genre: *Juice, Boyz N the Hood, Sugar Hill, New Jack City*—and *King of New York*, which was unfairly overlooked when it was released in 1990 but has become a cult favorite on video and cable. There's a lot of movie in this movie; you get the feeling the stellar cast had a great time making it under the direction of Guy Movie favorite Abel Ferrara, who has explored this territory often and to great success in gritty crime films such as *Bad Lieutenant* and *Fear City*, as well as the pilot for the television series *Crime Story*.

Christopher Walken practically parodies himself in the lead role as crime boss Frank White, who has just returned from a long stint in prison and is out to reclaim his share of the wildly lucrative drug trade. (His method for carving out a piece of the pie for himself is simple: Everyone else gets killed.) Among his chief soldiers is Laurence Fishburne, who has gold front teeth and a gold rope the size of a python around his neck and goes by the name of Jimmy Jump; and Theresa Randle, who wears deadly miniskirts and stiletto heels but also has the ability to pop up through a limousine's moonroof and wipe out half of Chinatown with an Uzi.

As soon as Frank is released from prison he takes up residence in a huge suite at the Plaza Hotel, where his crack staff (pun intended) alternates between laboring over their computers and snorting cocaine off each other's bodies. (There are *no* unattractive women in this movie; even when an actress has just one line, e.g., "Frank White—I've heard a lot about you, and it's all bad," the woman uttering the line is Vanessa Angel, the babe of desire in movies such as *Kingpin* and *Spies Like Us*.) He also spends a lot of time attempting to ingratiate himself into New York society—attending theater openings and black-tie benefits, announcing his plans to put $16 million into a hospital in the South Bronx, wining and dining with the likes of columnist Pete Hamill, playing himself in a cameo.

Not that any of this fools the cops, foremost among them Wesley Snipes and David Caruso, partners who bend the law to their liking when they're unable to nail Frank using conventional police methods. As the orange-haired Caruso puts it, "We make, what, $36,500 a year to risk our lives every night of the week, while Frank gets rich killing people."

Of course, Frank has his own code of conduct: "I never killed anyone who didn't deserve it."

The budget for blood squibs, pretend guns, and smashed cars for this movie must have been well over $1 million. Every ten minutes or so there's another breathtaking gunfight or chase scene, often bathed in blue light and set to the beat of the pulsating soundtrack. My favorite is the Chinatown massacre, because even though bullets are flying from all directions, Frank White calmly strolls through the chaos with AK-47 in hand. He knows he won't get hit. He's Christopher Walken, dammit, and he's got Movie Star Immunity.

Lonely Are the Brave

Unrated, 107 min., 1962
Director: David Miller
Screenplay: Dalton Trumbo, based on the novel *Brave Cowboy* by Edward Abbey
Starring: Kirk Douglas, Walter Matthau, Gena Rowlands, Caroll O'Connor, George Kennedy
Drinking: ★★★★
Fights: ★★★
Male bonding: ★★★★
Memorable dialogue: ★★★

The best performance Kirk Douglas ever gave is in one of his lesser-known films. *Lonely Are the Brave* is a small, modern Western that appeals to the rebel free spirit that lurks in all guys (with the possible exception of Al Gore.) Shot in black and white and infused with an overwhelming feeling of melancholy, *Lonely Are the Brave* is for those occasional moments when guys are feeling a bit introspective. (I have an inner cowboy spirit, dammit, even though I sell insurance and live in the suburbs!) A woman watching this movie might make fun of it—which is why any relationship should include two television sets and two VCRs.

Douglas plays Jack Burns, a handsome, cocky, good-natured cowboy who's completely out of place in a world of superhighways, jet planes, and fancy modern conveniences like the portable TV set and the toaster oven. Jack was a hero in the Korean War, but that was a decade ago, and he's been lost ever since then, picking up work as a cowhand here and there, sometimes getting into a little trouble and sometimes finding himself behind bars. Crossing New Mexico on his faithful horse, Whiskey, Jack often has to calm his steed as they wait patiently on the side of an expressway while the cars and trucks zoom by. (One of the truck drivers he encounters is played by Caroll "Archie Bunker" O'Connor.)

One morning Jack shows up on the doorstep of a beautiful blonde, played by Gena Rowlands. Turns out her husband, Jack's best friend, is in

Killer Scenes

Women love to talk about great love scenes in the movies. Clark Gable carrying Vivien Leigh up the stairs in *Gone With the Wind,* Kevin Costner painting Susan Sarandon's toenails in *Bull Durham,* Robert Redford kissing Barbra Streisand in *The Way We Were,* crap like that. You always see montages of these clinches on specials celebrating "the magic of Hollywood." There are books and videotapes celebrating the greatest love scenes in film. Usually they've got Bogie and Bergman in *Casablanca* on the cover.

What I'd like to see is a tribute to some of the best killing scenes in the movies. There are only so many ways you can film a couple making love—but there's no end to the ways you can snuff out a life. If you were to put together a collection of quality kills, you'd have to include these classics:

- James Caan does a macabre dance of death as he's hit with hundreds of bullets at a toll booth in *The Godfather.*
- Natasha Henstridge sticks her tongue right through a guy's head in *Species.*
- Nick Nolte shoots bad buy James Remar right between the eyes in *48 Hours.*
- Christopher Walken loses a game of Russian roulette in *The Deer Hunter.*
- Deborah Shelton gets drilled, literally, in *Body Double.*
- Janet Leigh is showered with attention from Anthony Perkins in *Psycho.*
- Warren Beatty and Faye Dunaway get ambushed in *Bonnie and Clyde.*
- Al Pacino's buddy gets chainsawed to pieces in *Scarface.*
- Jennifer Jason Leigh is literally pulled apart in *The Hitcher.*
- Steve Buscemi becomes fodder for the wood chipper in *Fargo.*
- John Travolta takes a nuclear missile to the gut in *Broken Arrow.*
- Jean Reno blows up himself—and Gary Oldman—in *The Professional.*
- Bruce Willis kills a guy with one punch in *The Last Boy Scout.*
- One of Sean Connery's romantic conquests is spray painted to death in *Goldfinger.*
- Robert De Niro beats a guy to death with a baseball bat in *The Untouchables.*
- John Amos takes an icicle to the eyeball in *Die Hard 2.*
- Eric Roberts poisons Burt Young in *The Pope of Greenwich Village.*
- Anthony Hopkins bites a prison guard in the face in *The Silence of the Lambs.*
- Mel Gibson is ripped to shreds in *Braveheart.*
- Standing atop a train about to go into a tunnel, Gene Hackman and Anne Archer duck in time—but the bad guy doesn't—in *Narrow Margin.*
- Feuding couple Michael Douglas and Kathleen Turner swing from a chandelier and then fall to their deaths in *The War of the Roses.*
- Sissy Spacek telekinetically takes out Piper Laurie in *Carrie.*
- Prison warden Tommy Lee Jones ends up as a head on a stick in the director's cut of *Natural Born Killers,* which also includes a scene of Woody Harrelson stabbing Ashley Judd with a pencil. Rent it today!

jail because he helped some illegal immigrant families find jobs and homes. It was a heroic, if stupid, deed.

"If it didn't take men to make babies, I wouldn't have anything to do with you," the gorgeous Gena says as she rustles up some grub for Jack, who obviously has more than a friendly history with her but is too much of a gentleman to make a move now that she's cast her lot with his former compadre.

Jack, who is such a master of his own destiny that he doesn't even carry any identification, concocts a scheme to get himself tossed into jail so he can spring his buddy. At the police station, the cop filling out the paperwork says, "Where do you live?"

"Anywhere I feel like," Jack responds.

Now that's a goddamn man's man. But that's also the kind of attitude that gets Jack into trouble with a sadistic prison guard played by George Kennedy, who beats the holy hell out of Jack just for the fun of it. ("I got rousted a little," is all Jack has to say about the bruises and cuts on his face when he returns to his cell.)

The prison break doesn't go as planned, but eventually Jack finds himself on the run, riding Whiskey into the mountains while a sympathetic sheriff (Walter Matthau in a dramatic role) oversees a massive, high-tech search.

We see what's going on here. Kirk Douglas is a 1960s Peter Pan, refusing to grow up and face the responsibilities of the real world. Matthau represents the grown-up world, acknowledging the allure of the lone-wolf lifestyle but insisting that everyone has to play by the same set of rules.

Now who do you think guys are going to root for?

Mad Max: Beyond Thunderdome

Rated PG-13, 107 min., 1985
Director: George Miller and George Ogilvie
Screenplay: George Miller and Terry Hayes
Starring: Mel Gibson, Tina Turner, Frank Thring Jr., Angelo Rossitto
Car chases: ****
Fights: ****
Male bonding: **
Memorable dialogue: ***

The reason I selected the third installment in the *Mad Max* series is simple: The second one was only pretty good and the first one absolutely *sucked*—not only was it badly dubbed, but Mel Gibson hadn't yet learned how to act and he doesn't even get very mad until the very end of the movie—but *Beyond Thunderdome* is an inspired piece of lunacy set in a murky future where everyone dresses like they're in a Pat Benatar video and talks like Dr. Seuss on LSD. "Two men enter, one man leaves, two men enter one man leaves!" "Bust a deal, get the wheel, bust a deal, get the wheel!" Like that.

Nobody ever calls Mad Max by his name in *Thunderdome*. The witch-like queen figure Auntie Entity (Tina Turner) calls him Raggedy Man, while the children who populate a remote valley near the desert think he is Captain Walker, the savior who will take them to "Tomorrow-morrow-land," where the buildings are tall and "everyone has videos."

But there are no more big cities. They were all wiped out in some sort of apocalyptic catastrophe, and those who survived are living in wild and dangerous places such as Bartertown, where slave labor is used to produce methane gas from pig shit, and disputes are settled in a wicker basket contraption known as Thunderdome.

There are no pastels in *Beyond Thunderdome*. Everything is gray and brown and grimy, and everyone looks as if they smell bad. This is one of those rare movies where the filmmakers succeed in creating an entire world unlike anything we've seen on the big screen; even the extras have shaved heads and weird makeup and medieval-punk costumes. Our man Max, with his Def Leppard hair and his seemingly endless arsenal of weapons, is obviously a cut above the grubby, thieving schemers who populate Bartertown, which is why Auntie Entity prevails upon him to duel to the death in Thunderdome with her rival Blaster, a hulking creature in an iron mask. As one of Auntie's henchmen tells Max, "[Blaster] can beat most men with his breath."

The fight between Max and Blaster is a banging, clanging, smashing dance of gore, as they bounce around Thunderdome on bungee cords and whack each other with knives, hatchets, cleavers, and chainsaws while the bloodthirsty citizens of Bartertown cling to the webbing of the inverted bowl. It's a wonder somebody hasn't turned the Thunderdome concept into a pay-per-view event in the real world.

Max's encounter with the chanting mud-faced children who think he's a prophet is a little loopy and confusing, but the action heats up again when he and the kids return to Bartertown to rescue a midget and duke it out with Auntie Entity. A portion of the desert has been conveniently pounded into an extended dirt track for the big finale of a chase scene involving plains, trains, and automobiles. "Ain't we a pair, Raggedy Man?" says Auntie Entity when they meet face-to-face for the last time. Indeed they are. When Tina sings "We Don't Need Another Hero" over the closing credits, she's absolutely right—who needs *another* hero when you've got the invincible Mad Max roaming this world?

The Magnificent Seven

Unrated, 126 min., 1960
Director: John Sturges, based on *The Seven Samurai* by Akira Kurosawa
Screenplay: William Roberts
Starring: Yul Brynner, Eli Wallach, Steve McQueen, Charles Bronson, Robert Vaughn, James Coburn
Drinking: ★★★
Fights: ★★★
Gunplay: ★★★★
Male bonding: ★★★★
Memorable dialogue: ★★★★

They say *The Seven Samurai* is a great movie but I wouldn't know. Guys don't do foreign movies, unless it's a karate flick where you don't care what the characters are saying, or maybe some Swedish porno film where everyone is speaking the universal language of love. But bad dubbing, or subtitles? No thank you. The only time guys want to see words on the TV screen is when *Monday Night Football* is telling us how many yards passing the Raiders had in the first half.

In a way, though, I have seen *The Seven Samurai*, because *The Magnificent Seven* is an American remake of that classic. (It's an American tradition to steal foreign movies, to wit, *Three Men and a Baby*, originally titled *Le Vehicle du Steve Guttenberg*.) In this version, Eli Wallach is the cruel bandit who terrorizes a village of gentle Mexican farmers who meekly surrender every time he rides into town, with a few boneheaded exceptions, such as the idiot with a machete who charges Wallach, only to be shot cold in his tracks.

"Stupid! Stupid!" bellows Wallach. No kidding. Knife-wielding guys in the movies never learn that they can't outrun a bullet.

Wallach commands a seemingly invincible band of thugs, maybe a hundred in all, but they face a serious challenge from a ragtag collection of drifters, headed by Steve McQueen and Yul Brynner, who was bald thirty years before Michael Jordan made it cool to be a chrome dome. McQueen is a gunman for hire, but these days it seems no one needs his services. Short on cash, he's thinking about taking a job in a grocery store—that is, until he walks into a saloon and orders a whiskey, which is what guys in the movies always order when they walk into saloons in the middle of the hot day.

As always, some young loudmouth in the bar challenges the mysterious stranger, with the words that always signify a character's imminent demise: "Let's see how fast you are!"

Well, he's plenty fast. He's Steve McQueen.

After McQueen takes care of the loudmouth, the villagers approach him and ask for his help in fighting Wallach. "He and his men, they steal our food, they leave us to starve," one of them says. "Not only that, but our women—"

Well, the movie was made in 1960. They can't say any more than that about what happens to the womenfolk.

In addition to McQueen and Brynner, *The Magnificent Seven* includes James Coburn as the fastest shot in the West, Robert Vaughn as a pretty boy gunman, Charles Bronson as Charles Bronson, and a couple of guys you never heard of. They ride into town to the famous Elmer Bernstein music that later became the Marlboro theme, and they teach the villagers how to defend themselves from the inevitable attack by Wallach and his men. For his part, Wallach views the uprising with philosophical amusement: "If God didn't want them sheared, he wouldn't have made them sheep!"

Because *The Magnificent Seven* is based on some legendary foreign film, it's more than just a standard Western about simple townsfolk learning to defend themselves against ruthless gunmen, with the help of a couple of movie stars. In fact, it's a movie about fatherhood, and what it takes to be a real man. The young boys in the village idolize McQueen, but he sets them straight, pointing out that he has no job, no wife, and no kids. And when one of the boys questions his own father's bravery, the previously mute Bronson delivers the longest and most emotional speech of his film career: "You think I'm brave because I carry a gun. Well, your fathers are brave because they carry responsibility!"

Deep.

Manhunter

Rated R, 100 min., 1986
Director: Michael Mann
Screenplay: Michael Mann, based on the novel *Red Dragon* by Thomas
  Harris
Starring: William Petersen, Dennis Farina, Tom Noonan, Joan Allen, Brian
  Cox
Explosions: ★★★
Gunplay: ★★★★
Memorable dialogue: ★★★

The FBI profiler needs to get inside the head of a serial killer known as the Tooth Fairy, so dubbed by the press because the maniac likes to take a bite out of his victims after he's slashed them to death. Who better to unlock the door to such an insane mind than another brilliant mass murderer with cannibalistic tendencies, this one behind bars?

So the agent, obviously haunted by personal demons stemming from previous encounters with the caged killer, walks the sterile corridor of the prison's ultramaximum security wing, finally reaching the cell at the very end of the hall, where the inmate is dressed all in white and has his back turned to his visitor.

The quietly insane murderer sniffs the air and says in a clipped, very civilized British accent, "That's the same atrocious aftershave you wore in court three years ago."

Boom. The FBI profiler is freakin' out.

If this sounds like an encounter with Dr. Hannibal "the Cannibal" Lecter, it is—only in this movie his name is spelled "Lecktor," and he's portrayed by the unknown Brian Cox rather than Academy Award–winner Anthony Hopkins.

Five years before *The Silence of the Lambs* turned Lecter into one of the most memorable killers in screen history, the nefarious doctor made his debut in *Manhunter,* a stylish and creepy suspense thriller directed by Michael Mann. William Petersen is Will Graham, the FBI agent who was responsible for capturing Lecktor and putting him behind bars—but not before the maniacal psychiatrist murdered nine people and succeeded in scrambling Will's brains so badly that Will has retired from the force and is now living in a fabulous beach house with a wife and kid who seem content to spend all their waking moments participating in a Hallmark card fantasy life. (The FBI must have a *really* good retirement plan for burned-out ex-agents.)

But that fantasy is jerked from beneath their bare feet when Will's old boss (Dennis Farina) enlists his services to track down the Tooth Fairy, who is killing entire families in a pattern dictated by lunar cycles. Will knows he'll have to contact the only man who will understand the inner workings of such a depraved soul, but he swears that this time he won't get caught in Lecktor's web.

No such luck. Soon he's knee-deep in a psychoanalytical quagmire created by the doctor, who haunts him with such questions as, "Dream much, Will?" knowing full well that Will is haunted by nightmares from past cases.

The gigantic, scary Tom Noonan (you might remember him as the hatchet-wielding maniac blown away by Schwarzenegger at the beginning of *The Last Action Hero*) is immensely effective as the Tooth Fairy, who takes time out from his killing spree to romance a blind coworker, played by Joan Allen. It's one of the weirdest courtship rituals you'll ever see, highlighted by a scene in which Joan gets turned on when she gets to caress a sedated Bengal tiger. (I'm not kidding.) As much as we'd like to see a happy ending to this love story, we're fairly certain that there's not much future in a relationship between a giant-sized serial killer and a blind, tiger-fondling woman. Besides, they work together, and we all know what a problem that can be!

When Will finally tracks down the Tooth Fairy, there's some great slow-motion, glass-shattering action, set to the tune of "Ina-Gadda-da-Vida" by Iron Butterfly, a surprisingly effective choice as background-killer music. *Manhunter* may not have Anthony Hopkins prattling on about eating someone's liver with some fava beans and a nice Chianti, but it's an eerie, unforgettable introduction to Dr. Hannibal Lecktor, no matter how you spell his name.

Mean Streets

Rated R, 110 min., 1973
Director: Martin Scorsese
Screenplay: Martin Scorsese and Mardik Martin
Starring: Harvey Keitel, Robert De Niro, Richard Romanus, Amy Robinson
Car chases: ★★★
Drinking: ★★★★
Fights: ★★★★
Gunplay: ★★★
Male bonding: ★★★★
Memorable dialogue: ★★★★
Nudity: ★★★

Before *Taxi Driver*, before *Raging Bull* and *Goodfellas* and *Casino*, Martin Scorsese and Robert De Niro teamed up for *Mean Streets*, an unpolished little gem of a movie about a couple of small-time hoods knocking around New York's Little Italy in the early 1970s. It's a brutal, foulnatured hoot.

Harvey Keitel, who probably looked like he was forty when he was in the second grade, stars as Charlie, a lapsed Catholic who collects money for his gangster uncle but dreams of taking over an Italian restaurant. Charlie's fatal flaw is his friendship with Johnny Boy, an energetic jerk played by the stick-skinny De Niro in a career-making role. Charlie is in love with Johnny Boy's younger sister, Theresa, but he doesn't want anyone in the neighborhood to know about it because in this macho environment, treating a woman with respect and kindness would be a sign of weakness. (Theresa is epileptic, and the guys in the neighborhood are so thick-headed they think this means she's retarded.)

His uncle tells Charlie he's got to sever ties with the volatile Johnny Boy if he wants to rise in the ranks, but Charlie just can't seem to wash his hands of the little creep. One minute he's got his hands around Johnny Boy's neck, the next minute they're all drinking shots and toasting the chicks. Here's Johnny Boy in the back room of the bar, sincerely telling Charlie how he feels about one of the girls waiting for them out front: "She's very nice, very nice. I want to bang her like crazy."

That's about as close to romance as you're going to get in *Mean Streets*.

The dialogue throughout the film is priceless, almost a parody of tough-guy talk, as when Johnny Boy gets confused about the nickname of one of the local goons and Charlie has to explain, "Joey Scala *is* Joey Clams, they're the same person!" Everyone is a "mook" or a "fucking moron," and everyone has a Mob name like Frankie Bones or Jimmy

Sparks. These guys barely scam enough money to go to the movies, but they sure do have the act down. They spend their days lurking in the back rooms of pool halls and taverns and strip clubs, hanging on the street corner, getting into messy fights with guys who owe them money. When they're not duking it out with their rivals they're pounding on each other.

This being a Scorsese movie, there are cool director–guy touches everywhere. When the characters appear for the first time, the action freezes momentarily and their names are superimposed on the screen: "Tony," "Michael," etc. (You never get anyone named "Miles" or "Lance" in a Scorsese film.) Religious imagery abounds. The bar is lit in hellish tones of red, and there are images of Jesus in nearly every scene; in fact, there are probably more crucifixes in *Mean Streets* than in *The Exorcist*. Scorsese occasionally uses slow motion, just as he does in *Goodfellas* and *Raging Bull*, and he peppers the soundtrack with pop tunes such as "Be My Baby" and "Jumping Jack Flash." The movie crackles.

Life closes in on Johnny Boy when he refuses to pay off a local loan shark, but before the violent climax, there's a quiet moment when Theresa asks Charlie to show a little sensitivity by revealing some of his favorite things in life.

"I like spaghetti with clam sauce, Francis of Assisi, chicken with lemon and garlic, John Wayne, and I like you," says Charlie.

"Saint Francis didn't run numbers," Theresa replies.

Good point.

Modern Romance

Rated R, 102 min., 1981
Director: Albert Brooks
Screenplay: Albert Brooks and Monica Johnson
Starring: Albert Brooks, Kathryn Harrold, Bruno Kirby, and George Kennedy
as George Kennedy
Drinking: **
Male bonding: **
Memorable dialogue: ****
Nudity: ***

This is one of the few romantic comedies told from the guy's point of view, and it's our good fortune that the guy is Albert Brooks, one of the funniest damn human beings of this century. (Who knows how he would have stacked up against the funniest people of, say, the sixteenth century. There were a lot of good comic minds working back then.) In the

semiautobiographical *Modern Romance,* the neurotic, cloying but ultimately sympathetic Brooks plays the neurotic, cloying but ultimately
sympathetic Robert, a film editor involved in a loving and somewhat
twisted relationship with the beautiful Mary, played by Kathryn Harrold.
The film begins with Robert once again breaking off their relationship,
launching a series of scenes in which he goes through rituals familiar to
every guy who's ever wavered between commitment and the urge to
break free.

Gooped up on a Quaalude, Robert works his Rolodex, calling women he
barely remembers and asking them out. Determined to make a fresh start,
he visits a sporting goods store and explains to the salesman, "I just broke
up with someone and I want to start a new life and I think running should
be a major part of it." (The salesman is Albert's brother, Bob Einstein, better known as Super Dave Osborne.) His first postrelationship date is trun-
cated when Michael Jackson's "She's out of My Life" comes on the radio,
reminding him of how much he misses his ex-girlfriend.

It takes Robert only twenty-four hours to realize he's made a grave mistake. He can't live without Mary. So of course he does that stupid guy
thing where he calls her at work and hangs up, calls her home machine
and doesn't leave a message, drives by her house, even leaves corny gifts
on her front stoop. When Robert and the reluctant Mary do reunite, the
"makeup sex" is great but the problems remain. Robert is still a jealous,

possessive idiot who takes one look at the not-at-all-revealing skirt Mary is going to wear to work and says, "We have to do some sewing here."

Interspersed with the relationship scenes are some hilarious bits about the film industry. The director James L. Brooks appears as the director of a low-budget sci-fi movie starring George Kennedy, who does a fine job of playing himself in the movie. As the editor of the movie, Robert and his trusty assistant (yep, that's a very young Bruno Kirby) have to work around the pretentious dweeb of a director and the blowhard star. The scene where they attempt to use a sound effect known as Hulk Running to duplicate Kennedy's footsteps is brilliant and fall-down funny.

The heart of the film, though, is the relationship between Robert and Mary. Guys will wince in recognition at the scenes where Robert sneaks a peek at Mary's phone bill and wonders who the hell she was talking to in New York for two hours at a time. They'll nod knowingly when Robert responds to Mary's attempt to dump him by saying, "Marry me." And they'll be all too familiar with Robert's irrational fits of jealousy, and his sickeningly saccharine attempts to return to Mary's good graces. What a wimp, what a waffler.

What a guy's guy.

Monty Python and the Holy Grail

Rated PG, 90 min., 1975
Director: Terry Gilliam and Terry Jones
Screenplay: John Cleese, Graham Chapman, Terry Jones, Michael Palin, Eric Idle, and Terry Gilliam
Starring: John Cleese, Graham Chapman, Terry Jones, Michael Palin, Eric Idle, and Terry Gilliam
Fights: ****
Male bonding: ***
Memorable dialogue: ****

While on his quest to find knights for his round table, King Arthur comes across a dark warrior in a remote forest who refuses to let him cross a bridge. Soon they're engaged in a furious sword fight. *Swoosh!* The king cuts off his adversary's arm. *Slash!* There goes the other arm. Blood is gushing from the warrior's arm sockets and he is utterly incapable of defending himself, yet he continues to insult King Arthur as he tries to kick him.

"You haven't got any arms!" the king points out.

"Ah, it's just a flesh wound!" comes the reply. Even after the good king has slashed off the man's legs, the hapless (not to mention arm-

less and legless) torso-with-head continues to hurl insults and challenges. Only when the king rides off does the warrior grudgingly concede he may not have won: "All right, we'll call it a draw."

Guys love that scene from *Monty Python and the Holy Grail*. They also love the scene where a man walks through a village while pushing a wheel barrow filled with decaying bodies while chanting, "Bring out your dead, bring out your dead"— almost as much as they love the scene where the king is insulted by a French guard who tells him, "I fart in your general direction." If there are gals who dig this stuff, they must live in England because I've never encountered a female Pythonite in America. The peculiar, leering, scatological brand of humor practiced by the Monty Python ensemble has spawned a large and fiercely devoted cult of fans— nearly all of them male. In fact I'm not sure I'd trust a woman who said she was a big fan of the Lumberjack sketch, or the twisted cartoons of Terry Gilliam.

Monty Python and the Holy Grail is the first original feature-length film from the popular English troupe, and they didn't waste a lot of time with a lot of plot or character development. The story of King Arthur's quest for the Holy Grail is really an excuse for a series of hilarious and very silly sketches that satirize religious oppression, the English class system, and pompous educators, among other targets. After the Knights of the Round Table split up—to increase the odds of finding the Holy Grail, and, more important, to set up a series of showcase sketches for each member of the Python troupe—we're treated to one wonderfully offensive segment after another. This movie uses spurting blood to comic effect like no film before or since.

---

*Note: *Monty Python and the Holy Grail* is set in 932 A.D. Who says guys don't like period pieces?

Some Python fans will tell you the Trojan Rabbit is the high point of the movie; others will argue for the scene where Sir Lancelot slaughters several dozen wedding guests during an ill-fated rescue mission. Then there are those who prefer the Knights Who Say "Nee!" and their demand that King Arthur present them with a gift offering of a "shrubbery." My preference is for the adventures of Sir Galahad the Chaste, who finds himself in a castle populated by "six scores of blondes and brunettes, all between the ages of sixteen and nineteen and a half." When good Sir Galahad discovers he has been tricked into believing the women have possession of the Holy Grail, they say he must administer the only acceptable punishment: "A good spanking, followed by oral sex." Alas, Sir Galahad is "saved" by his colleagues who drag him from the castle, telling him he must have been in great peril.

"Let me go back and face the peril!" wails Sir Galahad, echoing the sentiments of guys everywhere.

National Lampoon's Animal House

Rated R, 109 min., 1978
Director: John Landis
Screenplay: Harold Ramis
Starring: John Belushi, Tim Matheson, Peter Riegert, Karen Allen, Tom Hulce, John Vernon, Stephen Furst, Verna Bloom
Car chases: ★★★
Drinking: ★★★★
Fistfights: ★★
Male bonding: ★★★★
Memorable dialogue: ★★★★
Nudity: ★★★★

This is the goddamn funniest movie ever made and if you don't think so, you can flip ahead right now and read about the Gal Movies because you're not welcome here any longer. How can you not love *Animal House?* Everyone associated with it should win that lifetime achievement thingee, what's it called, the Amy Irving Award.

In the twenty-one years since it was released, *Animal House* has proven to be the rare comedy that improves with time. The film's legacy has been tainted because it spawned an entire industry of derivative movies and sitcoms, and our collective memory tends to lump them all together. But experience *Animal House* again, with fresh eyes and ears, as I did. Listening to the crackling dialogue; appreciating the timeless, Harpo Marx–like performance from the late great John Belushi, enjoying the smart-ass confidence of Tim Matheson and Peter Riegert in the dual high points of their careers; and lusting after the freckle-faced, elfin beauty of Karen Allen, I teared up like a soap opera actress. WHY CAN'T THEY MAKE CLASSIC COMEDIES LIKE THIS ANYMORE, DAMMIT!?

For the recovering alcoholics who have forgotten and the very young who don't know, *Animal House* is a toga party of a movie celebrating the antics of a rogue fraternity at the fictional Faber College in the early 1960s. Much to the dismay of the craggy-faced Dean Wormer (John Vernon does a great job because he plays it straight, giving the movie a sacred cow to tip over again and again), ROTC maniac Douglas Neidermeyer, and straight-laced kiss-ass Greg Marmalade, the Delta House is a belching, noxious, gaseous blight on the campus, filled with beer-guzzling lechers and career students who don't even bother to declare a major. They have names like Bluto, Boone, Pinto, Flounder, and D-Day. (In fact, virtually everyone in the movie—even minor characters such as Fawn Leibowitz and Mandy Pepperidge—has a name out of *Mad* magazine). They spend every waking moment drinking, womanizing, dancing, singing, eating, or cheating on their tests, and with the possible exception of the drinking, they're not really very good at any of these things, which makes it all the more entertaining.

If you were to compile a montage of *Animal House* highlights, you'd have to show the whole movie. From the opening scene where Kent Dorfman says, "Excuse me, sir, is this the Delta House?" and the eyebrow-twitching Belushi replies with evil understatement, "Sure, come on in," we know we're in for a devilishly funny ride.

You can't underestimate the influence of this film on guy culture. Toga parties enjoyed a revival because of *Animal House*. The fictional, but now real, Otis Day and the Knights have a career because of this movie. For twenty years, DJs at wedding receptions have played "Shout!" while formally dressed guests mimicked the dance steps from the film. And of course, any guy worth his guyness can recites snippets of dialogue from the movie, including:

"Food fight!"

"Thank you sir, may I have another?"

"Fat, drunk, and stupid is no way to go through life, son."

"Christ, seven years of college down the drain."

"Over? Nothing is over, until we decide it is! Was it over when the Germans bombed Pearl Harbor? No! And it ain't over now!"

Thank God they never made a sequel to *Animal House*. You can't improve upon perfection.

The Natural

Rated PG, 134 min., 1984
Director: Barry Levinson
Screenplay: Roger Towne and Phil Dusenberry, based on the novel by
  Bernard Malamud
Starring: Robert Redford, Glenn Close, Robert Duvall, Wilford Brimley,
  Richard Farnsworth, Michael Madsen, Kim Basinger, Joe Don Baker, Barbara Hershey
Drinking: **
Gunplay: **
Male bonding: ****
Memorable dialogue: ****

What *Cinderella* is for women, *The Natural* is for men—an old-fashioned fable about a forgotten nobody who is given one last dream of a chance to grab the golden fantasy. Guys who will sit through *Sophie's Choice* dry-eyed and bored, muttering, "What's with Meryl Streep and all the accents?" while their girlfriends give them dirty looks, will weep unashamedly at the glorious, scoreboard-smashing home runs belted by Roy Hobbs in *The Natural*. That's right, the long ball is much more emotionally effective than some dead-kid movie. When Roy's manager says, "Get in there and knock the cover off the ball," he does—literally. Now *that's* moving.

Most early baseball movies sucked, mainly because the actors playing the ballplayers were incredibly bad athletes. Gary Cooper ran like he was afraid of getting his shoes dirty in *Pride of the Yankees*, and Anthony Perkins threw like a sissy in *Fear Strikes Out*. I don't know what the hell William Bendix thought he was doing in *The Babe Ruth Story*, but it wasn't playing baseball. Robert Redford, however, is a former college-level ballplayer with a smooth swing and an easy throwing motion, so we can believe him in the role of an earnest and greatly gifted ballplayer from the heartland. Roy's legend is born when he faces off against the Babe Ruth–like Whammer in an impromptu contest outside a county fair; he requires just three pitches to strike out the arrogant home run king. As the sun covers the fairgrounds in a heavenly glow and the Randy Newman score swells to a crescendo, apple-cheeked youngsters surround Roy and beg for his autograph while a mysterious, raven-haired beauty (Barbara Hershey) looks on with hunger in her eyes. The future belongs to Roy Hobbs; as he puts it, "I want to walk down the street and hear people say, 'There goes Roy Hobbs, the best there ever was.'"

A shocking encounter with the dark-haired woman robs him of that future, and the next time we see Roy it's sixteen years later and he's of the age when most men retire. Nevertheless, he's going to give it one more shot with the woeful New York Knights, who are populated by a bunch of jinxed ballplayers such as Bump Bailey (Michael Madsen), a dimwitted outfielder with a disconcerting habit of running into outfield walls head-first.

Almost everyone Roy encounters has a comic-book name. Kim Basinger is a devious temptress named Memo Paris, while Robert Duvall hams it up as nosy sportswriter Max Mercy, who's sure Roy is harboring a dark secret. Roy also has to contend with the nefarious team owner (Robert Prosky) and a professional gambler (Darren McGavin), both of whom would bene-fit financially if the Knights were to lose the championship. But how can the Knights lose when Roy Hobbs is lifting slow-motion home runs deep into the stratosphere?

The only thing standing between this movie and perfection is Glenn Close, a Gal Movie star if there ever was one, as the woman of Roy's dreams. She wears big white hats and she's bathed in saintly backlight-ing, but she still looks like a mean substitute teacher and not the kind of woman who inspires you to hit home runs. Guys would take Barbara Hershey or Kim Basinger any day, even if there's a chance they might shoot you.

Near Dark

Rated R, 95 min., 1987
Director: Kathryn Bigelow
Screenplay: Eric Red and Kathryn Bigelow
Starring: Adrian Pasdar, Jenny Wright, Lance Henriksen, Bill Paxton
Car chases: ***
Drinking: ****
Explosions: ***
Fights: ****
Memorable dialogue: ***

The Lost Boys notwithstanding, *Near Dark* is the best modern erotic teen-vampire flick of 1987. Directed by Kathryn Bigelow (*Point Break, Blue Steel*), who's more of a man than most of the sissy male directors in Hollywood, and featuring a pulsating score from the synthesizer-driven Tangerine Dream (they also provided the score for *Thief* and *Risky Business*), this film is more invigorating than drinking a shot of tequila and falling facedown in a snowbed. Mike Tyson *wishes* he could pack so many bites and fights into a single evening.

The only weak link in *Near Dark* is lead hunk Adrian Pasdar as a horny young cowboy named Caleb, who is torn between the love he has for his father and his sister, and the blood bond he feels with the vampires who have taken him under their wings, so to speak. Pasdar conveys emotion by raising or lowering his voice without ever changing the expression on his Guess? jeans model face; he seems incapable of giving anything re-sembling an actual performance. (This may be why it would be extremely difficult for you to name any other Adrian Pasdar films since 1987.) For-tunately for the viewer, Pasdar doesn't have to do much more than make out with the gaminlike Jenny Wright (as Mae, a young vampire who still has a bit of a human heart) and occasionally do battle with some of Jenny's vampire friends, including the skull-faced Lance Henriksen as lead vampire Jesse and the pumpkin-headed Bill Paxton, who's much more interesting as a lusty bloodsucker than he is as an astronaut (*Apollo 13*) or a tornado-chaser (*Twister*). Note to Bill Paxton: Play more rotten apples, it'll extend your career. Paxton's greatest moment in *Near Dark* comes when he stands atop a bar and does a series of whirling kicks, his jangling spurs slashing a bartender's throat with the pinpoint accuracy of Zorro. After guzzling a pint or two from the dead man's neck, the blood-splattered Paxton grins like an insane circus clown and says, "Finger lickin' good!"

That moment comes in the middle of an extended, extremely gory, and quite artsy sequence set in a redneck bar somewhere in Texas. The whole vampire family is hungry, and they take turns slashing up various bikers and bar employees while a techno-rock version of "Fever" plays softly on the jukebox. Henriksen orders a beer mug and tells the confused waitress he doesn't want any beer—just the glass. When he cuddles up to the frightened gal, telling her how soft her skin is, his jealous vampire-girlfriend slashes the waitress's throat from ear to ear and Henriksen holds out the mug until it's filled with her fresh blood.

Caleb has been bitten by Mae and he's become quite the nocturnal creature, but he's still somewhat human and he's on kind of a vampire probation deal, so he shows mercy for the lone survivor of the tavern massacre. Unfortunately for our cold-blooded friends, the kid goes straight to the cops, who surround the vampires' motel and blast away, the bullet holes shooting deadly rays of sunlight into the dark room.

There's more—much more—including some exquisite shots of burning flesh, and more than a few moments of erotic bloodsucking. *Near Dark* is also something of a love story, if you can believe it. Not that you're going to be able to convince too many chicks to sit through that tavern sequence.

North Dallas Forty

Rated R, 117 min., 1979
Director: Ted Kotcheff
Screenplay: Frank Yablans and Ted Kotcheff and Peter Gent, based on the novel by Gent
Starring: Nick Nolte, Mac Davis, Dayle Haddon, Charles Durning, G. D. Spradlin, Dabney Coleman, Bo Svenson
Drinking: ****
Fights: ***
Male bonding: ****
Memorable dialogue: ****
Nudity: ***

Any guy who ever played football at any level will watch *North Dallas Forty* and nod knowingly at the realistic banter in the locker room, the painfully familiar scenes of the athletes doing anything and everything to combat their pain and the humiliating moments when the coach chews out somebody in front of the rest of the team. Any gal who watches *North Dallas Forty* will hang her head in shame for the opposite gender. Witness the moment at a wild team party when a Neanderthal offensive lineman named Jo Bob is introduced to Miss Farm Implement of the Year and tells her in all sincerity, "I have never seen titties like yours. Can I show your titties to my buddy O. W.?"

North Dallas Forty: It's realistic.

The game of professional football has changed a lot since 1979, but the core ideas in this film still hold true. The athletes get all the glory, but management uses every ounce of their beings and then casts them aside to make room for the next bunch of prized beefcake. Once a player turns thirty, he's old. It's a business.

Nick Nolte gives one of the great performances of his career as Phil Elliott, a battered but still valuable wide receiver for the North Dallas Bulls who has "the best hands in the league," as his Landry-like coach puts it, but also has a serious attitude problem. Elliott's downfall is that he just wants to play football without having to bother with all the corporate nonsense, but he's learning that leaving pieces of his body "on fields from [Dallas] to Pittsburgh" isn't enough. When he finally figures that out, things go from bad to worse. "We're not the team," he tells his coach during a disciplinary meeting with the board of directors. "*They're* the team. We're just the equipment! We're the helmets and the jockstraps."

Based on the novel by ex–Dallas Cowboy Peter Gent, *North Dallas Forty* captures the essence of a pro football player's life. The games take only three hours; the rest of the week during the season is devoted to film-watching sessions, indoor practices, weight training, whirlpools, partying with "dollies," and ingesting massive amounts of mind-altering, body-numbing substances designed to ease the pain. Even when Phil is getting treatment for his mushy knee, he's got a Budweiser in one hand and a joint in the other. This movie is a long way from *Knute Rockne: All-American*, or any of those other corny, crappy football movies from the black-and-white era.

It also helps that Nolte and Mac Davis (of all people) as the charismatic, Don Meredith–like quarterback Max, actually look like they can play football. The same goes for Bo Svenson as offensive lineman Jo Bob, and of course the late John Matuszak, who played for the Raiders and other teams, as his best friend, O. W. Shaddock. The Tooz also had some acting ability, showcased in a locker room speech after his line coach chastises him for behaving like a rah-rah high school player and not a professional doing his job.

"I don't want a job, I want to play football, asshole!" says O.W. "Every time we call it a game, you call it a business, and every time we call it a business, you call it a game! All you coaches are chickenshit cocksuckers!"

There's a big game near the end of *North Dallas Forty*, but we're not really rooting for the North Dallas Bulls—we're rooting for Phil. In one of those old-fashioned football movies, Phil would catch the winning touchdown pass and he'd get a big hug from the father-figure coach. To say that doesn't happen here is an understatement.

Not that Phil's a loser. He just figures out he's playing a game he has no chance of winning.

My Idea of Hell

by Laurie Viera

I know there are some women who like football, but I'm not one of them. I suspect that a lot of those women are just faking it out of some kind of fear of abandonment. But don't take my word for it—just watch *When Harry Met Sally . . .* if you doubt how good we can be at faking things.

I never could understand the male fascination with watching a bunch of uniformed guys built like major appliances grunting and crashing into one another. I mean, what's the point? I remember when I lived in San Francisco and the 49ers played the Super Bowl. I spent that afternoon in a nearly empty movie theater watching two black-and-white classics while my then-husband drank himself silly at some corporate tent party in the stadium parking lot. The streets of the city were so deserted that day, it felt like the aftermath of a nuclear holocaust. Has the whole world gone mad, I wondered?

So have a little pity, guys. It's bad enough that we have to endure *Monday Night Football* blaring from your TVs and a living room littered with junk food wrappers and beer bottles all winter long. Don't bring home *North Dallas Forty* from the video store, too. Women have been known to turn homicidal when pushed that far, and I've no doubt that a jury would be sympathetic. After all, I lived in San Francisco, the city where people get away with murder because they ate too many Twinkies.

Ocean's 11

Unrated, 148 min., 1960
Director: Lewis Milestone
Screenplay: Harry Brown and Charles Lederer
Starring: Frank Sinatra, Sammy Davis Jr., Dean Martin, Peter Lawford, Cesar Romero, Angie Dickinson
Drinking: ****
Fights: ***
Male bonding: ****
Memorable dialogue: ****

They wear black suits and skinny black ties, they walk down the street exuding cool, and they're planning a complicated heist.

They are the Reservoir Dudes.

The legend of the Rat Pack was cemented with *Ocean's 11*, which just might be the swingin'-est, kickiest, jazziest caper flick of all time. Watching this classic is like taking a two-hour time trip to an era when highballs and cigarettes were practically considered healthful, and you could call a broad a broad and maybe even slap her on the rump without finding yourself in front of a Senate Committee on Sexual Harrassment. Every frame of *Ocean's 11* is politically incorrect, which is the primary reason why guys love it and women think it's about as relevant as a 1958 issue of *Playboy* magazine.

Frank Sinatra is Danny Ocean, an irresistible schemer who swaggers into the movie in an orange sweater, pouring himself the first of at least a dozen hard drinks he seems to consume every day as if they were iced tea. (Everybody in this movie drinks heavily, at all hours. With the notable exception of an hilarious cameo by Shirley MacLaine, they never get drunk.) Watching a bodacious babe giving Peter Lawford a massage, he cocks an eyebrow and says, "If you're not careful, buddy boy, she'll rub you out."

Danny is recruiting Lawford—and the rest of his former army buddies—to swoop down on Las Vegas on New Year's Eve and knock off five casinos simultaneously. The way Danny figures it, each member of Ocean's 11 could realize a cool million bucks from the heist, if all goes according to plan. He doesn't have much trouble getting the guys to go along with the plan, because, after all, who says no to Frank Sinatra?

Throwing only a slight crimp into the plan is Angie Dickinson as Danny's estranged wife, who at one point actually tells him, "You could never love a woman like you love danger."

Oh, man. Most guys go their entire life without hearing a woman tell them that. Sinatra probably heard it once a week.

Danny's best friend is played by Dean Martin, who looks as if he wandered onto the movie set straight from the stage at the Sands. Cupping a cig and swishing his martini glass around, Dino explains his plan for a better world: "Repeal the Fourteenth and Twentieth Amendments. Take the vote away from women and make slaves of them." Enlightened!

Dean and Sammy Davis, Jr., each manage to work in a musical number, but Frank never sings, which was surely his decision. ("I'm *acting* here. If people want to hear me sing they can come to Vegas and pay for it!") Also making appearances are Joey Bishop as a former prizefighter, Norman *"Three's Company"* Fell, and Red Skelton in a cameo as Red Skelton. But the strongest performance is turned in by future Joker Cesar Romero as a big-time crook who's engaged to marry Lawford's rich mother.

The heist itself isn't quite as much fun as the buildup, but there's a nifty twist of an ending, and you've got to keep watching for the in joke during the final credits, when Sinatra and company stride down the Strip—right past the gigantic billboard for the Sands that lists the names of the stars then appearing in the main showroom: Frank Sinatra, Dean Martin, Sammy Davis, Jr., Joey Bishop, and Peter Lawford.

Guy-Movie Frauds!

They may seem like quintessential Guy Movies to the untrained observer, but each of the following flicks is at best gender-neutral and at worst a Gal Movie in disguise.

Braveheart. On the surface, this seems like the best Guy Movie in recent years. The plot: Mel Gibson paints his face blue like a North Carolina Tar Heel fanatic and screams like a maniac as he kills hundreds of enemies in a wonderfully gory film about the life and (quite gruesome) death of Scottish legend William Wallace. With all the maiming and stabbing and killing, this seems like such a Guy Movie—but don't forget *why* William Wallace turns into such a murdering machine in the first place. It's all because of a chick! Only after his young wife is murdered does Wallace have any interest in fighting for Scotland's freedom. This is the kind of movie where old buddies say hello by hurling rocks at each other, but remember—if William Wallace hadn't been all bummed out over his dead wife, he would have gone through life as "Tenderheart."

Rocky. Another sappy love story disguised as a Guy Movie. Rocky Balboa, the thick-headed lunk from the streets of Philadelphia, goes the distance with Apollo Creed not because he's a tough guy but because he wants to impress Adrian. Watch the original *Rocky* again and you realize there are more scenes of Rocky courting Adrian than fighting in the ring.

Private Parts. Here at Guy Movie headquarters, we listen to Howard Stern every day, not only for the constant stream of laughs but for his refreshingly brutal candor when it comes to any gender-related issue. We also enjoyed *Private Parts*, but we cannot in good conscience call it a Guy Movie, not when so much of the story is about the love affair between Howard and his wife, Allison. Many women had to be dragged into the theater to see *Private Parts*, but most of them emerged with comments like, "That was really a sweet movie," and, "I didn't know it was going to be a love story." No doubt Howard has a great Guy Movie in him, *Private Parts*, however, was not that movie.

Body Heat. Willam Hurt and Ted Danson are outstanding as a couple of minor league lawyers. The sex scenes with Kathleen Turner are among the finest to be found in a major motion picture. Mickey Rourke has a great cameo as an arsonist who jams along with Bob Seger's "Feel Like a Number" while he teaches Hurt how to set fire to a building. Richard Crenna is terrific as the millionaire attorney murder victim who almost deserves to get bashed to death with a baseball bat. Why, then, is this not a Guy Movie? Because our boy Hurt is the dupe who winds up in prison, while the evil Turner sips tropical drinks on the beach, that's why!

Top Gun. Oh please. Just because Tom Cruise and friends happen to be fighter pilots doesn't make this a Guy Movie. If there's any doubt in your mind about the real target audience for this film, I refer you to the volleyball sequence in which a shirtless Cruise and three other bare-chested boys hop around *in slow motion* while the camera lingers on their sweaty torsos. For further discussion of the real meaning of *Top Gun,* check out the Quentin Tarantino scene in *Sleep with Me,* in which Tarantino makes a convincing argument that the entire film is about a man's struggle with his sexuality.

Not that there's anything wrong with that.

The Professional

Rated R, 112 min., 1994
Director: Luc Besson
Screenplay: Luc Besson
Starring: Jean Reno, Natalie Portman, Gary Oldman, Danny Aiello
Explosions: ★★★★
Gunplay: ★★★★
Male bonding: ★★★
Memorable dialogue: ★★★★

> MATILDA
> You mean you're a hit man?
> LEON
> Yeah.
> MATILDA
> Cool.

Leon is a hulking, brooding figure who likes to drink milk and favors a wardrobe of weird round sunglasses, an odd little stocking cap, and pants that are four inches too short for him. He's also an illiterate mope who seems to think very carefully before responding to even the most innocuous of questions. You'd take one look at Leon and you wouldn't hire him to sweep floors in a fast food joint, but that's okay, he's got a steady job— as a "cleaner," i.e., professional hit man. Leon might not be able to spell his own name, but he's a one-man SWAT team capable of taking out a dozen men, which is exactly what he does at the beginning of *The Professional.* (When he finishes the job he takes the subway home and relaxes by tending to his plants and watching Gene Kelly movies.)

When Leon kills, it is a thing of beauty to watch. And we don't even feel bad for his victims because they're low-life drug dealers and murderers. Heck, if Leon were a bit smarter he could run for mayor of New York.

The bulk of Leon's work comes from Tony, a mob boss played by Danny Aiello, in one of his extremely rare turns as a mafioso. Tony recognizes that Leon couldn't tie his own shoes without some help, so he hangs onto Leon's money for him and tries to help him understand some of the realities of life in New York City. (Leon is from somewhere else—France?—but we're not sure where.) You get the sense Leon is perfectly content with his uncomplicated hit man existence, but his life is turned upside down when a crooked cop (Gary Oldman) and his henchmen assassinate everyone who lives next door—with the exception of the disturbingly precocious twelve-year-old girl named Matilda, who escapes the hit and moves in with Leon, who isn't socially skilled enough to send her on her way.

Matilda is played by Natalie Portman with Lolita-esque flair. Her relationship with Leon invites comparisons to the Jodie Foster–Robert De Niro pairing in *Taxi Driver*, and the sexual undertones here are unmistakable, but somehow this comes across as an admittedly weird but also gentle and almost touching union. As Matilda teaches Leon to read and Leon teaches Matilda how to be a professional killer, they each learn the meaning of family-type love for the first time.

But don't worry, this isn't some weird precious European artsy film. Director Luc Besson made *La Femme Nikita*, which also dealt with young females who are trained to kill, and he infuses *The Professional* with the same operatic glorification of flying bullets and flying bodies. Gary Oldman is allowed to go over the top—way over the top—as the dirty cop Stansfield, who tells a fellow officer, "Bring me everyone!" when he decides it's time to go after Leon. When the associate innocently asks, "What do you mean, everyone?" Oldman nearly shatters our eardrums with "EVERYONE!!!!"

It's only a slight exaggeration. The final confrontation pits several dozen members of the New York City Police Department against Leon, and it's a fair fight. There are at least two moments when you're sure you know how it's going to turn out—but don't be so sure. Besson isn't a slave to conventional Hollywood endings, which may be one of the reasons why *The Professional* didn't attract a large audience when it was released in 1994. That's too bad, because it is one killer of a Guy Movie.

Raging Bull

Rated R, 128 min., 1980
Director: Martin Scorsese
Screenplay: Paul Schrader and Mardik Martin
Starring: Robert De Niro, Joe Pesci, Cathy Moriarty, Nicholas Colasanto,
  Frank Vincent
Drinking: ★★★★
Fights: ★★★★
Male bonding: ★★★★
Memorable dialogue: ★★★★

Millions of guys know millions of guys who talk like the guys in *Raging Bull*. Rough guys who insert the "f-word" into every sentence, who mangle the language as they fumble about to explain what they're feeling, who eventually resort to using their fists to express themselves because that's really the only way they know how to make a point. Nearly two decades after *Raging Bull* was released, would-be toughsters all over the country continue to ape the comically Neanderthal conversational style of Robert De Niro and Joe Pesci as the LaMotta brothers. Here's Jake LaMotta asking little brother Joey about Vickie (Cathy Moriarty), a fifteen-year-old temptress who's lolling by the pool in their Bronx neighborhood, causing all the men to trip over their tongues:

> JAKE:
> You bang her?
> JOEY:
> No.
> JAKE:
> Tell the truth.
> JOEY:
> I just told you the truth! I tell you the truth the first time, you
> don't have to ask me again. I never do that, I always tell the truth,
> if I did it you would know.

When Joey admits he took her out but she wouldn't do anything, Jake leans back in satisfaction and says, "Naturally. She knew better, she knew you were an animal."

And that's one of the more tender moments shared by the boys.

What everyone first mentions about *Raging Bull* are the explosive fight scenes, which seem more painfully realistic because they're shot in black and white, often in super-slow motion, as bone-crunching ballets. More than a dozen of Jake LaMotta's middleweight fights from the 1940s and 1950s are chronicled here, with particular attention paid to LaMotta's epic battles with Sugar Ray Robinson. ("No other fighter will go near them," explains the ring announcer, "so they fight each other, three weeks apart.") Yet as great as those fight scenes are, it's the dialogue that elevates *Raging Bull* to the very top of any list of great Guy Movies.

"Don't overcook it," Jake says to his first wife as she grills him a steak. "You overcook it, it's no good. Defeats its own purpose."

Later, when Joey keeps asking Jake the same question in different ways, Jake explodes: "What am I, the circus over here?" He also asks Joey when he and Vickie became such "ah-*thar*-itics" on everything.

And when Jake once again obsesses to Joey about his wife's imagined infidelities, he stands all fat and stupid in front of the TV set and says in a quietly menacing tone, "I heard some things. I heard things, Joey." That line has been repeated by so many De Niro imitators that it's in danger of becoming his "You dirty rat!" or "My dear, I don't give a damn." I heard some things. I heard things, Joey.

Jake is a tremendous fighter who rises to the middleweight championship, but he's never able to savor his triumph because of his inherent lack of trust in almost everyone he meets, and his insanely jealous treatment of his wife. If she so much as approaches another guy, Jake yanks her aside and interrogates her about every word that was spoken, every thought that might have popped into her head. No matter what she says, it's not going to satisfy him. He's one sick rockhead.

De Niro put on something like sixty pounds to capture the rotund essence of Jake in his down years, but if anything that stunt takes away from his performance. Instead of concentrating on Jake's pathetic slide to the gutter, we're all saying, "Damn! Look how fat De Niro got for this role! He must have been guzzling Bosco!"

Nevertheless, *Raging Bull* stands as a classic. That it lost the Academy Award as Best Picture to *Ordinary People*, a weepy soap opera starring Donald Sutherland and Mary Tyler Moore as sweater-clad wealthy jerks who wish Timothy Hutton had drowned instead of his cuter and more well-adjusted younger brother, is a great injustice. I don't know how it happened but *I heard some things*.

Red River

Unrated, 133 min., 1948
Director: Howard Hawks
Screenplay: Borden Chase and Charles Schnee, based on a story by Chase
Starring: John Wayne, Montgomery Clift, Joanne Dru, Walter Brennan, John Ireland
Drinking: ★★★
Fights: ★★★★
Gunplay: ★★★★
Male bonding: ★★★★
Memorable dialogue: ★★★★

John Wayne and Montgomery Clift couldn't have been more different, as actors and as men. Wayne was a no-frills kind of guy, a hulking brute who probably never put the toilet seat down in his life, while Clift was a tortured pretty boy who wanted to be "just friends" with Elizabeth Taylor when she was the most desirable woman in the world. Monty and the Duke were never going to be drinking buddies in real life, but in the great Howard Hawks film *Red River*, they made for an unforgettable team.

Red River is *Mutiny on the Bounty* in the Old West, with Wayne as the Captain Bligh character and Clift as the dashing Fletcher Christian. In this version the Duke plays Thomas Dunson, a stubborn, rough-hearted cattle rancher who loved only one woman in his life—a gal who was killed by Indians when he left her behind with the wagon trail while he and his trusty sidekick (Walter Brennan, of course) blazed on ahead.

"You need what a woman can give you to do what you have to do," Dunson's woman had told him, but he brushed her aside, telling her he'd send for her later. The decision haunts him for the rest of his life and leaves him with a heart of stone.

Not long after that tragedy, Dunson semi-adopts Matt, a boy he finds wandering in the Texas wilderness—a boy who grows up to be Montgomery Clift. After fifteen years of struggling to make it in Texas, Dunson asks Matt to join him on a 1,000-mile cattle drive to Missouri, where there's great demand for beef. Along the way, they have to fight tomahawk-wielding, war-whooping studio Indians, who, of course, are no match for the Duke and Monty, the two best shots in the West. Of more concern than the occasional Indian attack is Dunson himself, a hard-drinking, hard-driving perfectionist who relentlessly pushes his men to the brink of mutiny. Some quit, while others directly challenge Dunson. He almost kills one upstart, but Matt fires more quickly, wounding the man instead.

"Why, you'd a shot him between the eyes," says Matt.

"Just as sure as you're standing there," replies Dunson.

The father figure and the young man have a bitter parting of the ways, with Dunson swearing to kill Matt some day if it's the last thing he ever does. Right around that time Matt meets and falls in love with the spunky Tess (played by the fabulously beautiful Joanne Dru), who doesn't even flinch when she takes an arrow through the shoulder. Watch for the scene where Dru and Clift are sitting against a rock, and Dru takes the traditional male romantic role, playing with Clift's face and making the first move while the handsome cowpoke babbles on, oblivious at first to the woman who is throwing herself at him. For 1948, it was quite a daring role reversal.

Lore has it that Wayne didn't much care for Clift and his prissy Method ways, and the big fistfight between the two of them looked so realistic because it went beyond the choreographed punches. A half-century later, it doesn't much matter. The important, lasting result is a classic Guy Movie.

Reservoir Dogs

Rated R, 99 min., 1992
Director: Quentin Tarantino
Screenplay: Quentin Tarantino
Starring: Harvey Keitel, Tim Roth, Michael Madsen, Lawrence Tierney, Steve Buscemi, Quentin Tarantino, Chris Penn
Car chases: ★★★
Gunplay: ★★★★
Male bonding: ★★★★
Memorable dialogue: ★★★★

Women don't exist in the world of the *Reservoir Dogs*. A waitress serves breakfast to the band of fast-talking crooks as they plan a diamond heist, and a female carjacking target pulls out a gun and shoots one of the robbers before she is blown away—and that's about it. Neither one of these minor characters has a single line of dialogue; we don't even get a good look at their faces. They exist on the very fringes of this guys' world. Then again, there's not much room for a woman to get a word in edgewise when Mr. Pink, Mr. Blue, Mr. Brown, and the rest of the color-coded bad guys are endlessly punching the air with hilariously obscene dialogue about such topics as the real meaning of Madonna's "Like a Virgin," the pros and cons of leaving a tip, and who played the title character in the 1970s detective series *Get Christie Love.*

When *Reservoir Dogs* was released in 1992, it singed the screen and announced the arrival of a major, pioneering voice in the world of Guy Movies—Quentin Tarantino, the jabbering maniac who specializes in plots that fold over like an omelet, with main ingredients of blood, male bonding, and intense conversations about the popular culture. With a snap of his fingers, Tarantino shifts the action from a chuckle-filled bull session in a breakfast diner to the backseat of a car, where a man who is covered with blood screams in pain and fights for his life. It's ballsy, inventive filmmaking, and it spawned a whole generation of Tarantino-wannabes, none of whom can match the original.

Reservoir Dogs is the story of a robbery gone wrong. Gravel-voiced crime boss Joe Cabot (Lawrence Tierney) has assembled a team of professional gunmen who are known to one another only by those literally colorful names—Michael Madsen is Mr. Blonde, Harvey Keitel is Mr. White, Tim Roth is Mr. Orange, and much to his dismay, Steve Buscemi is Mr. Pink. When Mr. Pink asks why he can't have a cooler color, Joe replies, "Because I tried that once and you get four guys all fightin' over who gets to be Mr. Black. . . . You're lucky you ain't Mr. Yella."

Most of the action takes place in an abandoned warehouse where the team is supposed to meet after the robbery, with flashbacks showing how Joe put together the gang and how the holdup went wrong. Tarantino fanatics, take note of the references made during the meetings in Joe's office. Mr. Blonde, we learn, is Vic Vega—perhaps he's cousins with the John Travolta character of Vincent Vega from *Pulp Fiction*. When Joe asks about Mr. Blonde's parole officer, Mr. Blonde says the guy's name is Scagnetti— the last name of the Tim Sizemore character in *Natural Born Killers*, for which Tarantino wrote the original screenplay. And Mr. White talks of his former partner, Alabama, and what a good gal she was. Alabama shows up again in *True Romance*, another Tarantino-scripted classic.

Every dog has his day in this movie, as Tarantino gives each of the main actors some juicy dialogue. The all-star cast is uniformly excellent, but the most memorable of all is Michael Madsen as the soda-sipping psychopath Mr. Blonde, who listens to a frightening rant from Mr. White and simply says, "Are you going to bark all day, little doggie, or are you going to bite?" Mr. Blonde also has the only musical dance number in *Reservoir Dogs*, when he shuffles around with a straight razor to the tune of "Stuck in the Middle with You" as he tortures a cop strapped into a chair.

The body count in *Reservoir Dogs* negates the opportunity for any kind of a sequel. However, a *prequel* about Mr. White and his cohorts—well, guys can only hope.

Risky Business

Rated R, 96 min., 1983
Director: Paul Brickman
Screenplay: Paul Brickman
Starring: Tom Cruise, Rebecca DeMornay, Joe Pantoliano, Bronson Pinchot, Curtis Armstrong
Car chases: ****
Drinking: ****
Male bonding: ***
Memorable dialogue: ****
Nudity: ****

Risky Business is the *Citizen Kane* of horny teenager movies. From that opening sequence when Tom Cruise's Joel tells us, "The dream is always the same," and his fantasy about a naked woman segues into a nightmare about missing his college exams, we know this isn't a typical teen-sex movie (not that there's anything wrong with typical teen-sex movies), this is an *artsy* teen-sex movie, with fancy music and decent acting and the very classy and quite naked Rebecca DeMornay. Four stars! Two thumbs up—way up!

The philosophy of *Risky Business* is summed up by Joel's friend Miles (Curtis Armstrong, who went on to utter the immortal line, "We've got bush!" as Booger in *Revenge of the Nerds*). After Joel tells Miles he's afraid to do anything that will jeopardize his future, Miles tells him, "Sometimes you gotta say, 'What the fuck.' Make your move."

Joel lives on the North Shore near Chicago with his wealthy, semi-clueless parents, who leave him in charge of the house for the weekend. "Just use your best judgment," his mother tells him. "You know we trust you."

His best judgment includes taking the forbidden Porsche for a wild ride, eating a frozen dinner washed down by Jack Daniels', dancing around in his underwear to "Old Time Rock and Roll" by Bob Seger, and calling up a prostitute who turns out to be a black man in drag. He/she immediately realizes he/she is not what Joel wants, so he/she gives him a phone number and says, "Ask for Lana. It's what you want. It's what every white boy off the lake wants."

Enter Lana (DeMornay). She stands in the open doorway as the leaves from the patio blow all around her and the Tangerine Dream score heats up, raising her skirt to reveal her perfect underwear-less body as Joel hugs her like, well, like a teenager hugging a beautiful naked hooker. Lana mounts Joel on the staircase while the camera pans to photos of Joel as a little boy, and we know we're watching one great movie, even as we yell for the camera to pan back to the staircase action.

Adding great spice to the action is Joe Pantoliano as Guido, a pimp who is not too thrilled that Lana and her girlfriends are now hanging out with Joel and his hormonally crazed classmates. He wants Lana back, and he's not about to let some North Shore kid steal his business. During a chase through the streets of Chicago, Miles screams, "I don't believe this, I've got a midterm tomorrow and I'm being chased by Guido the killer pimp!"

There are a number of indelible scenes in *Risky Business*, including Joel's underwear dance, the chase scenes, the big party at Joel's house, and of course the L train sex with Lana, to the tune of Phil Collins's "In the Air Tonight." But what really makes this a classic Guy Movie is the dialogue, the great one-liners, as when a Princeton recruiter tells Joel he's not exactly Ivy League material, and Joel dons the Ray-Bans and says, "Looks like the University of Illinois!", or a Porsche dealer working on the waterlogged car says, "Who's the U-boat commander?" And then there's Joel's presentation to the future businessmen's club, as he explains his money-making project: "My name is Joel Goodson. I deal in human fulfillment. I grossed over $8,000 in one night."

Hollywood just doesn't make too many films about a teenage boy who becomes a successful pimp while falling in love with a hooker. God bless the 1980s.

Saturday Night Fever

Rated R, 118 min., 1977
Director: John Badham
Screenplay: Norman Wexler, based on a story by Nik Cohn
Starring: John Travolta, Karen Lynn Gorney, Donna Pescow
Drinking: ★★★
Fights: ★★★
Male bonding: ★★★★
Memorable dialogue: ★★★★
Nudity: ★★★

Yeah I know there's disco dancing in this movie but the guys doing the dancing usually have cuts on their faces because they've been in nasty rough fights, and they're guzzling booze and getting lucky with the broads between dances so it's not like this is a freakin' musical or anything, all right? In fact, *Saturday Night Fever* is more of a comedy—intentional and otherwise—than a dance movie or a love story.

Take the dinner scene, in which John Travolta's Tony Manero wears a sheet around his polyester shirt so he doesn't spill spaghetti sauce on it. Every time someone at the table offers an opinion it turns into a fight, with family members throwing meatballs around and slapping one another stupid.

"No hitting, no slapping at the dinner table, that's the rule," says Tony's caricature of an Italian mother, who crosses herself every time she mentions Tony's brother, Father Frank the priest.

"Watch the hair," Tony says to his unemployed bum of a father. "You know, I work on my hair a long time, and you hit it. He hits my hair."

Hilarious.

Tony and his Brooklyn buddies—played by a bunch of actors who pretty much disappeared from sight after this movie—work in crappy jobs all week, saving their money so they can blow it on a Saturday night at Odyssey 2000, a glittery disco where the music of the Bee Gees and the Trampps ("Burn baby burn, disco inferno," whatever the hell that means) bangs off the walls and the dance floor lights up like a Twister game on mescaline. Tony is the king of the disco because he looks like Al Pacino and he can dance up a storm, and he has something resembling a brain compared to the apes who follow him around. All the girls want to dance with him and sleep with him, in that order—and while Tony doesn't particularly care about his sex mates, he's very selective about his dance partner.

Which leads us to Karen Lynn Gorney, who really screws up any serious intentions this movie might have had with her gum-cracking portrayal of Stephanie, a Brooklyn girl who thinks she's escaped from Brooklyn because she has a job as a secretary in Manhattan, on the fringes of the artistic community. ("I had lunch with Laurence Olivier," she says to Tony, who doesn't recognize the name until she mentions the Polaroid commercials he's done.) Stephanie is supposed to be this graceful young dancing babe, but Gorney is a rather clunky, thirtyish woman who is lucky to just hang on for dear life in her dance scenes with Travolta. The fact that we never saw her in any film of consequence after the megasuccess of *Saturday Night Fever* tells us everything we need to know.

If you haven't seen this movie in a while you may have forgotten that there are nearly as many sex scenes as dance moments. One of the boys has a loud tryst in the car while his buddies impatiently wait in the cold; after a screaming climax, he kisses his partner and says, "What was your name again?" And then there's Tony's make-out scene with Annette, played by the soon-to-be-pudgy Donna Pescow, aka TV's *Angie*. As they fumble with their clothes and Annette tells Tony not to bother with a condom, he says, "What do you got, the IOU, that thing?" There's also a cameo from another future TV star, Fran "*The Nanny*" Drescher, who cups Tony's ass and says, "Are you as good in bed as you are on the dance floor?"

Forget about the white suit and the Bee Gees, this is a Guy Movie all the way.

Scanners

Rated R, 102 min., 1981
Director: David Cronenberg
Screenplay: David Cronenberg
Starring: Stephen Lack, Jennifer O'Neill, Patrick McGoohan, Michael Ironside
Car chases: ***
Explosions: ****
Fights: ****
Gunplay: ***
Male bonding: ***

Thirteen minutes into *Scanners*, a head explodes. Literally. It inflates like a balloon, throbs like a broken toe, and then *kaboom!* it shatters in a gory storm of blood and bones and brain tissue, sending some viewers (gals) to the bathroom and others (guys) to the remote control so they can rewind and watch that scene again.

In its own way, the exploding-head scene is just as groundbreaking as the burning of Atlanta in *Gone With the Wind*. We'd never seen anything quite like it. If you erased the other 101 minutes of *Scanners* and you were left with a one-minute movie showing that head exploding, it would still be worthy of inclusion as a Guy Movie. In the last decade and a half there have been great strides made in special effects technology, but the exploding-head scene is still one of the most shocking and goriest scenes of all time. Even when you freeze the picture and advance it a frame at a time—and trust me, you'll want to do that—it's a stunning effect.

Scanners comes from the sick mind of David Cronenberg, who has also made movies about twisted twin gynecologists, people who turn into flies, and videocassettes that emerge from human torsos. A "scanner" is a telepathically gifted individual who can manipulate thoughts and actions through the power of the mind—to the point where you can even burst someone's head like a pinata if you really concentrate. There are 236 known scanners in the world, most of them "pathetic, social misfits" who are "unstable and unreliable," as a doctor explains it. How did they get this way? Could be "radiation, ESP, or a derangement of the synapses."

Whatever. The cool thing is, a head explodes.

The scariest scanner of them all is Darryl, played by the always-creepy Michael Ironside, who delights in creating bloody havoc wherever he goes. When Darryl was twenty-two he had a hole drilled in his head "to let the people out," but it didn't work. He can still hear what everyone is thinking, he can still climb inside their minds and control their thoughts and actions, he can still make people kill themselves. Rather than fight his demons, he's come to embrace them. Darryl's dream is to take over the planet so he can "bring the world of 'normals' to their knees!"

Darryl's chief rival is Cameron (Stephen Lack), a scanner who would like to use his power for the good of humanity. Cameron hooks up with the beautiful Jennifer O'Neill as Kim, who gets to utter such lines as "Now I know what it feels like to die," and, "We're the dream and he's the nightmare." Kim introduces Cameron to group self-therapy for scanners who would like to harness their abilities, leading to a scene where a bunch of scanners have to throw themselves around like Jerry Lewis in the last hours of his Labor Day telethon. It's Method acting run amok.

The plot of *Scanners*, such as it is, can be confusing at times, what with all the psychological and scientific mumbo-jumbo. Not that it matters when you've got a final battle between the top scanners kicked off by one of the harshest threats ever uttered on film: "I'm going to suck your brain dry!"

Scarface

Rated R, 170 min., 1983
Director: Brian DePalma
Screenplay: Oliver Stone
Starring: Al Pacino, Steven Bauer, Michelle Pfeiffer, Mary Elizabeth Mastrantonio, Robert Loggia
Car chases: **
Drinking: ****
Explosions: ***
Fights: ****
Gunplay: ****
Male bonding: ****
Memorable dialogue: ****
Nudity: **

When Al Pacino is good, he's very, very good. But when Al Pacino is bad, he's even better. In movies such as the aforementioned *Heat, Dog Day Afternoon, Scent of a Woman,* and *Devil's Advocate,* Pacino hams it up so much you almost expect the overacting police to show up and cart him away. The other actors just stand around like the Bulls used to do when Michael Jordan was in his prime. *Who knows where he's going, just get out of his way!*

This is the way it goes for nearly three hours in Brian DePalma's lush, rich, ridiculous, and revolting epic *Scarface,* a cocaine-soaked update of the old Paul Muni film about a low-level gangster who kills his way to the top of the crime world. There are a lot of other great actors in this movie and they all sweat and strain to keep up with Pacino, but in the end it's Pacino who stands alone as the king.

Then again, maybe he's standing alone because he's killed everyone else.

"I'm Tony Montana, a political prisoner from Coo-bah!" exclaims a man-tanned Pacino when he arrives in a detention camp in Miami, circa 1980. After barely surviving an encounter with a chainsaw-wielding coke dealer, Tony begins to make his mark as a criminal. Within a year he and his sidekick Manny (Steven Bauer) have risen from dishwashers to high-level thugs working for the loud and sloppy drug kingpin Frank Lopez (Robert Loggia), who has acquired a number of treasures with the millions he has made selling cocaine. Foremost among those treasures is Michelle Pfeiffer's Elvira, an ice-cold bimbo with birdlike shoulders who has a perpetually bored expression on her face, even when she's snorting coke or dancing in one of the brassy nightclubs where Frank and his boys like to hang out.

Tony, who tools around in town in a canary-yellow Cadillac with leopard-print seats, doesn't care that Elvira belongs to the boss. He wants Elvira, even though she tells him she has no interest in some guy who just fell off a banana boat.

"Banana boat!" says Tony. "Choo got the wrong guy. I don't come off no banana boat, okay?"

Try as she might, Elvira can't resist the cigar-chomping clown. Why, they might even have kids some day—"as long as there's a nurse" to take care of them, says Elvira.

The only woman Tony finds more enticing than Elvira is his own sister, Gina, played by the very long-named Mary Elizabeth Mastrantonio, who sports a bigger, bouncier Afro than Dr. J. in his prime. This whole weird incest thing is never really explained in *Scarface*; it's just there as an excuse for Tony to fly into a rage whenever any man even thinks about putting his hands on Gina.

Tony's rise to the top is splattered with blood, and his downward spiral is fueled by evil cocaine. He violates one of Frank's cardinal rules of drug dealing—"never get high on your own stash"—in a big way, keeping heaping piles of "yayo" stashed in gold containers throughout his monumentally tasteless mansion.

In the extended siege that is the climax to *Scarface*; Pacino wields a gun bigger than he is, screaming "How choo like that!" as he wipes out dozens of attackers.

"I'm Tony Montana!" he tells us, as if we didn't know by now.

Slap Shot

Rated R, 122 min., 1977
Director: George Roy Hill
Screenplay: Nancy Dowd
Starring: Paul Newman, Michael Ontkean, Strother Martin, Lindsay Crouse
Drinking: ***
Fights: ****
Male bonding: ****
Memorable dialogue: ****
Nudity: ***

Paul Newman's career is filled with great Guy Movies from *Somebody up There Likes Me* to *Cool Hand Luke* to *Butch Cassidy and the Sundance Kid* to *The Color of Money*, but the best of 'em all is *Slap Shot*, an unbelievably profane and violent comedy set in the gritty, blue-collar world of minor league hockey, where the men are animals and the women are tougher than beef jerky. Wearing a mind-boggling array of 1977-hipster clothes (including a pair of leather pants if you can believe it), Newman eats up the screen as the grizzled, booze-soaked but eternally optimistic player-coach Reggie Dunlop, who still believes that after all these years in the trenches, he's still one phone call away from coaching in the NHL. Never mind that his marriage is falling apart and he's old enough to be the father of everyone else on the team, never mind that his knees are like Jell-O—he's a hockey man. Wouldn't know how to do anything else. Wouldn't want to.

While waiting for that eternal pro dream to come true, Dunlop is helming the decidedly minor league Charleston Chiefs, a lousy team in a dying town. Rumor has it that the steel mill is going to be shut down any day now—and if half the city is out of work, the already sparse crowds will surely dwindle to nothing, giving the mysterious owner of the Chiefs an excuse to fold the franchise at the end of the season, unless she can find a buyer willing to take over the team and move it out of town. Adding to Reggie's headaches are the three new additions to his team, foisted upon him by penny-pinching team president Joe McGrath. (He's played by the oily Strother Martin, the same guy who told Cool Hand Luke, "What we have here is . . . failure to communicate.") The Hanson brothers are long-haired goons with glasses as thick as the ice they skate on, and they seem to have the mentality of very small children. After watching them unpack suitcases filled with trains and remote-control cars, Reggie storms into McGrath's office and says, "Are you crazy? Those guys are retards! They brought their fucking *toys* with them!"

Reggie keeps the Hanson brothers on the bench for as long as possible, but when he finally inserts them into another lost cause of a game, it's one of the most exhilarating moments in sports movie history. The Hansons are brutal idiots who really don't care about putting the puck into the net—they just want to make their opponents bleed, and they do so with unfettered glee. With Reggie's encouragement, nearly every member of the Chiefs joins the goon squad, and soon the team is on a winning streak that will take them all the way to the championship game. Reggie even goes on the local radio station one afternoon and puts a $100 bounty on a goon from another team.

When *Slap Shot* was released in 1977, there was a lot of controversy over all the foul language, although I find Newman's clothing more shocking. (A white turtleneck with a big honkin' necklace, are you kidding me?) Obscene dialogue has been commonplace in the two decades since then, but few movies contain such creative swearing.

Not only that, but *Slap Shot* has a patriotic heart. Witness the scene where a nervous ref skates up to one of the Hanson brothers during the "Star-Spangled Banner" and warns him that he won't tolerate any unnecessary rough stuff.

"I'm listening to the fucking song!" screams the Hanson brother.

Here's to the land of the free and the home of the brave.

Stripes

Rated R, 105 min., 1981
Director: Ivan Reitman
Screenplay: Dan Goldberg, Len Blum, and Harold Ramis
Starring: Bill Murray, Harold Ramis, John Candy, Warren Oates, Judge Reinhold, P. J. Soles, Sean Young, John Larroquette
Car chases: ★★★
Drinking: ★★★★
Explosions: ★★★
Fights: ★★★★
Gunplay: ★★
Male bonding: ★★★★
Memorable dialogue: ★★★★
Nudity: ★★★★

Bill Murray is the patron goof of every guy who ever mouthed off in class or roped his buddies into participating in elaborate schemes concocted to avoid anything resembling actual work or requiring physical exertion. In his early films such as *Meatballs*, *Ghostbusters*, and *Stripes*, Murray played basically the same character: the charming smart-ass, a sloppy Peter Pan with a crooked grin and a quick wit. Some women find this character to be annoying and creepy; others think he's irresistibly cute.

Men love him. He appeals to the inner malcontent in all of us.

In *Stripes*, Murray is John Winger, a sad-sack cab driver who loses his job, his car, and his girlfriend all in one day. Out of money and out of options, John and his best buddy Russell Ziskey (Harold Ramis, he of the thick glasses and even thicker hair) wander into the local recruiting center for the army. After all, as the TV ads tell them, it's not just a job, it's an adventure.

"Now there's a couple of questions I have to ask you," says the recruiting officer. "Are either of you homosexuals?"

"You mean, like flaming?" deadpans Winger.

"No, we're not homosexuals," says Ziskey, "but we are willing to learn."

Thus begins their "Be All You Can Be" adventure. John and Russell are assigned to the Bravo company, a collection of castoffs and oddballs who are whipped into semishape by the rigid Sergeant Hulka (the late Warren Oates). In a bull session on the eve of basic training, each of the soldiers has to talk a little bit about himself.

"Chicks dig me," says Winger, "because I rarely wear underwear, and when I do, it's usually something unusual."

John Candy is Ox, a chain-smoking lug who has joined the army because he wants to lose weight. "And you've got what, a six- to-eight-week training program, a real tough one, which is perfect for me!"

There's also a cow-loving country boy named Lee Harvey, and a dark-eyed loon who says, "My name is Francis Sawyer, but everybody calls me Psycho. Any of you guys call me Francis, and I'll kill ya."

The meandering plot follows our boys through the basic training experience and then to an overseas mission, where they're assigned to the top-secret "EM50" project—a ridiculous "urban assault vehicle" that looks like an RV with armor plating and big machine guns. When everybody in the company except John and Russell are captured by Czechoslovakian forces, John says they've gotta climb aboard the EM50 and go after their buddies—but Russell has his reservations. What if this rescue mission escalates into a miniwar?

"It's Czechoslovakia, it's like going to Wisconsin!" argues John.

Also along for the ride are a couple of dishy MPs played by P. J. Soles and Sean Young, back when she was pretty and not completely bonkers. (The scene with Murray and Soles and a spatula has been aped by millions of guys, much to the befuddlement of millions of gals.) Like *Animal House* and *Caddyshack*, *Stripes* isn't really concerned with telling a story; the laughs come from a series of loosely connected sketches, and when they hit the ninety-minute mark, it's time to blow up a few things and run the credits.

If only Merchant and Ivory would follow the same philosophy.

"Lighten up, Francis"–Guy Movie One-Liners

Ask a guy to pick up a gallon of milk on his way home from work, and you might as well head to the store right now to get it yourself because you know he's going to forget about it. Ask a guy what day of the week it was when he met his wife, and he'll look at you like you're insane. Day of the week? He can't even remember what year it was.

But if you ask a guy to repeat what Warren Oates said in *Stripes* to the soldier who insisted everyone call him Psycho rather than his real name, the guy will immediately tell you exactly what Warren Oates said:

"Lighten up, Francis."

And then he'll shed a tear for the late great Warren Oates.

There are dozens of memorable guy-movie one-liners rattling around in every man's head, including these all-time classics:

- "I'll be back."—Arnold Schwarzenegger in *The Terminator*
- "I'm too old for this shit."—Danny Glover in *Lethal Weapon*
- "I heard some things. I heard things, Joey."—Robert De Niro in *Raging Bull*
- "Our fugitive's name is . . . Dr. Richard Kimball."—Tommy Lee Jones in *The Fugitive*
- "Luca Brasi swims with the fishes."—James Caan in *The Godfather*
- "I'll bet you're a big Lee Marvin fan, aren't you?"—Michael Madsen in *Reservoir Dogs*
- "I coulda been somebody . . . I coulda been a contender."—Marlon Brando in *On the Waterfront*
- "If it were me, I'd bet everything. But that's me, I'm an aggressive gambler, Mr. Vegas."—John Candy in *Stripes*
- "Funny? Funny how? Like I'm a clown, I'm here to amuse you?"—Joe Pesci in *Goodfellas*
- "What are you going to do—arrest me for smoking?"—Sharon Stone in *Basic Instinct*
- "That'll be the day."—John Wayne in *The Searchers*
- "Don't you look at me!"—Dennis Hopper in *Blue Velvet*
- "Get your hands off me, you damn dirty apes!"—Charlton Heston in *Planet of the Apes*
- "You're going to need a bigger boat."—Roy Scheider in *Jaws*
- "Blessed is he who in the name of charity and goodwill shepherds the weak through the Valley of Darkness, for he is truly his brother's keeper and the finder of lost children."—Samuel L. Jackson in *Pulp Fiction*
- "Yippee ki-yay, motherfucker."—Bruce Willis in *Die Hard*
- "Go ahead. Make my day."—Clint Eastwood in *Sudden Impact*

- "Go ahead. Make my day."—Clint Eastwood in *Sudden Impact*
- "I bury those cock-a-roaches! What did they ever do for us?"—Al Pacino in *Scarface*
- "Here's Johnny!"—Jack Nicholson in *The Shining*
- "We're on a mission from God."—Dan Aykroyd in *The Blues Brothers*
- "Is it safe?"—Laurence Olivier to Dustin Hoffman in *Marathon Man*
- "I love the smell of napalm in the morning."—Robert Duvall in *Apocalypse Now*
- "Gimme back my son!"—Mel Gibson in *Ransom*
- "Badges! We ain't got no badges. We don't need no badges. I don't got to show you no stinkin' badges."—Mexican federale in *Treasure of the Sierra Madre*
- "You're money, baby!"—Vince Vaughn in *Swingers*

The Terminator

Rated R, 108 min., 1984
Director: James Cameron
Screenplay: James Cameron and Gale Anne Hurd
Starring: Arnold Schwarzenegger, Michael Biehn, Linda Hamilton, Paul Winfield, Lance Henriksen
Car chases: ★★★★
Explosions: ★★★★
Fights: ★★★★
Gunplay: ★★★★
Memorable dialogue: ★★★★
Nudity: ★★★

Who knows why a trained-killer cyborg from the future would have an Austrian accent, but why quibble when the half man, half machine in question is played by none other than Ah-nold Schwarzenegger, one of the finest actors in the history of motion pictures. This is the film that made Arnold a huge international star and propelled him to the top of the action-movie heap for the next decade, and rightfully so. Wearing those wraparound sunglasses, clomping around in jackboots, and uttering just a few key phrases—including the immortal, "I'll be back"—Arnold created one of the greatest Guy Movie bad guys ever. In fact, you have to keep reminding yourself that Arnold *is* the bad guy, and Michael Biehn's Reese is the hero of the film.

The film opens with a naked Terminator arriving in Los Angeles in 1984, having traveled all the way from 2029 so he can kill Sarah Connor (Linda Hamilton) in order to prevent her from one day giving birth to the son who will become the leader of the human revolution against the

machine-dominated society. "Sort of a retroactive abortion," explains a psychiatrist who thinks Reese and Sarah are nuts.

Reese has followed the Terminator into the present. His mission is to kill the Terminator, so the Terminator won't kill Sarah, so Sarah can give birth to John, who is the one who sent Reese into the present in order to kill the Terminator. But don't worry if you can't follow all that, there are explosions every ten minutes to keep you entertained.

Within minutes of his arrival, the Terminator has executed a gang of punks (including Bill Paxton, with a blue-haired Coolio look) and has armed himself with a cache of weapons. He blows away two other women who are unfortunate enough to have been named Sarah Connor and executes a number of innocent bystanders along the way as he relentlessly stalks Sarah number three, who is in police custody. After the Terminator destroys the police station, killing veteran character actors Paul Winfield and Lance Henriksen, Reese helps her escape, and tries to explain all that futuristic gobbledygook to her while protecting her from the unstoppable cyborg.

"He's a model 101 cybernetic organism—part man, part machine," says Reese. "One of the hunter-killers built in automated factories."

"In the future?" says Sarah.

"One possible future," replies Reese. In other words, the future is fluid and can be changed, depending on what happens between Reese, Sarah, and the Terminator. Talk about your love triangles!

Director James Cameron has a wonderfully unflinching touch, as in the scene where the Terminator takes an X-Acto knife to his own arm and eyeball as he does a little home repair. He also gives the supposedly emotion-free Terminator a sense of humor, as when the nosy super in the building knocks on the Terminator's door and says, "Hey buddy, you got a dead cat in there or what?"

The Terminator's scanning device runs down a number of possible replies, including a simple "Yes" or "No," but he opts for the most colorful option: "Fuck you, asshole."

Cameron infuses *The Terminator* with deep messages and he's clever enough to leave just enough room for the great sequel that will follow, but when he ladles up the philosophy he does so with heaping portions of guts and gore and fireballs. Even if you don't entirely buy the time-travel premise, *The Terminator* rocks.

Ah-nold

by Laurie Viera

I'm sure at some point, Rich will make his not-at-all homoerotic tribute to Arnold Schwarzenegger. Before he can do that, I'd like to give you my "Three Reasons Why Ah-nold's Movies Annoy Women."

Reason # 1: The Accent: We often find a foreign accent sexy, but on Arnold it's just plain ludicrous. Why? Because he keeps playing characters with distinctly American names, like Harry Tasker, his secret agent role in *True Lies*. Then there was Doug Quaid, Arnold's alias in *Total Recall*. Those names just don't fit with a man who sounds like he should be wearing lederhosen while chugging beers in an Austrian pub.

Reason #2: The Portrayal of Women: We've come a long way, right? As if! In the world view of Arnold films, we are reduced to one of the following roles:

The attractive victim in need of Arnold's special brand of carnage-laden rescue, like Vanessa Williams in *Eraser*.

The tough-as-nails heroine with masculine biceps, like Linda Hamilton's sinewy character in *Terminator 2, Judgment Day*. In the first *Terminator* film, she was a more softly curved version of the above attractive victim, except in that film she was terrorized, rather than rescued by the nearly mute slab of a man.

Then there's every husband's revenge fantasy: the naughty wife who gets her comeuppance. In *True Lies*, Arnold blackmails on-screen wife Jamie Lee Curtis into doing a striptease for a "stranger," who's really Arnold's character. This is supposed to afford her a bit of excitement as well as teach her a lesson for contemplating an affair, even though her character is constantly neglected and lied to by Arnold.

And let's not forget Sharon Stone in *Total Recall*, whose duplicitous dealings earn her a bullet in the head from outraged hubby Arnold, who instructs her corpse to "Consider that a divorce." His character sure saved a bundle on lawyers.

Reason #3: The Dialogue: Arnold's most adept at spouting cute one-liner sound bites that cut nicely into the movie trailers. It's no doubt a toss-up between a line of dialogue and a Neanderthal grunt, or maybe longer sentences would be just too difficult to decipher, due to—you guessed it—Reason #1: The Accent. Arnold's most memorable bit of verbalizing was the erudite gem, "Fuck you, asshole," in *The Terminator*. Too bad they couldn't use that one in the preview.

Arnold Schwarzenegger:
An Appreciation

"Grant me one request!" barks Arnold Schwarzenegger in *Conan the Barbarian,* one of his first big hits. "Grant me—"

Grant him what? Acting lessons? A better haircut? A dialect coach?

No! Grant him "revenge!"

And revenge he gets in that bloody masterpiece. Wielding a sword the size of an airplane wing, Conan slices and dices his way to Guy Movie immortality in that 1982 flick, which also starred James Earl Jones as a ruthless pillager with a really cool helmet, and Sandahl Bergman as the woman who takes off her shirt and makes love to Conan even though he has bigger breasts than she does.

Even before *Conan the Barbarian,* muscleheads knew Arnold as the legendary bodybuilder from the 1977 documentary *Pumping Iron,* in which he psyched out such humorless competitors as Lou *"The Incredible Hulk"* Ferrigno on his way to yet another Mr. Olympia title. Here was a guy who was built like a tree trunk but didn't take himself seriously; he was obviously using his bodybuilding career as a springboard to something more. Even if we could barely understand what Ah-nold was saying with that thick Austrian accent, we knew this guy could become a force in Hollywood.

Guy Movie Rule #1: You don't necessarily have to be able to talk to become a superstar.

After *Conan,* Arnold starred in a series of violent, action-packed thrillers, including *Conan the Destroyer, Red Sonja, Commando, Predator, Red Heat, Raw Deal, The Running Man, Total Recall,* and of course the two *Terminator* movies. You could tell he was having a great time flexing his muscles, chomping cigars, shooting guns, throwing knives, punching out stuntmen, and occasionally pawing a willing young thing. Other actors might suffer for their art, but Arnold was clearly enjoying his rise to the top. Off-screen, he never complained about the trappings of stardom or the pressures of fame or the "grind" of making a movie or any of that crap. Whether he was hanging out at a Republican convention, marrying Maria Shriver (much to the horror of the Kennedy family), or puffing a stogie at another Planet Hollywood opening, Arnold was reveling in his unlikely reign as the biggest star in Hollywood. He was like the foreign exchange student who is voted homecoming king. The Guy Movie Hall of Fame had to raise its ceiling just to make room for Arnold's statue.

Not that there haven't been some dark moments. Perhaps softened by marriage, Schwarzenegger started making movies that were practically cuddly. In *Kindergarten Cop* and *Twins* and even *The Last Action Hero,* Arnold was no longer winking at the camera—he was mugging like one of the Three Stooges. Instead of ripping men's hearts out and blowing them to smithereens, he was lifting them off their feet with one hand or trying out lame catchphrases like "big mistake." Instead of rolling around with seminaked babes ten minutes after meeting them, he was *courting* them—holding their hands and sending them flowers. The family-friendly Arnold was still more entertaining than, say, a Daniel Day-Lewis or a Mandy Patinkin.

Arnold rebounded in 1994 when he reteamed with director James Cameron for *True Lies,* which was filled with explosions and airplane stunts, and even featured a gratuitous striptease scene starring Jamie Lee Curtis. There were a few too many wisecracks from Tom Arnold as the comedic sidekick, but the kills-per-minute ratio ranked right up there with the best of the early Arnold.

But later that same year, Arnold hit an all-time low with *Junior,* a supposed comedy about the world's first pregnant man. The sight of Arnold giving birth was more horrifying than the alien popping out of John Hurt's stomach in *Alien.* Adding to the debacle was the presence of Gal Movie superstar Emma Thompson as Arnold's love interest. What in the world was he thinking?

At this point I wondered if we'd lost Arnold forever, if he'd gone over to the other side. Maybe next he'd be showing up as a footman in a MerchantIvory film, or deaf-mute in a movie by the creators of *The Piano.* But he came back strong with the gratuitously violent *Eraser,* costarring the great James Caan and the beautiful Vanessa Williams. It was vintage Arnold—the kind of movie where he takes a spike through the right hand and a bullet to the left shoulder, but shrugs off those injuries and is still able to throw the bad guys around as if they were no heavier than Tickle Me Elmo dolls. He also shoots an alligator and says, "You're luggage!" Not as good as when he killed his wife Sharon Stone in *Total Recall* and said, "Consider that a divorce," but a heckuva lot better than, "I'm going into labor!"

84 Charing Cross Road

Director: David Jones

Screenplay: Hugh Whitemore, based on the book by Helene Hanff, originally adapted for the stage by James Roose Evans

Starring: Anne Bancroft, Anthony Hopkins, Judi Dench, Jean De Baer, Maurice Denham, Eleanor David, Mercedes Ruehl, Daniel Gerroll, Wendy Morgan, Ian McNeice, J. Smith Cameron, Tom Isbell

1986, 100 min., PG

Romance: **

Tears: ***

Heartthrob men: **

Smart-ass women: ****

So who's the heartthrob in this picture? Anthony Hopkins, that's who. What is it about that guy that makes him so, well, doable? He's certainly not conventionally sexy like that other irresistible senior, Sean Connery. Yet despite that balding pate, that British reserve, and that face that bears a faint resemblance to the Pillsbury doughboy, I just want to have his children. There, I've said it. Hopkins's acting is as piercing and brilliant as his lovely blue eyes, and even though he once portrayed that Martha Stewart of human flesh-eaters, Hannibal Lecter, I can't help but think of him as a helluva nice guy. When he plays a romantic lead, it's always as a shy, polite, and very English gentleman. And despite rumors to the contrary, we gals like gentlemen. Yes, I could gaze into Anthony Hopkins's baby blues forever.

So could Helene Hanff (Anne Bancroft), who falls for him without even seeing those periwinkle orbs. A sassy, tough-talking writer with an insatiable hunger for classic and affordable English literature—a taste that can scarcely be satisfied in 1949 New York City—Helene forms a most unlikely epistolary friendship with Frank Doel, the reserved English bookseller (played by Hopkins, of course) who fills her orders from his quaint little antiquarian bookshop on London's Charing Cross Road. Their literary—and deeply intimate—friendship spans two decades of letters that go back and forth from New York and London.

Not much of a story, you might think. But oh, how wrong you are. For this film celebrates literature, love, the deeper attachments that transcend physical chemistry, the generosity of spirit that transcends continents and cultural differences, and the sadly lost art of letter writing. And don't give me that puzzled look just because letter writing has found a shadow of a renaissance in our E-mail and fax culture. It's not the same, I tell you. Women know this, but since the time of Cyrano, most men have become completely clueless about the power of the handwritten letter. This film is also very much about the love of books as objects themselves, and repeated viewings are akin to curling up with a beloved book you've read over and over again.

Helene's letters to Doel, with their cynical humor and their love of literature, and their occasional food packages for the meat-and-produce-rationed postwar Brits, become an anticipated treat that touches the lives of all who labor among the dusty shelves of Marks & Co. Her missives range from ecstatic praise like, "Your Stevenson is so fine it embarrasses my orange crate bookshelves" to diatribes such as, "Sloth! I could rot over here before you send me anything to read!" And she often looks directly into the camera to remark on things like the "Dear Madam" that opens the letter Doel pens to accompany his very first shipment to her:

"I hope 'Madam' doesn't mean over there what it means over here," says Helene.

Maybe I adore this film because I'm a hopeless romantic nerd who once worked in an antiquarian bookstore. Maybe it's because the contrast between the sharp-tongued Bancroft and the oh-so-genteel Hopkins is oh-so-amusing. Or maybe it's because the king of flatulence humor, Mel Brooks, is the executive producer.

Don't even think about putting off renting this film, because seeing it will make you think twice about putting off things you really want to do.

All About Eve

Director: Joseph L. Mankiewicz
Screenplay: Joseph L. Mankiewicz, based on a short story called "The Wisdom of Eve" in *International Cosmopolitan* magazine, May 1946
Starring: Bette Davis, Anne Baxter, George Sanders, Celeste Holm, Gary Merrill, Hugh Marlowe, Thelma Ritter, Marilyn Monroe
1950, 138 min., unrated
Great clothes: ★★★★
Romance: ★★★
Smart-ass women: ★★★★

"Fasten your seat belts. It's going to be a bumpy night."

That's Bette Davis as diva theatrical actress Margo Channing, slugging martinis as she prepares to wreak jealous havoc at boyfriend Bill's welcome home birthday party. And that's an apt description of the melodramatic, wryly amusing ride you'll take when you strap yourself in to watch *All About Eve.*

So what's Margo, undisputed star of the New York theater, surrounded by friends and her loving director boyfriend, got to be jealous about? Eve, that's who. Eve, the devoted young fan who's charmed all and sundry around Margo and has become her live-in personal assistant.

Ever wonder why women always seem to know in their guts when a sweet, pretty young thing is really an evil queen offering you a poisoned apple? Or why men seem blissfully oblivious to anything lurking behind that darling face?

Well, as Margo says to Bill (Gary Merrill) when he dismisses her dawning suspicion of Eve as "paranoiac insecurity," "It's obvious you're not a woman."

And like Mankiewicz's other tribute to the intricacies of women, *A Letter to Three Wives*, *All About Eve* is all about women. We can be your best friend—or your worst nightmare. And we know, despite how men might scoff at our much-maligned women's intuition, that our guts are the best friends we have. And our own insecurities can be our worst enemies.

Despite boyfriend Bill's steadfast loyalty, Margo can't deal with the fact that he's eight years her junior. After several martinis, she confides in playwright friend Lloyd Richards (Hugh Marlowe) that she's attained the dreaded age of forty.

"Bill's thirty-two," she slurs. "He looks thirty-two. He looked it five years ago. He'll look it twenty years from now. I hate men."

The script is chock full of pointed rejoinders and juicy barbs, all delivered by an astounding cast of believable characters. There's deliciously wicked George Sanders, who plays the acid-tongued theatrical columnist Addison DeWitt. And there's my favorite movie maid Thelma Ritter, who's the first to see behind Eve's demure facade. There's super-gal Celeste Holm, who plays Margo's devoted best girlfriend. And then there's Anne Baxter, who pulls off Eve's labyrinthine character with nothing short of brilliance. There's even a tiny role for a very young Marilyn Monroe, who plays the dimwitted starlet Miss Casswell, described by Sanders as "a graduate of the Copacabaña School of Dramatic Art."

And besides Oscars won for Best Picture, Best Screenplay, Best Director, and Best Supporting Actor (George Sanders), there's to-die-for clothes that'll make you hit your nearest vintage clothing store for a fix.

All This, and Heaven, Too

Director: Anatole Litvak
Screenplay: Casey Robinson, from a novel by Rachel Field
Starring: Bette Davis, Charles Boyer, Jeffrey Lynn, Barbara O'Neil, Virginia
Weidler, Harry Davenport, Helen Westley, June Lockhart, Anne Todd,
Richard Nichols
1940, 141 min., unrated
Heartthrob men: ***
Romance: ****
Tears: ***

Before there was Nannygate, movies and novels made nannies into a veritable icon of female culture. Some of these nannies took their power back, like the one who worked for Robin Williams and not only went on to replace his wife, but also to produce non-nanny-oriented movies. There are, of course, the more extreme cases, like Rebecca DeMornay in *The Hand That Rocks the Cradle* and Bette Davis herself in the creepy title role of the 1965 film *The Nanny*. This is what happens when you don't check references. But my favorite sort of nannies are those long-suffering, selfless creatures who lust after their married employers, like Jane Eyre and a very young Bette Davis in *All This, and Heaven, Too.* If you're partial to that kinder, gentler breed of nannies, this movie's for you. It's also the perfect movie to sit home alone and watch on major holidays while your lover spends his with his wife and children. So snuggle up with a jumbo box of Kleenex and a half gallon of Ben & Jerry's. And don't worry, you'll lose about five pounds of water weight no matter what you eat.

Young, pretty Henriette Deluzy-Desportes (Bette Davis) is all a-flutter when she's hired to be the governess for the adorable children of the handsome, wealthy Duc de Praslin (Charles Boyer). At first, you might wonder whether you've just tuned into a reunion of the cast of *Gone With the Wind.* The duc's nightmare of a wife, who alternates between cruelty and self-humiliation in her vain attempts to lure the duc into the marital bed, is played by Barbara O'Neil (Scarlett O'Hara's mom). And the kindly valet who warns Bette about the dangers of working for this twisted family is played by Harry Davenport (*GWTW*'s Dr. Mead). Bette herself vied for the role of Scarlett O'Hara. To further disorient you, the role of the duc's eldest daughter is played by a very young June Lockhart, but luckily she's too girlish to be mistaken for Lassie's mother.

The duc's children are transformed by Bette's kindness, as the only interest their spiteful, neurotic mother has in them is their living proof that she actually slept with her husband at least four times. A doting father, the duc is instantly taken with his kids' kindly caretaker. She feels compassion for his plight as the man who is married to the mother of all wives who don't understand their husbands. And before long, the two of them look upon each other with unspoken but undeniable love. Boyer is so endearing in this film, one can hardly connect him with the creep who drove Ingrid Bergman to insanity in *Gaslight*.

Insane herself with jealousy, the duchesse is convinced that an affair is afoot. And when she's out of town and the duc squires Bette and one of his daughters to the theater, Parisian tongues start wagging. So not only does the duchesse determine to rid her palatial home of that sweet young baby-sitting thing, she also vows to ruin her life. Everyone's so darn convinced that Bette and Boyer are doing the wild thing, you wish they'd just go ahead and do it.

Here's a little taste to whet your appetite for tears to come. As Bette's friend the Reverend Henry Field (Jeffrey Lynn) says to her in her darkest hour, "All ministers have their faiths, and most of them preach that one must endure with patience the miseries of this world in order to earn happiness in another. But I believe that no matter what our despair, there is a heaven on this earth for each of us, if we can only find it."

Amen.

What's the Deal with This Bette Davis Thing?

by Richard Roeper

Women of all ages love Bette Davis. Right after a little toddler girl learns to say "Mommy!" and "Daddy!" and "Let's go shopping," she'll utter the phrase, "I sure do like Bette Davis." Then, seventy-five years later, when that little girl has grown into a tired old woman, she'll sigh and say, "One of the great pleasures of my life has been watching the films of Bette Davis."

No man has ever said that.

What is the deal with this Bette Davis thing? Why do women think she's great? Maybe it's because Bette Davis was never all that great-looking, though women will try to argue otherwise. Maybe it's because Bette Davis always seems to be picking on some guy, or duking it out emotionally with some classically beautiful babe. All I know is, Bette Davis reminds me of those female gym teachers who hated the boys and was very protective of the girls. She's scary.

The American President

Director: Rob Reiner
Screenplay: Aaron Sorkin
Starring: Michael Douglas, Annette Bening, Martin Sheen, Michael J. Fox, Anna Deavere Smith, Samantha Mathis, Shawna Waldron, Richard Dreyfuss, David Paymer, Nina Siemaszko
1995, 114 min., PG-13
Great clothes: **
Heartthrob men: ***
Romance: ****
Smart-ass women: ***

Ever since I saw more than I ever wanted to see of Michael Douglas's posterior in that misogyny-fest *Basic Instinct,* I'd have put my money on Dan Quayle's spelling abilities before I'd ever bet on Douglas as a believably wholesome leading man. But that was before I'd seen *The American President.* And this film has done much more than restore my faith in Michael Douglas: It made me believe once again in the fairy tale of a principled American leader.

Wrap up that delicious fancy in a modern-day Cinderella story, complete with the incomparable Annette Bening dancing at the ball, and you've got a film that'll defrost the jaded heart of any contemporary American gal.

President Andrew Shepard (Douglas) is exactly what a woman dreams of when she casts her vote. He's smart, he's dedicated, he's got integrity, and he's cute. He's never served in the military, an obvious parallel to Bill Clinton. But unlike Bill, there are no Paula Joneses, Gennifer Flowerses, or Monica Lewinskys tumbling out of closets. Frankly, I'm one of those people who doesn't care whom the President screws, just so long as it's not the American people. This fictional President is single, a widower who wonders if he would've made it to the White House had the tragic death of his wife not made character assassination a dicey proposition for his opponents.

Now it's an election year once again, and the people care very much about whom the President screws. It seems that Shepard finds himself facing a drop in his 63 percent approval rating, all because he falls for lovely, sassy environmental lobbyist Sydney Ellen Wade (Bening). And who can blame him? For one, it's lonely at the top. Shepard can't even get his chief of staff, A.J. (Martin Sheen), who was once the best man at his wedding, to call him Andy when they're alone together. Also, Shepard's smitten by

Sydney, who stands up to him at their very first meeting regarding an environmental bill she's pushing, despite her awe at finding herself face-to-face with the most powerful man in the world.

That night, when he's playing pool alone with A.J., Shepard awkwardly broaches the subject of seeing Sydney again.

"She didn't say anything about me?" asks Shepard.

"Well, no, sir," deadpans A.J., "but I could pass her a note before study hall."

Despite his staff's fears and the fact that the most powerful man in the world can't even get it together to order flowers, Shepard courts Sydney. And the press, fueled by the venom of conservative opposition leader Senator Rumson (a convincingly slimy Richard Dreyfuss), has a feeding frenzy. With her career now at stake and Shepard's approval rating plunging, Sydney reluctantly tries to break it off, but the President is determined to have a private life with the woman he loves despite all the hoopla. Whatta guy.

And whatta gal. Sydney is no passive Cinderella. She can be all innocence and confusion in one moment, all fire and brilliance in the next.

It's a fabulous love story laced with witty repartee and scathingly ironic political commentary. And the cast, from Michael J. Fox as a hilarious Stephanopoulos clone to Shawna Waldron as the wise-beyond-her-years first child, is a blast.

The Americanization of Emily

Director: Arthur Hiller
Screenplay: Paddy Chayefsky
Starring: James Garner, Julie Andrews, Melvyn Douglas, James Coburn, Joyce Grenfell
1964, 117 min., unrated
Heartthrob men: ★★★★
Romance: ★★★
Smart-ass women: ★★

If you swooned over James Garner's plaid polyester–clad bod on that seventies TV show *The Rockford Files*, just wait'll you see him play a convincingly romantic lead in *The Americanization of Emily*. Now Julie Andrews I could usually do without, because she always reminds me of that prelude-to-a-lobotomy song "Edelweiss" from *The Sound of Music*. But when you see her shine as the sassy, sexually liberated Emily in this film, you'll forget she once left the convent for an even drearier fate as a Von Trapp family singer.

As Lt. Commander Charlie Madison of the U.S. Navy, Garner looks a bit bewildered when he first meets Emily and his friendly pat on the derriere is met with an outraged slap on the kisser. Oh, well. England may be in the throes of the Second World War during the tense weeks before D-day, but Charlie's got more important concerns. His job in the navy is something like those lackeys who have to root out all the green jelly beans from the candy dish in the rock star's dressing room, except that Charlie's pretty high up on the navy food chain. His raison d'être is to keep his master, Admiral Jessup (Melvyn Douglas), in luxury. For the admiral, Charlie procures the best food and liquor from the black market, the cushiest hotel rooms, and the prettiest girls from the British army's motor pool. And in return for an expensive dress, a few Hershey bars, and maybe even a bottle of French perfume, most of the girls are happy to show up at Charlie's swank admiral-hosted soirees for dinner, cards, and "a little mauling."

Emily's smug, British sense of fair play is disgusted by such excess, especially at a time when most English families have endured food rationing for years. But when Charlie calls her a prig, Emily is hurt. After all, as she later confides to a female coworker, she'd bestowed numerous mercy humps upon wounded soldiers while working at an army hospital. At the time, her husband had just been killed in action, and she "was overwhelmed with tenderness for all dying men."

Determined to prove she's a good sport—although not a slut—Emily haughtily agrees to attend one of Charlie's parties—for cards only and wearing her own dress, thank you very much. But Charlie is stung by her imperious perception of him as a typically hedonistic American, and he lets her have it.

"We crass Americans didn't introduce war into your little island," declares Charlie. "This war, Miss Barham, to which we Americans are so insensitive, is the result of two thousand years of European greed, barbarism, superstition, and stupidity. Don't blame it on our Coca-Cola bottles. Europe was a going brothel long before we came to town."

That's it. She's hooked. Actually, Charlie's quite attractive and really not a bad sort after all, even if he is American. Besides, his noncombat status is the most appealing thing about him to a woman who's lost a husband, father, and a brother in the war. Charlie doesn't even want to be in battle. After surviving Guadalcanal, his self-proclaimed religion is unabashed cowardice. Hell, he's the most antiwar soldier you've ever seen. And this is the most provocatively antiwar movie to predate Vietnam I've ever seen. Why, there's not a chance in hell that Charlie could become a casualty.

Until Charlie's mentally unhinged admiral decides that in order to boost the navy's importance in the eyes of the military powers-that-be, "The first dead man on Omaha Beach must be a sailor." And guess whom he orders to capture that event on film?

Garner and Andrews are splendidly witty; Melvyn Douglas a perfect personification of war's institutionalized madness. Joyce Grenfell is delightfully dotty as Emily's mom. And James Coburn, as gung-ho Lt. Commander "Bus" Cummings, is a ten on the hunk meter.

Auntie Mame

Director: Morton DaCosta
Screenplay: Betty Comden and Adolph Green, adapted from the play by Jerome Lawrence and Robert E. Lee; based on the novel by Patrick Dennis
Starring: Rosalind Russell, Forrest Tucker, Coral Browne, Fred Clark, Roger Smith, Patric Knowles, Peggy Cass, Joanna Barnes, Pippa Scott, Lee Patrick, Willard Waterman, Connie Gilchrist
1958, 143 min., unrated
Great clothes: ****
Romance: **
Smart-ass women: ****
Tears: **

They just don't make movies like they used to. Gone are the days when child bartenders, gut-wrenching hangovers, liquid lunches, and slurred speech spelled comedy. You'll just have to check your nineties sensibilities at the door and see *Auntie Mame* to get a taste of these nostalgic delights.

In this genuinely funny and touching story, little Patrick Dennis, a shy, sheltered orphan, unexpectedly comes to live with his affluent bohemian Auntie Mame (Rosalind Russell). One of her continuous, mid-Prohibition cocktail parties is in full swing, and although she's never before laid eyes on her new charge, it's love at first sight.

Patrick immediately gets a lesson on how to mix the perfect martini for Mame's endless array of artistic and intellectual guests. From them, he learns lots of new words, like "heterosexual" and "libido." But most important, from his big-hearted Auntie Mame he learns how to love, how to open his mind, and how to embrace life to the fullest.

Enter the staunchly conservative Mr. Babcock of the Knickerbocker Bank, who is Patrick's trustee and thinks the boy's free-thinking guardian has come straight out of hell. Mr. Babcock probably would have financed a sequel to *Auntie Mame,* one in which Patrick, now about forty, is attending his first AA meeting. Fearful that Babcock will take Patrick away from her if she continues to violate the rules of the trust, Mame bamboozles the banker into believing she's enrolled Patrick in a conservative private school. But when Babcock does a little checking and finds Patrick at a progressive—and nudist—school in the Village, it's off to a "restricted" and "exclusive" boarding school for Mame's "little love." She's so heartbroken she doesn't even care when the stock market crashes that very same day and wipes out her fortune.

You'll adore Rosalind Russell as the wildly eccentric Mame, a woman whose ever-changing hair color and outfits would spark envy in the heart of any fashion-conscious transvestite. My favorite of one of her many pathetic attempts to earn a living after the crash is her stint as a switchboard operator whose pronunciation of her firm's multisyllabic name sounds like Lucille Ball doing a Vita-Meta-Vegamin commercial.

Why do I adore *Auntie Mame*? Because Mame is woman at her life-affirming, powerful—and feminine—best. She's determined that Patrick won't grow up buying into the bigotry and snobbishness he learns at school, and does her best to make sure his vacations at home keep at least one of his feet in her open-minded and often outrageous world. Mame can work her magic on anyone, even Agnes Gooch, the dowdy, bespectacled secretary hired to type up her memoirs.

"Live!" she tells Agnes. "That's the message! Life is a banquet and most poor suckers are starving to death!"

Beaches

Director: Garry Marshall
Screenplay: Mary Agnes Donoghue, based on the novel by Iris Rainer Dart
Starring: Bette Midler, Barbara Hershey, John Heard, Spalding Gray, Lainie Kazan, Victoria-Grace Johnston (and Mayim Bialik and Marcie Leeds, who play Midler and Hershey as children)
1988, 123 min., PG-13
Heartthrob men: **
Romance: **
Smart-ass women: ***
Tears: **

For someone who considers herself to be a woman of sophisticated tastes, this mainstream studio tearjerker is a guilty pleasure. Perhaps it's because, like Bette Midler's character, CC Bloom, I grew up in New York in a working-class Jewish family, and living in California makes me homesick for stuff like Lainie Kazan (who plays her mother Leona) complaining in a nasal Bronx twang that she's "schvitzing" from the heat (translation: sweating). Perhaps it's also because, like CC, I've always had a morbid curiosity about upper-class WASPs like her best friend Hillary Whitney (Barbara Hershey). Such exotic creatures. What do they do at those Junior League meetings? And why do they have so many forks on the table?

Midler's and Hershey's characters meet by chance on an Atlantic City beach at the tender age of eleven. CC is a precocious child singer who lives in the Bronx with her bossy stage mother. CC's extremely talented but not conventionally pretty—a shortcoming that haunts her all her life. Hillary is a beautiful, wealthy, and privileged child from San Francisco, and instantly wins CC's heart by admiring her talent. The two girls become pen pals, fascinated by the gulf between their two worlds. They finally meet up again when, as young women, CC is a struggling singer scraping by delivering singing telegrams in a dreadful bunny costume, and Hillary shows up in New York determined to break out of her staid lifestyle as a lawyer.

Bette is enchantingly wicked as the self-absorbed but big-hearted CC, and Barbara is perfect as the vulnerable goddess. She'd also be every bit as gorgeous, even without those Julia Roberts–like lips, which were as initially confusing to behold as Julia was the first time I saw her without her trademark curls.

The two totally dissimilar girls have a friendship made in heaven, until competition in the form of John Heard, a handsome theater director, enters the picture. CC may have astounding talent that will skyrocket her to success, but she'll never be the man-magnet that Hillary is. And she'll never have her well-bred taste in clothes, either.

At one low point in the women's friendship, Bette whines to John Heard, "What would I do without a best friend?"

"You have me," he offers.

"It's not the same," she says.

Ain't it the truth, gals. There's nothing like a best girlfriend—that heart that comforts, that shoulder to cry on, and those eyes you want to scratch out in an occasional fit of jealous rage.

Be prepared to laugh, but have a big box of tissues on hand as well, even if you think you're immune to films that deteriorate into the disease-of-the week genre. And be forewarned: Chances are you'll be belting out the "Wind Beneath My Wings" in the shower despite all your efforts at self-control and complaints from your neighbors.

Guilty Pleasures

Beaches is one of my guilty pleasures, but there are so many more. These are the movies your film-buff friends will scoff at. You'll agree with them, but you'll rent them anyway, probably alone. If you're lucky enough to have a friend like my gal-pal Mary Hagen, who shares my passion for no-brainers despite her fancy education, you'll find someone with whom you can share the fun. Here's a few that Mary and I love:

Midnight Lace, an unintentionally comic thriller. It stars Rex Harrison and that queen of squeaky-clean, Doris Day, who plays a hysterically screaming victim while prancing around in leopard pillbox hats and other campy vintage wear.

Gidget and *Gidget Goes to Rome,* ridiculously unlikely teen romances that are so sweet you'll probably break out in an adult case of acne. Mary also highly recommends *Gidget Goes Hawaiian.* I haven't seen that one yet, but Mary's taste is always impeccable.

Two Susan Hayward sob-fests, *Back Street* and *I Want to Live!* In the first, Hayward desperately tries to cope with her love for a married man. In the second, she desperately tries to avoid execution. You'll be desperately trying to stem the saline tide.

Valley of the Dolls, a cinematic soap opera in which Barbara Parkins champions virginity, Patty Duke rips a wig off the head of Susan Hayward, Sharon Tate firms up her bosom, and everyone gets hammered.

The Best Years of Our Lives

Director: William Wyler
Screenplay: Robert E. Sherwood, from a novel by MacKinlay Kantor
Starring: Myrna Loy, Fredric March, Dana Andrews, Teresa Wright, Harold
Russell, Cathy O'Donnell, Virginia Mayo, Hoagy Carmichael
1946, 170 min., unrated
Heartthrob men: **
Romance: ***
Tears: ****

Forget about ambushes, bombing raids, bloody campaigns, and triple-digit body counts. We'll leave those questionable pleasures to the war movies guys crave. This is a film about the aftermath of war, made

decades before Jane Fonda welcomed Jon Voight home from Vietnam, and way ahead of its time. It's *The Best Years of Our Lives*, an unforgettably poignant coming-home story that won Academy honors for Best Picture of 1946. In other words, it's a sure-fire tearjerker.

World War II is over, and three servicemen, strangers to one another, catch an air force flight back to their midwestern hometown of Boone City. Drawn together by their hopes and fears about coming home, the three forge an instant friendship. Glamour-boy bombardier Fred (Dana Andrews) may have a chest full of ribbons, but what awaits him back home is hardly a hero's welcome. The only job he can get is his former gig at a drugstore lunch counter, and his shallow peroxide blonde of a wife (Virginia Mayo) isn't exactly keen on living on a budget. You'll simply love to hate her; Madonna could've dedicated the song "Material Girl" to that trashy dame.

Then there's Homer Parrish (Harold Russell), a sailor returning to a loving family and fiancée (Cathy O'Donnell). There's just one small problem: He's got hooks now instead of hands. He's sure his bride-to-be will be grateful when he lets her off the hook . . . anyway, you know what I mean. (By the way, this gifted actor really had lost his hands and won a special Oscar for this role.)

Finally, there's Sergeant Al Stephenson (Fredric March), who is thrilled to be back in the arms of wife Millie (Myrna Loy), but not so sure he'll fit back into his old life as a stuffy, conservative banker.

When Al takes up a new post as a loan officer for returning vets, his boss Mr. Milton is miffed that Al grants a farm loan to a penniless ex-soldier named Novak. After all, Novak has neither security nor collateral. But Al takes a stand. His time in the trenches has taught him how to "tell which ones you could count on."

"I tell you that this man Novak is okay," says Al. "His collateral is in his hands and in his heart and in his guts."

I tried that one the last time I applied for another credit card, but evidently the man I spoke to hadn't seen this film.

No one can understand the pain of the memories these men carry back with them—and the harsh realities of readjusting to civilian life. No one but the women who help them heal, soothe their night terrors, and offer them unconditional acceptance. These women play a crucial role in this film, and a crucial role in the aftermath of war. Few films in those days exposed how war changes people forever—not just those who fought it, but those to whom they return. This one does it beautifully.

Myrna Loy's at her consummate best as the good sport who puts up with Al's postwar excessive partying. Like Robinson Crusoe counting off his days on that deserted island, Myrna stoically counts off Al's cocktails at a company banquet at which he is to give a speech. Their daughter, Peggy, (Teresa Wright) is just what Dana Andrews needs as the reality of his sham of a marriage sets in, although Al doesn't quite envision home wrecker as an acceptable career choice for his child. And Homer's girl Wilma is determined to prove she's ready for life with a handicapped man, despite his stubborn efforts to shut her out.

And by the way, Teresa Wright, the sweet young thing who plays Al's daughter, recently made a comeback as a sweet old lady in Francis Ford Coppola's *The Rainmaker*.

The Big Easy

Director: Jim McBride
Screenplay: Daniel Petrie, Jr.
Starring: Dennis Quaid, Ellen Barkin, Ned Beatty, John Goodman, Grace
   Zabriskie, Lisa Jane Persky, Tom O'Brien
1987, 101 min., R
Heartthrob men: ****
Romance: ***
Smart-ass women: ***

Once, years ago, I met Dennis Quaid. Well, I didn't exactly have a conversation with him. I was filling in for a hotshot Hollywood producer's regular assistant, and Dennis Quaid walked into the office. He smiled that devilishly boyish trademark grin at me and said, "Hi, I'm Dennis." No shit, I thought, as my knees shook and I weakly smiled back. Hollywood "insider" protocol prevented me from jumping up and down and screaming like some hausfrau game show contestant. But what a devastatingly sexy man. I'll never forget that moment. Why don't we see more of you these days, Dennis?

The Big Easy stars Dennis Quaid as a romantic lead. Reason enough to rent this film at least once a month. But then, as if you need more motivation than that, it's set in decadent, steamy New Orleans. Locals I've met in New Orleans scoff at *The Big Easy* as a stereotypical tourist's view of their city. But to me, New Orleans will always be linked in my mind with the three essential ingredients for personal happiness: great music, raw oysters, and the six-pack on Dennis Quaid's inimitable stomach.

Oh, I almost forgot, there's sex, too. Both Dennis and Ellen Barkin, the object of his attentions, simply ooze sexuality. It's actually quite amusing to watch Barkin try to play a straight-arrow district attorney who's investigating New Orleans police corruption and trying very hard to steer clear of police lieutenant Dennis's spicy Cajun charms. Even in a prim gray suit with her hair done up in a modest chignon, Ellen might as well be wearing spandex. I adore Ellen Barkin, who embodies everything that's come-hither about a woman. And together she and Dennis have a chemistry that'll fog up your TV screen in the hottest half-clothed sex scene in cinematic history. Guys might feel cheated that Dennis is the one who's shirtless, but that's their tough luck.

In midseduction, Dennis is called away on police business.

"It's okay," Ellen says shyly, "I never did have much luck with sex anyway."

"Your luck's about to change, chére," says the ever-confident Quaid. For all you purists, there's even a story, a good one. Ellen's D.A. character is hot on the trail of the killer of a New Orleans gang lord. Dennis is supposed to help in the investigation, but Ellen's frankly disgusted at first sight by Dennis's blatant and unapologetic exploitation of his badge. He parks at fire hydrants, takes free meals at restaurants, but hey, that's just the way things are done in the Big Easy. What Ellen doesn't know is that Dennis's whole precinct pads their paychecks with what they euphemistically term the "widows and orphans fund," and what Dennis doesn't know is that he has finally met his match.

Bram Stoker's Dracula

Director: Francis Ford Coppola
Screenplay: James V. Hart, based on the novel by Bram Stoker
Starring: Gary Oldman, Winona Ryder, Anthony Hopkins, Keanu Reeves, Sadie Frost, Tom Waits, Richard E. Grant, Cary Elwes, Bill Campbell
1992, 128 min., R
Great clothes: ★★★★
Heartthrob men: ★★★★
Romance: ★★★★

Ask just about any guy what they thought of Gary Oldman as a casting choice for the role of Dracula. Are you kidding me, they'll say? He's not attractive enough. Why didn't they cast someone who's actually good-looking? Someone like, say, Keanu Reeves.

I take exception to such opinions, as obviously did the very wise Francis Ford Coppola. Gary Oldman may not be classically handsome, but, girl, is he sexy. Sure, there are times in the film when he parades around in a white wig that brings to mind a geriatric Mickey Mouse. And when he dons those cloven hooves or that bat creature thing it is admittedly far from a fashion statement. But when he's in his youthful, well-fed vampire guise with those cute little Lennon-esque sunglasses, Oldman has an irresistible, magnetic energy that just makes you want to rip your own bodice from your heaving bosom and offer him your blood to drink. Never has bloodsucking been more erotic. Never has undead been more enchanting.

Keanu's in this film, too, and yes, he's got a nice face. His natural

woodenness even lends a clear sense of virtual reality to the role of Jonathan Harker, the prim legal clerk to whom leading lady Winona Ryder (Mina) is betrothed. While Jonathan is in Dracula's castle helping him close escrow, Dracula notices Mina's picture in Jonathan's room. She is the image of the beloved wife he lost in the fifteenth century, a tragic event that first incited him to have a taste for blood. Count Oldman knows this cannot be a coincidence, and vows to win Mina for himself, while we girls pray that his pursuit might spare her from a lifetime of matrimony to a boring mortal.

This is not just your usual horror film: it is a sweeping, operatic romance about grand passions and great clothes. The costumes are baroque hybrids of English and Japanese fashion. The sets are stunning. The haunting score and the gorgeously moody cinematography will hook you from the prologue right through to the end. The film's also a clever commentary on the shadow side of sexuality and the all too prevalent relationship between sex and diseases that are carried by the blood.

As Von Helsing (Anthony Hopkins), a benignly mad metaphysician who leads the crusade to destroy Dracula, comments:

"The very name 'venereal diseases,' the diseases of Venus, imputes to them divine origin, and they are involved in that sex problem about which the ethics and ideals of Christian civilization are concerned. In fact, civilization and 'syphilization' have advanced together."

The rest of the supporting cast are superb. There's Sadie Frost playing Lucy, a hormonally charged virgin who serves as an appetizer for the blood-and-love-starved Dracula. And there's also a handsome trio of Lucy's lovestruck suitors: Arthur (Cary Elwes), a pretty boy aristocrat; Quincy (Bill Campbell), a strapping Texan; and Jack (Richard E. Grant), a morphine-addicted shrink whose most interesting patient is an insect-eating insane asylum inmate played by Tom Waits. As good things seem to come in threes in this film, there's also a troika of bare-breasted, blood-sucking incubi to whom Dracula offers Keanu as a snack.

Speaking of food, a glass of red goes very nicely with this film.

Chapter Two
Director: Robert Moore
Screenplay: Neil Simon
Starring: James Caan, Marsha Mason, Valerie Harper, Joseph Bologna
1979, 124 min., PG
Heartthrob men: **
Romance: ***
Smart-ass women: ***
Tears: **

If you thought James Caan was hot as the schlong-wielding Sonny Corleone in *The Godfather*, you'll feel much better about yourself for loving him in *Chapter Two*. In this Neil Simon treat, Caan is adorably vulnerable as George, a writer who hasn't quite recovered from the death of his wife. As Jennie, Caan's love interest, Marsha Mason does a fine job, even if she is a bit too perky at times. Nonetheless, her character takes the stand-by-your-man stance to a level that few of us mortals could ever hope to do.

When the story opens, neither George nor Jennie are looking for love. The death of George's beloved wife isn't the sole cause of his posttraumatic state. He's also shell-shocked after surviving a series of disastrous blind dates with creatures sporting names like Bambi, thanks to his well meaning but terminally philandering brother, Leo (Joseph Bologna). As for Jennie, starting a relationship is the last thing on her mind. She's trying to revive her dormant acting career, now that she's freshly divorced from an insensitive jock. But despite all their efforts to resist a Leoengineered blind date, a series of mishaps and clever one-liners brings George and Jennie together anyway.

In one of the best first dates ever seen in any film or other plane of reality, George and Jennie check each other out and . . . surprise, surprise: They really like what they see. Here's a little taste of the kind of intergender honesty this scene exemplifies:

GEORGE

No matter how old or experienced you are, the process never seems to get any easier, does it?

JENNIE

What process?

GEORGE

Um, mating.

JENNIE

Mating? My God, is that what we're doing?

GEORGE

The first thing I did when you passed was inhale, got a whiff of your fragrance. I don't know if you're aware of it or not, but in our particular species the sense of smell is a determining factor in sexual attraction.

JENNIE

This is just a guess, but do you write for *Field and Stream?*

After nine whole days together, George and Jennie realize they're in love. Of course, that's when George's grief and guilt blast out of his psychic hiding place. Both of them are scared shitless, but they decide to get married anyway. Target date: their two-week anniversary. And the same fellow, George's brother, Leo, who was dying to see these two pair up, starts to think that adjoining rooms in a local mental health facility might have been a better option.

As Jennie doggedly takes on the ghosts of George's past, it's suspense, tears, and laughs right through to the end. Does she lack pride and have a Teflon-coated ego, or can a woman's love really heal her man's grief for another? You decide.

Basically, *Chapter Two* is a lesson in how fearlessness, honesty, and Neil Simon's witty repartee can pay off in our romantic lives. If only I could hire him to ghostwrite my real-life conversations.

If you get the urge for a midviewing snack, try toasting marshmallows over a roaring fire fueled by one of those books on how to deceive your way into a man's heart. And while you're at it, toss one of those puppies to Valerie Harper, who plays Jennie's best friend, Faye. She's fabulous and beautiful as always, but looks like she may have gone a bit overboard in the dieting department. Maybe it's a Rhoda Morgenstern thing.

Dangerous Liaisons

Director: Stephen Frears
Screenplay: Christopher Hampton, based on his play, and adapted from the novel *Les Liaisons Dangereuses* by Choderlos de Laclos.
Starring: Glenn Close, John Malkovich, Michelle Pfeiffer, Swoosie Kurtz, Keanu Reeves, Mildred Natwick, Uma Thurman
1988, 120 min., R
Great clothes: ****
Heartthrob men: **
Romance: ***
Smart-ass women: ****

Ever feel guilty about your nastiest fantasies? Like turning the lover who dumped you into road kill, seducing your husband's best friend, or slapping the face of that syrupy-sweet co-worker who's just too damn perky in the morning?

Fear not. I have a solution to your moral dilemma. Rent *Dangerous Liaisons* and watch it alone. Then you'll be able to delight unabashedly in the evil conspiracies of the two main characters, for whom guilt just isn't a concept.

You might think of Glenn Close and John Malkovich, who play the leading roles with nothing short of genius, as being fairly average-looking people. But in *Dangerous Liaisons*, you'll believe they are the hottest stud and studette to ever mince through an eighteenth-century Parisian drawing room and summon demons into the lives of everyone around them.

A self-described "virtuoso of deceit" whose credo is "win or die," Glenn's character, the Marquise de Merteuil, has elevated dishonesty and seduction to an art form. After all, life as an ordinary eighteenth-century Frenchwoman would have been just too darned confining. Too many men ordering you around and telling you when it's okay to open your legs. But thanks to her world-class talents for all forms of manipulation and emotional blackmail, the marquise can have any man she wants and society is never the wiser.

There's only one person with whom the marquise can candidly gloat

over her triumphs—only one person who is her peer—and that's her male counterpart, the lady-killing Vicomte de Valmont (Malkovich).

The marquise has just learned of an opportunity to destroy an ex-lover who once spurned her for another woman—but she needs a lethal weapon like Valmont to carry it out. It seems that her hated ex-lover plans to wed sixteen-year-old convent-reared Cecile (a dazzling and very young Uma Thurman). That very same ex prizes virginity above all else in a prospective bride, and so, the marquise asks, would Valmont to be so kind as to deflower the dim-witted girl? Unfortunately, such prospects only bore Valmont, as the task would be far too easy. He's a master of seduction, and a master must hone his skills to stay on top. (Pun definitely intended.) His chosen prey is, instead, the breathtakingly beautiful Madame de Tourvel (a marvelous Michelle Pfeiffer), whose deliciously challenging combination of qualities include virtue, religious piety, and marital fidelity.

Says Valmont:

"I want her to believe in God and virtue and the sanctity of marriage and still not be able to stop herself. I want the excitement of watching her betray everything that's most important to her. Surely you understand that? I thought betrayal was your favorite word."

"No, no . . ." says the marquise thoughtfully. "Cruelty. I always think that has a nobler ring to it."

The spider's web that the marquise and Valmont spin grows more and more complex, and the fun ever more wonderfully wicked. Close and Malkovich are irresistibly ruthless, fascinating to watch as they slither through their own and everyone else's romantic entanglements like serpents in human form. They do what you and I would never dare to do.

So go ahead, indulge in a guilt-free viewing. You can always go to confession tomorrow.

Dial "M" for Murder

Director: Alfred Hitchcock
Screenplay: Frederick Knott, adapted from his play
Starring: Grace Kelly, Ray Milland, Robert Cummings, John Williams
1954, 123 min., unrated
Romance: **

"You're the only person I can trust."

How sweet the sound of those words from your partner in love and life. Not so in Alfred Hitchcock's ironically chilling *Dial "M" for Murder*. Ray Milland's character, Tony, delivers this line to the only person he feels he can trust—the man he has just hired to murder his trusting wife, Margo.

We women all have this fear that the man we trust will turn out to be our worst nightmare. After all, all men are dogs, right? Liars, drunks, beaters, cheaters. Of course, a few of us occasionally stoop to their level and get a little nooky on the side. But for that we should be punished, shouldn't we? After all, aren't we all vying for the crown of the queen of mea culpa? Even if we had good reason to cheat in the first place?

As the quintessential master of irony, Hitchcock opens by carefully confusing the audience as to just how trustworthy and sympathetic a character Margo is. When we meet Margo, elegantly played by lovely Grace Kelly, we learn that she's an Englishwoman married to retired tennis star Ray Milland. We also learn she's been having a clandestine affair with a man who is definitely not a dog—American crime novel writer Mark Halliday (Robert Cummings). When boyfriend finds himself in London and stops in for a quick rendezvous with Grace, she explains her dilemma: Hubby's been ever so much nicer and more attentive lately. So she feels it's only right to give her marriage another shot.

But what she doesn't know is this: Ray's reformed ways are all a ruse to throw her off the track. He knows all about her affair with Mark, and he not only intends to punish her for her infidelity, but also to inherit her sizable bank account in the process.

Ray Milland is splendidly diabolical as the wronged husband whose motivations for engineering Grace's demise are greed as well as revenge. Hell, he probably only married her for her money anyway, we say to ourselves as the consciousness of Grace's infidelity fades in the face of Ray's ruthlessness. This bastard truly enjoys devising the whole elaborate, seemingly flawless plan for Grace's murder, from blackmailing his chosen assassin into service, to playing the reformed neglectful husband to an unsuspecting Grace and new buddy to her visiting ex-lover. Ray is solicitous, kind, and considerate to Grace—in short, he's a lot like Ted Bundy.

"Good-bye, dear," he says to Grace, and kisses her full on the mouth as he is about to leave their apartment for a stag party with her unsuspecting lover, Mark—knowing full well that this good-bye will hopefully be his last. It's truly a delight to watch him, whether he's sweetly talking to Grace on the phone while the assassin rehearses the crime in the background, or when he's coolly sweating out a solution to a foiled plan.

The interactions are all wonderfully British in a mannered sort of way with everyone wearing their polite social masks, even when lives are hanging in the balance and you're sitting on the edge of your seat wiping sweat from your brow. But when Chief Inspector Hubbard (John Williams) comes on the scene with his posh accent, soft heart, and dogged determination to sniff out the truth, the fun truly begins.

A Self-Help Moment

Any of you gals shopping for the perfect man? Forget anything anyone's ever told you. Instead, remember what you do when you're in the market for any big-ticket item. Make a shopping list.

Sometimes watching movies helps you figure out what you want. Here's what I came up with for my idea of Mr. Right:

- The face and physique of Greg Wise in *Sense and Sensibility* (all right, I'm shallow, it's the first thing on my list)
- The shy sexiness and career mentoring of Gabriel Byrne in *Little Women*
- The courtliness of Anthony Hopkins in *84 Charing Cross Road*
- The irresistible wit of Billy Crystal in *When Harry Met Sally . . .*
- The sexual magnetism Gary Oldman has in *Dracula* (no, not the cloven-hooved version, the youthful persona with the John Lennon glasses)
- The biting wit and loyal friendship of Rupert Everett in *My Best Friend's Wedding* (who cares if he's gay, this is a fantasy list)
- The gigantic personality and presence of Gerard Depardieu in *Green Card*
- The well-defined tummy and arrogant smirk of Dennis Quaid in *The Big Easy*
- The fidelity and deep, come-hither voice of *Sense and Sensibility's* Alan Rickman—even if he's reading the phone book
- The ability to look as good in a loincloth as Daniel Day-Lewis does in *Last of the Mohicans*

The Double Life of Veronique
(La Double Vie de Veronique)

Director: Krysztof Kieslowski
Screenplay: Krysztof Kieslowski and Krysztof Piesiewicz
Starring: Irene Jacob, Phillipe Volter, Aleksander Bardini, Claude Duneton, Halina Gryglaszewska, Kalina Jedrusik, Jerry Gudejko, Wladyslaw Kowalski
1991, 96 min., R, French and Polish with English subtitles.
Heartthrob men: **
Romance: ***
Tears: **

I still haven't come to terms with the fact that the master of dramatic subtlety and understatement, director Krysztof Kieslowski, has left this life. I am grateful that he left behind one of the few, very few films that I would call perfect—*The Double Life of Veronique*. This is one of those blissful experiences where film really does feel like a fine work of art, yet without the emperor's-new-clothes pretensions I often find in so-called serious works of cinematic brilliance. This one shows how the art of cinema can be entertaining and absorbing at the same time.

The story centers around two young women who are strangers to each other, yet are physically identical. One, Weronika, lives in Poland; the other, Veronique, lives in France. Think of it as an artsy take on the *Patty Duke Show*. After all, all art is derivative, and Kieslowski may have been unconsciously influenced by poorly dubbed sixties sitcoms imported from the good old U.S. of A.

But enough film theory. Both Weronika and Veronique are classical singers, both had mothers who died when they were young, both seem robust but have frail health. And both are played by the luminously talented Irene Jacob, who will always be the object of my envy for getting closer to Laurence Fishburne's so-fine body (in *Othello*) than I could ever hope to do.

Weronika leaves behind her boyfriend Antek (Jerry Gudejko) to enter into a singing competition in Krakow. She has the most hauntingly beautiful, almost otherworldly voice you've ever heard. "I have a strange feeling," she tells her father, "I'm not alone in the world." This feeling doesn't creep her out or anything, mind you, it makes her feel comforted.

In Krakow, Weronika gets a fleeting glimpse of her double, Veronique, who is staring out from the window of a school tour bus. As the bus whisks her away, Veronique snaps a photo of Weronika—without even realizing she's her double—as she's too caught up in a student demonstration raging in the background.

Weronika wins the singing competition, but as she makes her Krakow debut before a packed concert hall, tragedy strikes.

At that same moment, in France, Veronique weeps without knowing why. And also without knowing why, she decides to give up singing. Then she becomes fascinated from afar with a children's book author who's also a puppeteer. (Perhaps more writers should consider augmenting their income in this growing field.) Anyway, it's a mutual fascination as he slowly lures her into his net with cryptic and whimsical clues.

My advice is to see this film at least two times: once to enjoy the story and soak in the lush imagery; the second and subsequent times to let the underlying themes sink in and resonate on more and more levels. For me, this film is about rebirth and transformations. It's about using reality to create art. It's even about parallel realities, and it could be about angels. I find something new in this dreamlike cinematic experience every time I see it. In fact, the last time I viewed it, I realized that in France, even classically trained singers smoke cigarettes like they're going out of style.

So what makes this a women's film other than an astonishingly intelligent female lead playing two women? The director. Kieslowski not only loves women, he reveres them in all their strength, in all their vulnerabilities, and in all the strength of their vulnerabilities. And let's face it, it's also a women's film because your average football-watching, Howard Stern–listening male weighs his film hero's strengths and vulnerabilities by weapon size and body count. And in case you haven't noticed, he usually isn't hot for reading subtitles. Unless he's hot for you and hoping that feigned interest in French cinema will get him past the portals of your panties.

Enchanted April

Director: Mike Newell
Screenplay: Peter Barnes, from the novel by Elizabeth von Arnim
Starring: Miranda Richardson, Josie Lawrence, Polly Walker, Joan Plowright, Alfred Molina, Michael Kitchen, Jim Broadbent
1992, 93 min., PG
Great clothes: ★★★
Romance: ★★★
Tears: ★★

Have you looked at your checkbook lately and tearfully concluded you just can't take that idyllic vacation you've been dreaming about? Don't fret, my dears, you can always rent *Enchanted April*. It's ever so easy on the bank balance, and I swear, afterwards you'll feel as refreshed and renewed as someone who just spent a month in the country. Besides, there's no jet lag.

Now imagine the dreary, rainy wintry London of the 1920s. Lottie (Josie Lawrence), a childlike, innocent eccentric who "sees inside people" and believes she sees long-dead "immortals" like Keats crossing the street from time to time—in other words, delightfully mad—spots an ad in a newspaper and instantly obsesses on it. The ad proclaims the availability of a medieval castle for rent on the Italian Riviera. Lottie hasn't a clue about most things, let alone how she's going to get there, especially with her dull, self-centered, and penny-pinching hubby Mellersh (Alfred Molina) standing in the way, but she won't rest until she makes it happen.

She does have a nest egg, however, and if she can only get a few ladies to share in the expenses . . . Her first reluctant convert is an acquaintance named Rose (Miranda Richardson), who is in an equally passionless marriage to Frederick (Jim Broadbent). Pale, demure Rose and red-faced, lusty Frederick couldn't be more mismatched, she with the "face of a disappointed Madonna," and he with his profession writing racy books under a pseudonym. Lottie and Rose find two strangers to share their holiday: Mrs. Fisher (Joan Plowright), a crusty old widow who wishes "to sit in the shade and remember better times and better men," and the stunningly gorgeous Lady Caroline Desta (Polly Walker), who longs to get away from the crashing boredom of life as a man magnet. Oh, Lady Caroline, how I can relate! If only she knew that the wife of one of her most ardent fans—a man she knows only by his nom de plume—was none other than Rose.

Though they arrive at night in a driving rain, Lottie and Rose wake up to a fairyland filled with fragrant flowers, and the shimmering sea beckoning beyond. Dreary London, disappointing husbands, and nagging suitors couldn't be farther from the present reality.

"This place makes me feel flooded with love," declares Lottie.

Even the pompously bossy Mrs. Fisher falls under the spell of her surroundings, and is won over by Lottie's persistent, if daft, kindness. Lottie is determined that Mellersh should come and share her joy, and determined that Rose should persuade her husband to join them, too. Uh, oh, Lady Caroline, I see a soap opera in the making.

Even if you're not dying to fly off to Europe or Hawaii or wherever, if you're a hopeful romantic who wants to believe in the transformational power of love, this film will make you believe.

Gas Food Lodging

Director: Allison Anders
Screenplay: Allison Anders, based on the novel *Don't Look and It Won't Hurt* by Richard Peck
Starring: Brooke Adams, Ione Skye, Fairuza Balk, James Brolin, Jacob Vargas, Robert Knepper, David Lansbury, Chris Mulkey, Donovan Leitch, Nina Berlanger, Adam Biesk
1991, 102 min., R
Heartthrob men: ★★★
Romance: ★★
Smart-ass women: ★★

Fairuza Balk may be young, but she already has an amazing range. I believed her when she played a dim-bulb, lamb-to-the-slaughter virgin in *Valmont* just as much as when she played a sinister, modern-day Wicked Witch of the West in *The Craft*. Fairuza may not have gotten top billing in *Gas Food Lodging*, but to me, she's the main attraction.

In this film, Fairuza plays Shade, a sweet, quirky adolescent who lives with mom and big sis in a remote New Mexico trailer park. Shade innocently hopes to become the girl of best friend Darius's dreams, but Darius's dreams are of becoming a girl himself—Olivia Newton-John, to be exact. To escape her white-bread existence, Shade spends solitary afternoons watching Spanish-language films starring her favorite actress. As she devours these romantic melodramas, she also dreams of love—not for herself, but for her single mom, Nora, a waitress in the local greasy spoon. Nora (Brooke Adams) has gone through legions of suitors since her deadbeat husband left when the girls were still in diapers. While Shade longs for her real father, she'll settle for a substitute as kind and generous as the ex-flame of Nora's who let Shade and her sister, Trudi, go wild on a K-Mart shopping spree.

As for Trudi (Ione Skye), she's only seventeen, but already busy cementing her reputation as the foulest-mouthed slut in town. Trudi's behavior drives Nora crazy, but her mean-spirited attitude and willingness to bed half the population hides her own dark secrets and lack of self-worth.

Gas Food Lodging is about three women who seek healing from rejection—rejection by the man who was the father to two and the husband to one, and for Shade and Trudi, rejection by the young men in their lives.

"When someone rejects you," says Shade, "they say that it's not personal. But who are they kidding? It's as personal as it can get."

These three women may be very different, but they're all searching for the same thing—love—and they just might find it in the most unexpected places. Shade faces the inevitable rebuff from her effeminate buddy, but will she open her eyes to Javier (Jacob Vargas), the irresistible projectionist in the movie theater? Trudi's just been dumped by her latest lay, but will her newfound infatuation with a sexy geologist (an oxymoronic concept made believable through actor Robert Knepper) turn out to be another one-night stand? Nora's finally rid herself of married lover Raymond, but will she succumb to the charms of a satellite dish salesman with the unlikely moniker of Hamlet Humphrey? And what happens when Nora's ex-husband (James Brolin) unexpectedly resurfaces?

It's fun, it's touching, and it'll give you a whole new perspective on trailer park living.

The Ghost and Mrs. Muir

Director: Joseph L. Mankiewicz
Screenplay: Philip Dunne, from the novel by R. A. Dick
Starring: Gene Tierney, Rex Harrison, George Sanders, Natalie Wood, Edna Best, Vanessa Brown, Anna Lee, Robert Coote
1947, 104 min., unrated
Heartthrob men: ★★★★
Smart-ass women: ★★★★
Romance: ★★★★
Tears: ★★★★

Decades before Demi Moore and Patrick Swayze explored the joys of ectoplasmic erotica in Ghost, Gene Tierney and Rex Harrison heated up the screen in The Ghost and Mrs. Muir. Sure, we never get to see the ghost and Mrs. Muir do it, because they meet when Rex is already of the more vaporous persuasion. Nonetheless, it's an enchanting and moving love story.

If only real, live, breathing men could all be as sexy and as vital as Mrs. Muir's ghost! If only all women could be as calm, brave, and self-assured as Gene Tierney's Lucy Muir. Granted, she doesn't have to contend with his snoring, his obsession with Monday Night Football, and his drinking straight out of the milk carton. Ghosts don't do those things, at least not in turn-of-the-century England, where our story takes place.

When Lucy Muir, a beautiful young widow, escapes from the clutches of her tiresome in-laws and takes up residence in a windswept cottage on the English seacoast with her daughter, Anna, and her devoted maid, Martha, the former owner and current resident ghost is furious. He's managed to scare every other prospective tenant away, but Lucy will not be deterred. She stands up to the hot-tempered ghost of Captain Greg (Rex Harrison), try as he might to frighten her. Not only does she win his respect by refusing to be intimidated, she wins his heart because she loves his house every bit as much as he did. The fact that Lucy is a gorgeous woman doesn't hurt either.

So they call a shaky sort of truce, but have much to get used to, sharing the same master bedroom and all. The ghost really loses it when Lucy cuts down the tree that obscured the view from the bedroom window, but Lucy gives him a properly British set-down.

"Captain Greg, if you insist on haunting me," she says, "you might as well be more agreeable about it."

What's a ghost to do? So a bit later, he tries his hand at a compliment, noticing that Lucy's just come out of mourning. But when she thanks him politely, he growls:

"Much better than smothering yourself in all that ugly black crepe!"

"I happen to have been wearing mourning for my husband."

"Whom you didn't love!"

"How dare you say that!" she cries.

"Because it's true," says the ghost. "You were fond of him perhaps, but you didn't love him."

Poor Lucy. She can't hide the truth, especially not from a ghost. And now that she's finally found love, it's with a spirit. I guess we can't expect one man to fulfill all our needs. Either he's got a great body but bores you to death, or he's got a great mind but has no body at all.

Gene Tierney is luminous; Rex Harrison is deliciously male; a very young Natalie Wood is adorable as Lucy's daughter, Anna; and George Sanders stirs up things masterfully as a rival for Lucy's affections. It's amazingly romantic, sparkles with wit, and never fails to make me sob no matter how many times I see it.

Telltale Signs You're Watching a Guy Movie

by Richard Roeper

Guy Movies are incredibly easy to spot. All you have to do is look for these red flags.

- If a woman is thrown up against a wall by a coworker and has her shirt ripped off, and she responds by moaning with desire rather than filing a sexual harassment suit, you're watching a Guy Movie.
- If men are in a bar drinking shots of tequila and licking the salt off the necks of silicone-enhanced women who have no speaking roles in the film, you're watching a Guy Movie.
- If the opening credits roll to the sound of a military drum cadence, you're watching a Guy Movie.
- If a naked woman is murdered by an unseen stranger in the first five minutes of a film, you're watching a Guy Movie.
- If a woman undresses near a window while one or more horny young men snicker in the bushes, you're watching a Guy Movie.
- If anyone dies in slow motion, you're watching a Guy Movie.
- If more than one car is demolished in any scene, you're watching a Guy Movie.
- If there's a scene where the hero gets stitched up without benefit of anesthetic, it's a Guy Movie.
- If the word *threesome* is used in any context, it's a Guy Movie.
- If any of the following actors appears in the film, odds are you're watching a Guy Movie.

Danny Aiello	Chevy Chase
Dan Aykroyd	Rae Dawn Chong
Joe Don Baker	Jamie Lee Curtis
John Belushi	Robert De Niro
Linda Blair	Brian Dennehy
Humphrey Bogart	Bo Derek
Charles Bronson	Bruce Dern
Albert Brooks	Danny DeVito
Mel Brooks	Robert Duvall
James Caan	Clint Eastwood
John Candy	Chris Farley
Jim Carrey	Glenn Ford
Phoebe Cates	Harrison Ford
Jackie Chan	James Garner

Harrison Ford	Joe Pesci
Andy Garcia	William L. Petersen
James Garner	Richard Pryor
Pam Grier	Burt Reynolds
Sterling Hayden	Eric Roberts
Samuel L. Jackson	Mickey Rourke
Harvey Keitel	Arnold Schwarzenegger
George Kennedy	Steven Seagal
Michael Madsen	Frank Sinatra
Dean Martin	Wesley Snipes
Steve Martin	Paul Sorvino
Lee Marvin	Sylvester Stallone
Steve McQueen	Sharon Stone
Robert Mitchum	Jean-Claude Van Damme
Eddie Murphy	Christopher Walken
Bill Murray	Fred Ward
Jack Nicholson	John Wayne
Chuck Norris	Raquel Welch
Al Pacino	James Woods
Jack Palance	

Gloria

Director: John Cassavetes
Screenplay: John Cassavetes
Starring: Gena Rowlands, John Adames, Buck Henry, Julie Carmen
1980, 123 min., PG
Smart-ass women: ★★★★
Tears: ★★

What becomes an action hero the most? Toughness. Fearlessness. Big guns. Feminine allure. No, it's not Arnold in drag, it's a woman. Not just any woman, you see, but a break-the-mold, all-woman kind of woman that only Gena Rowlands can play. (No offense, Sharon Stone, you're good, but there will never be another Gena. Just can't be done. Give it up with those remakes, girl. In the meantime, Gena, I bow down before you.)

She's blond, she's beautiful, and she makes Dirty Harry look like Snow White. She's Gloria, fortysomething ex-mob-girlfriend now retired to a quite life with her kitty and a closetful of clothes in her comfy apartment in a lousy neighborhood. She doesn't want trouble, and she doesn't like kids. She gets both when Phil enters the picture.

Phil is the six-year-old neighbor boy who is thrust into her reluctant care when his terrified father (Buck Henry), an accountant for the mob, realizes his employers are about to blow his brains out because he kept a ledger of their doings as insurance. So Buck shoves Phil, clutching the precious ledger, into Gloria's apartment. And within seconds, Phil's entire family is dead—and Gloria's the only one who can save his precocious little ass. She's worked hard for a little bit of peace and quiet, and a kid marked for death is the last thing she needs. But what can she do? She can't let the kid die. And she sure as hell can't let the mob find him in her apartment. So this unwilling but stalwart hero single-handedly takes on the bad guys, complaining every inch of the way.

Gloria and Phil go on the run, hiding out in borrowed flats and cheap hotel rooms. She can't even fry an egg, let alone be a mom to an orphaned boy with a price on his head. And she can't go to the cops, being an ex-con herself with ties to the mob. The very thugs who are hunting for Phil are her friends, and every second she keeps the boy with her she makes them a dangerous enemy. But try as she might to get rid of the kid and make him leave, little Phil sticks fast, motivated by much more than his need to survive. He's got a big old crush on his big blond amazon protectress. And Gloria doesn't realize how attached she's become to Phil—until the mob surprises them on the street—and she blows them away.

But there's nothing sappy about the ensuing scene when they take flight from the carnage—Gloria wouldn't hear of it. And Phil's not your typical cute child actor, either. He's an ordinary-looking, real-life working class kid (John Adames) from whom Cassavetes conjured an actor's debut performance you'll never forget, a tiny kid who's made his father's parting words, "Be a man. Always be tough," into a religion.

When Phil and Gloria finally find refuge in a flophouse, Phil lies beside her on the sagging bed, smitten with the woman who'd do murder for him.

"Have you ever been in love?" he asks her dreamily.

"Forget about it," she snaps. "I outweigh you by sixty pounds. So leave me alone."

Gloria is a gripping, suspenseful, heartstring-pulling treasure.

The Goodbye Girl

Director: Herbert Ross
Screenplay: Neil Simon
Starring: Richard Dreyfuss, Marsha Mason, Quinn Cummings, Barbara
  Rhoades, Paul Benedict
1977, 110 min., PG
Romance: ****
Smart-ass women: ****

He's the one. You've been wrong before, but this one's different. Sure, you spend most of your time listening to him whine. Sure, his libido isn't what it used to be. But that's because he feels like a failure, and sensitive artists need a lot of support from their women. You'll get him back on track; you know you will. You've even bought a copy (secretly, of course) of *Martha Stewart's Weddings*. But that nagging voice inside worries if you're tempting fate. Will he turn out to be like all the others, leaving you with a broken heart, an extra ten pounds, and a need to avenge yourself on every adult who pees standing up?

If any of this sounds familiar, you'll love *The Goodbye Girl*, whose leading female, Paula (Marsha Mason), has an uncanny ability to fall for self-centered actors who leave her behind. The first was her husband, who left her to brave single parenthood with precocious daughter Lucy (Quinn Cummings). The latest is her live-in boyfriend, who not only dumps her via letter, but also just happens not to mention that he's sublet their Manhattan apartment. So when the unsuspecting subletter, an obnoxiously egocentric actor named Elliot (Richard Dreyfuss) shows up with lease in hand, Paula does her hostile best to throw him out. She's unemployed and has a kid to feed and house. Besides, he's got three strikes against him: he's a man, he's an actor, and he's a friend of her ex. But Dreyfuss won't budge. He's paid his rent and is about to start rehearsals for his New York acting lead debut in an off-off-off Broadway production of *Richard III*. So the two call a temporary ceasefire: They'll share the place.

It's a match made in hell. She can't stand his late-night guitar-playing and crack-of-dawn chanting; he can't stand her verbal venom. But it's love at first sight for Elliot and Paula's kid, Lucy, who campaigns for Elliot to be Mom's next boyfriend. But Mom isn't going for it. Not only is she determined to hate him, she lets Lucy know he's not even her type.

" . . . your type never hangs around long enough to stay your type," says Lucy, who is ten going on thirty-seven.

Rooming isn't the only challenge this unlikely pair face. Paula's trying to resume her chorus line career after a two-year hiatus on the flab-inducing island of love's illusion. Elliot's trying to convince his insane director (Paul Benedict) that Richard III shouldn't be portrayed as a flaming drag queen. Watching Dreyfuss prance around the stage in the most ridiculously offensive take on Shakespeare you'll probably ever see is more than half the fun. In fact, watching Dreyfuss do anything in this film is pure delight, as he masters every aspect of his vain, eccentric, but generous and kind character with convincing finesse.

And guess what? He's so convincing that even Paula starts to like him, despite all her efforts to hate his thespian guts. And Elliot is in for what any man must face when he charms a scorned woman. After all, some-body's gotta pay.

Green Card

Director: Peter Weir
Screenplay: Peter Weir
Starring: Gerard Depardieu, Andie MacDowell, Bebe Neuwirth, Gregg
    Edelman, Robert Prosky, Ethan Phillips, Mary Louise Wilson, Ronald
    Guttman
1990, 107 min., PG-13
Heartthrob men: ★★★★
Romance: ★★★★
Tears: ★★

Life is full of choices. Take food, for instance. Do we want to eat a salad with low-fat dressing on the side, or would we rather have a hot fudge sundae? Men present similar choices. Would we rather be with the healthy, safe, white-bread thinking, tofu-eating, sex-on-Sundays Ameri-can man? Or would we like to take on the bad-boy, steak-scarfing, nicotine-breathing, sex-on-the-floor Eurotrash? *Green Card* is about those choices.

Andie MacDowell's character, Brontë, is a privileged horticulturist who volunteers her time bringing gardens to the poor of Manhattan. She needs a husband to land the apartment of her dreams, one that comes with a greenhouse. George (the gorgeously bulky Gerard Depardieu) is an unemployed composer from France. He needs a green card. A mutual friend (Ronald Guttman) arranges a marriage of convenience for these

two strangers, who hope never to see each other again. The Immigration and Naturalization Service hopes otherwise.

Brontë and George must prove to the INS that their marriage is legit, and have only two days to learn everything there is to know about each other. For both, the stakes are high: George can be deported, and she can lose her apartment, not to mention possible criminal prosecution. And if her veggie-chomping boyfriend (Gregg Edelman) finds out Brontë's got a man, let alone a husband, stashed away in her pad, she could lose even more.

As the unlikely pair team up to study each other's habits, mutual contempt builds to intensity. He's a meat-eating, caffeine-drinking, cigarette-smoking hedonist with a questionable past and a cynical present. She's a prim, repressed, plant-loving, do-gooder with a wimp of a boyfriend. But the looming interview with the INS forces them to put a positive spin on their differences as they weave a fabrication of their lives together. And as life imitates artifice, fascination and repressed lust build as well.

"He has passion. He eats life," says Brontë to her INS interrogator.

"She has peace. I don't have peace," says George to his.

Can they pull it off? If they do, what next?

Depardieu is, as always, incomparably talented and sexy. Andie Mac-Dowell gives her best performance and her best hair. And there's a gem of a supporting cast: Bebe Neuwirth shines as Brontë's spoiled-rich girl-friend who circles seductively around George. Ethan Phillips is slick as the INS dude whose beady, suspicious eyes are out to detect fraud. And Mary Louise Wilson as his female colleague mirrors us gals as her dreamy eyes eat up the couple's romantic tales of love at first sight.

Heartburn

Director: Mike Nichols
Screenplay: Nora Ephron, based on her novel
Starring: Meryl Streep, Jack Nicholson, Jeff Daniels, Stockard Channing, Richard Masur, Catherine O'Hara, Steven Hill, Milos Forman, Maureen Stapleton
1986, 108 min., R
Romance: **
Smart-ass women: ***

She's Rachel. He's Mark. She's a New York food columnist whose cooking would give Martha Stewart pause. He's a hotshot Washington political columnist whose amorous résumé would make Casanova blush. She's played by thespian metamorph Meryl Streep. He's played by thespian madman Jack Nicholson.

It's instant chemistry for these two, lubricated by Rachel's postcoital spaghetti carbonara. Enough to make even a rake like Mark propose marriage. She says yes, but has an anxiety attack just before the wedding ceremony. What if this marriage ends like her first one? So Mark's married friends Julie and Arthur tell her not to worry—she's the first woman Mark's ever treated like a human being. With such a vote of confidence, she takes the plunge. After all, they're in love. Or in lust. Or in caloric heaven. Or whatever.

The newlyweds begin married life with a home that becomes an endless renovation nightmare, and swiftly follow that with procreation. But despite all the chaos and sawdust, the lovebirds settle into their nest. Rachel happily immerses herself in the day-to-day minutiae of her role of wife and mother, a blissful domestic dream. Until one day she wakes up to the fact that Mark is cheating.

"Oh, Daddy, what am I gonna do?" Rachel whines to her father after fleeing back to New York with her toddler daughter and enormously pregnant belly in tow.

"There's nothing you can do," Daddy deadpans. "You want monogamy, marry a swan."

Mark wants her back. She wants her marriage back. But is that possible?

I have a friend, Esther Boynton, who says about men, "Once a philanderer, always a philanderer." But how do we deal with it? "Stand by your man," we're told. Don't ask questions. Pretend it isn't there—and maybe it'll just go away.

There's a darkly funny bit just after Rachel goes back to Washington to give Mark a second chance. She's on the phone with Julie (Stockard Channing), who has rallied to Rachel's side.

"Are you behaving yourself?" Julie asks.

Rachel reports with no more affect than a Stepford wife how she baked bread and hung curtains and made lots of special dinners for Mark. But what she's thinking is how she went through his wallet, scanned his dirty laundry for lipstick stains, and steamed open his credit card bills.

"I'm being very good," Rachel says.

"I'm proud of you," Julie says.

"I wish he were dead," Rachel says mildly.

"I know," Julie says just as blandly. "When Arthur was having his little affair, every time he got on a plane I would imagine the plane crash, the funeral, what I would wear at the funeral, flirting at the funeral, how soon I could start dating after the funeral."

"I know," sighs Rachel.

The whole film is a series of gems like this, all strung together in a free-flowing, almost documentary style. It's an unremarkable story told in a remarkable way. And there are lots of delicious cameos. Kevin Spacey, complete with punked-out red hair, makes a most unwelcome appearance at Rachel's group therapy session. Mercedes Ruehl is one of the group members. Yakov Smirnoff is the contractor from hell who oversees the remodeling of Mark and Rachel's house. And Milos Forman plays the live-in lover of Washington gossip queen Catherine O'Hara.

Jack and Meryl are amazing, as always. And she doesn't even have to use an accent.

By the way, in case you didn't know, she's based on Nora Ephron, and he's based on Carl Bernstein.

The Heiress

Director: William Wyler
Screenplay: Ruth Goetz and Augustus Goetz, adapted from their stage
   play, based on the novel *Washington Square* by Henry James
Starring: Olivia de Havilland, Montgomery Clift, Ralph Richardson, Miriam
   Hopkins, Vanessa Brown, Betty Linley
1949, 115 min., unrated
Great clothes: ★★★
Heartthrob men: ★★★
Romance: ★★★
Tears: ★★

If you think you have a serious self-image problem, take a look at *The Heiress*. Compared to main character Catherine Sloper, your ego probably needs its own apartment. You'll be amazed at how the magic of acting, directing, and some very unflattering hairstyles managed to transform the beautiful Olivia de Havilland into this drab nineteenth-century wallflower. Catherine may be filthy rich, and she may live in a palatial home overlooking New York's Washington Square Park, but the only praise she's ever received from her disapproving father is a sarcastic comment on her ability to "embroider neatly."

Shy, awkward, and endearingly guileless, Catherine tries in vain to please her father. For Dr. Austin Sloper, his daughter's deficiencies are nothing more than a painful reminder of his lovely and accomplished wife—who died giving birth to her. And when chided by his sister Elizabeth for expecting the plain, tongue-tied Catherine to resemble his idealized image of the woman who bore her, Austin is unmoved. He's simply incapable of speaking to his daughter with anything warmer than thinly veiled contempt. In short, you'll hate his guts.

Despite Catherine's claim to a vast inheritance, Austin has little hope of marrying off such ordinary offspring. Then, a miracle happens, or so it seems to Catherine and her hopelessly romantic aunt, an adorable Protestant yenta named Lavinia Penniman (Miriam Hopkins). That miracle is Morris Townsend (Montgomery Clift), a gorgeous, intelligent, and yes, penniless man who appears to have instantly fallen head over heels in love with the heiress. At first, the self-effacing Catherine is confused by his attentions—after all, she's been taught to think of herself as pond scum. Morris's ardor, however, inevitably prevails. Montgomery Clift is so irresistible, he could convince any woman to hike up her hoop skirts.

Austin, on the other hand, is convinced of only one thing—Morris is a fortune-hunter.

"How is it possible to protect such a willing victim?" he says to his sisters Lavinia and Elizabeth (Betty Linley).

"You will kill her if you deny her this marriage," Lavinia warns.

"You forget, I'm a doctor," says Austin. "People don't die of such things."

Olivia de Havilland is absolutely divine in this film. When she first says "I love you," to Morris, it's as if she can hardly believe she's saying these words to a real human being who actually loves her. She's been so starved for love all her life, she was hardly even aware of it. Until suddenly she finds herself with the answer to all her unspoken prayers . . . or is he?

If I were William Wyler, I would have reshot the ending. But don't worry, I won't spoil it for you. It's still a terrific movie. Deeply disturbing and wholly engaging, *The Heiress* will spark heated discussions about honesty, the choices we make, the true nature of at least one of the characters, and the relative merits of forgiveness or revenge.

La Femme Nikita

Director: Luc Besson
Screenplay: Luc Besson
Starring: Anne Parillaud, Jean-Hugues Anglade, Tcheky Karyo, Jeanne Moreau, Jean Reno
1991, 117 min., R, French with English subtitles
Great clothes: ★★★
Heartthrob men: ★★★
Romance: ★★★
Smart-ass women: ★★★★

Need I even mention that you shouldn't bother to see the English-language remake of *La Femme Nikita*, which practically duplicates, shot for shot, the French original and stars, of all people, Bridget Fonda? I love Bridget Fonda, but she's not exactly my idea of a tough girl. Granted, the remake also stars Gabriel Byrne, a stud in any language, but let's face it: These English-language remakes are really for the testosterone set who can't be bothered to read subtitles. Even my sister Felice Levine, who was once quoted as saying "I go to movies to watch and listen, not to read," has since seen the light. Anyway, there's a lot to be said for reading subtitles, especially if you live in an urban environment like I do. I like the fact that I didn't have the hit the pause button on *La Femme Nikita* when the L.A.P.D. helicopters made their nightly noise-polluting and dialogue-obliterating round of my neighborhood.

When we first meet lead character Nikita, played by the diminutive but believably dangerous Anne Parillaud, she's a violent druggie who's in dire need of a bath and a makeover. After cold-bloodedly killing a cop during a botched pharmacy heist, Nikita is sentenced to life imprisonment. Then she's given a choice: either death or recruitment into a secret government agency where she will be trained as an assassin and have a chance to "serve her country." It's not really much of a choice; after all, these shadowy spooks have already faked her death and would be more than happy to place a real corpse in her empty coffin. And the guy who recruits her, Bob (Tcheky Karyo), is not only convincing, he's gorgeous.

Nikita is far from compliant at first, biting martial arts instructors, giving her computer teacher a sadistic gift of a real mouse, and painting the walls of her room with graffiti. And, despite the patient efforts of Jeanne Moreau, who is supposed to school Nikita in the feminine arts of walking, talking, smiling, and looking seductive, Nikita shows little promise in wielding a mascara wand. I guess it makes sense for Nikita to have such a teacher. I'd never thought about it before, but some expert in masculinity probably taught those male action heroes how to master such essentials as grabbing their crotches, grunting in a threatening way, and streaking themselves with grime.

Spurred on by a death threat from the kindly Bob, Nikita finally applies herself to her studies. For three years, she trains to become a deadly weapon, and, with the help of Jeanne Moreau, one who can seduce her prey. Even Bob finds himself fighting off his attraction to her, and who can blame him? Nikita's probably the first woman he's ever met who can kick his ass.

Finally, Nikita is let out into the world with a new identity and a seemingly normal life, and the amazing Anne Parillaud turns this initially repulsive character into a charming and sympathetic figure who becomes a pawn in a bizarre and deadly game. She even acquires a sweet, romantic boyfriend (Jean-Hugues Anglade)—but always the knowledge that her controllers may call on her to pull a hit looms in the background. The pressure builds as her ever more suspicious boyfriend pushes for information about his mysterious lover, and the hits get more and more danger-ous.

Aside from being a powerful, passionate character study—something as unlikely to be found in a male-oriented action movie as polysyllabic words—*La Femme Nikita* offers us gals some sage advice from the lips of the regally beautiful Jeanne Moreau, "There are two things that have no limit: femininity and the means of taking advantage of it."

A Letter to Three Wives

Director: Joseph L. Mankiewicz
Screenplay: Joseph L. Mankiewicz
Adapted by Vera Caspary from a *Cosmopolitan* magazine novel by John Klempner
Starring: Ann Sothern, Linda Darnell, Jeanne Crain, Kirk Douglas, Paul Douglas, Jeffrey Lynn, Thelma Ritter
1949, 103 min., unrated
Heartthrob men: ★★★
Romance: ★★
Smart-ass women: ★★★★

Imagine getting a letter that ends like this:
"You see, girls, I've run off with one of your husbands."
Wouldn't it be enough to make you go postal? The three wives in the title roles may not run off to their nearest assault-weapons empo-rium, but they do spend one very miserable day sweating it out until they can discover which of their husbands has run off with Addie Ross.

We never actually see Addie Ross—we just hear her silky voice (that of Celeste Holm) narrating all. But seeing this woman is not important. For she symbolizes the elusive image we strive to imitate every time we buy a new dress or get our roots dyed. We (and the three wives) must en-dure a perpetual litany of Addie's virtues voiced by all three of the hus-bands. Addie's the epitome of grace, style, beauty, and class. She's the woman who has it all, and now she's got something else—one of her friends' husbands. But which one is it?

It could be Debby (Jeanne Crain), a poor farm girl fresh out of the navy when she married her well-to-do husband, Brad (Jeffrey Lynn). She still squirms at the memory of wearing her hideous mail-order

dress on her first night out as a newlywed to meet Brad's friends at his country club. Has he finally dumped her for a woman of his own class?

Then there's sultry Lora Mae (Linda Darnell), who managed to escape from a life on the wrong side of the tracks by manipulating the wealthy Porter Hollingsway (Paul Douglas) into marrying her. It was a mutually beneficial partnership: He wanted sex; she wanted money. And both of them hide their vulnerable hearts behind tough-talking exteriors. Lora Mae couldn't care less, she insists, if Porter ran off with Addie. But doth the lady protest too much?

My favorite of the three wives is Rita (Ann Sothern). Rita writes soap operas for a living and is the mother of twins (whom we never see). She also earns far more than her schoolteacher husband, George (Kirk Douglas in one of the best roles he's ever played). When George doesn't buy the scotch Rita requested for a dinner she's giving to suck up to her boss—a refrigerator-shaped woman named Mrs. Manley—Rita gets upset. Too expensive, George explains.

RITA

But the Manleys are a cinch to want scotch. People in show business, you know what I mean, those kind always drink scotch.

GEORGE

I know what you mean, but I wish you wouldn't say it in radio English:
that kind not *those kind.*

RITA

There are men who say *those kind* who earn $100,000 a year.

GEORGE

There are men who say "stick 'em up" who earn more. I don't expect to
do either.

RITA

Nor are you expected to pay for the scotch.

GEORGE

You're quite right. Funny how it slips my mind that in certain respects
I'm only the titular head of the house.

Fact is, although George's male ego might chafe from time to time, he's
sincerely grateful for the extra money his wife brings in. But he draws the
line when he realizes she wants him to land a high-paying job editing
radio soaps—a job he has no interest in acquiring. He's perfectly happy to
remain a schoolteacher, despite the meager rewards of his profession, and
despite his wife pointing out to him that teachers are quitting in droves
to take jobs that pay a decent living. Have Rita's complaints finally driv-
en him away?

I guess some things haven't changed much since 1949. You'll be surprised at just how much you can sink your teeth into the marital, gender, and class issues bandied about in this picture. You'll also have a
helluva good time trying to figure out which husband has flown the
coop.

The cast is simply marvelous, and includes one of my very favorite
uber-gals, Thelma Ritter, who, as usual, plays a wisecracking maid. If she
ever showed up to clean my apartment and dish out some insults, I'd die
a happy woman.

Dear Thelma

Why do I adore the late, great Thelma Ritter? Because every gal should have a Thelma in her life. Decidedly unglamorous and inevitably speaking with a grammar-slaying New York twang, her most well-known roles are an array of wisecracking maids, nurses, and gal Fridays who offer comic relief, cutting commentary, sage advice, and most importantly—uncompromising loyalty.

I don't know if anyone's written a biography of Thelma Ritter, but I'd be afraid to read one. What if the real Thelma wasn't the same gal I know and love? Hey, I know she's an actor. I know her films aren't real life. I'm not stupid. But to me, Thelma *is* her characters, and like Special Agent Fox Mulder, I want to believe.

More on the Thelma mystique:

- She's an undereducated working-class gal who's wiser than you are;
- She'll always tell you the truth, even if you're the queen of de-nial;
- She knew you when you drove a beat-up clunker and watched the country music channel for fashion tips—before you put on airs, flashed your plastic (cards or body parts), and lost your Brooklyn accent;
- She'll never take crap, not from you or anyone;
- Oh, yeah, she'll also clean your house, run your errands, and be the best friend you ever had.

Check her out in *All About Eve*, *A Letter to Three Wives*, and *Rear Window*. And if any of you know of a Thelma Ritter fan club, I'd like to run for president.

Little Women

Director: Gillian Armstrong
Screenplay: Robin Swicord, based on the novel by Louisa May Alcott
Starring: Susan Sarandon, Winona Ryder, Gabriel Byrne, Trini Alvarado, Samantha Mathis, Kirsten Dunst, Claire Danes, Christian Bale, Eric Stoltz, Mary Wickes
1994, 118 min., PG
Heartthrob men: ★★★★
Romance: ★★★★
Tears: ★★★★

Gillian Armstrong's vision of Louisa May Alcott's well-loved book is a tender portrait of four sisters emerging into womenhood in 1860s New England. Most importantly, it's done what no previous version has done before—it's given us Gabriel Byrne.

It's not easy being the daughters of free-thinking Transcendentalists without a penny to their name while surrounded by wealth and privilege. It's kind of like living in "Beverly Hills–adjacent," one of those euphemistic realtor terms for so close yet so far. Despite deprivation, the March sisters lovingly make their way through genteel poverty, illness, and their fears of growing up. Jo (Oscar-nominated Winona Ryder) is a tomboy who aspires to be a novelist. By the way, she's much better than June Allyson, her predecessor in the 1949 version. June looked like she was ready to leap out of the closet at any moment and start tuning up a Harley. Jo's older sister, Meg (Trini Alvarado), is a sweet, feminine thing who aspires to be a wife. Younger sister Beth (Claire Danes) is a shy, sickly angel who dreams of staying a child; and the youngest, Amy (Kirsten Dunst and Samantha Mathis), is a vain but adorable girl who dreams of romance and riches. Their solid but gentle backbone is their principled mother (Susan Sarandon) whom they affectionately dub "Marmee."

Oh, to have a mother figure like Marmee! Even if she does embarrass Meg by pontificating to prospective suitor Mr. Brooks (Eric Stoltz) about corsets and confining lives being the cause of feminine fainting spells. I know she'd be crestfallen if she ventured into the ladies' lingerie department today and saw those same corsets euphemistically renamed "body slimmers." Nonetheless, Marmee instills confidence and strength in her girls, all with a generous dose of unconditional love and unfailing optimism.

After Meg returns from a fancy ball in which the hostess exchanged Meg's plain frock for one of her own opulent ones, Meg sighs at the memory.

"It's nice to be praised and admired," Meg says. "I couldn't help but like it."

"Of course not," Sarandon gently replies. "I only care what you think of yourself. If you feel your value lies in being merely decorative, I fear that someday you might find yourself believing that's all that you really are. Time erodes such beauty, but what it cannot diminish is the wonderful workings of your mind, your humor, your kindness, and your moral courage. These are the things I cherish so in you."

I don't know about you, but a speech like that would be enough to make me consider canceling a facelift.

There's more than just the power and glory of the female in *Little Women*. There are also a couple of to-die-for male specimens in the form of Jo's would-be suitors Friedrich (Gabriel Byrne, of course) and Laurie (Christian Bale). And a gorgeous score whose swelling strains promise to wring out every available tear you've stored up for the occasion.

Mildred Pierce

Director: Michael Curtiz
Screenplay: Ranald MacDougall, based on the novel by James M. Cain
Starring: Joan Crawford, Ann Blyth, Zachary Scott, Eve Arden, Jack Carson, Butterfly McQueen, Bruce Bennett
1945, 109 min., unrated
Great clothes: ★★★
Romance: ★★
Smart-ass women: ★★★★

Picture real-life mother from hell Joan Crawford playing the martyred mama of a spoiled brat daughter. Need I say more? The funny thing is, her performance in the title role not only convinced me, it convinced the Academy to give her an Oscar for Best Actress.

Betrayal, lust, and padded shoulders abound in this noirish melodrama about a woman who overcomes poverty, divorce, and single-parenthood to forge a successful career for herself. But it's not for herself that she works so hard—it's for her self-centered, social-climbing daughter, Veda (Ann Blyth). And satisfying Veda is what Mildred lives for.

When she and hubby first split, Mildred works night and day slinging hash in a restaurant and baking cakes to sell from her home, all the while hiding her waitress uniform from the prying eyes of the snobby Veda. But the dirty secret soon comes out. So Mildred saves up enough money to open an instantly successful restaurant, hoping that Veda will approve. One restaurant turns into a thriving chain, but there's never enough money to satisfy Veda. What she thirsts for is social status—even if she has to do shots of mama's blood to get it.

Mildred's friend and real-estate deal maker Wally (Jack Carson) hopes to take up where ex-hubby left off, but Mildred falls instead for Monty Beragon, a ne'er-do-well playboy who looks like an ersatz Errol Flynn. Monty's got no money, but doesn't mind taking Mildred's. He's also got an old family name and social connections, enough to thrill Veda.

Wally's less than thrilled, so he unleashes his venom at Ida (Eve Arden), Mildred's tough-talking gal-pal and trusty restaurant manager.

"I hate all women," he proclaims. "Thank goodness you're not one."

Hit the pause button on romance when Mildred and Monty soon come to blows over Veda, whose devious social-climbing schemes have gone way out of control.

Ida steps in and offers Mildred her own special brand of parenting advice: "Personally, Veda's convinced me that alligators have the right idea. They eat their young."

If I were Mildred, I'd listen to Ida.

Mississippi Masala

Director: Mira Nair
Screenplay: Sooni Taraporevala
Starring: Denzel Washington, Sarita Choudhury, Roshan Seth, Sharmila
    Tagore, Charles S. Dutton, Joe Seneca, Konga Mbandu, Sahira Nair
1992, 117 min., R
Great clothes: **
Heartthrob men: ****
Romance: ****
Tears: ***

I don't know about you, but thoughts of the Deep South don't usually conjure up visions of Indian women in saris. That's one good reason to see *Mississippi Masala*, for its fascinating slice-of-life glimpse at one of the many little immigrant enclaves across America. While I can't deny the benefits of a little cross-cultural education, especially when it's served up in a touching story with a first-rate cast and an excellent woman director, for me there's a much more compelling reason to see this film over and over again. And that's the pure pleasure of watching a love scene featuring Denzel Washington in the altogether.

When our story opens, it's 1972, and the family of little Mina (Sahira Nair) are being cast out of their homeland in Uganda by the racist anti-Asian decrees of dictator Idi Amin. Mina's father, Jay (Roshan Seth), is bitter about the enforced exodus, and his boyhood best friend, Okelo (Konga Mbandu), wounds him to the core with his belief that "Africa is for Africans—black Africans."

Now it's 1990, and the family lives in an Indian-owned motel in small-town Mississippi. Jay, once wealthy, now ekes out a meager living for his family from a liquor store he and his wife, Kinnu (Sharmila Tagore), own. Jay is still bitter, still petitioning the Ugandan government for the right to reclaim his Ugandan home and property. Now twenty-four, Mina (Sarita Choudhury), spends her days cleaning rooms in the motel. Her parents hope she'll snare prized bachelor Harry Patel (Ashok Lath), but local gossips are convinced that a poor girl, and one with dark skin at that, hasn't a chance in hell.

Mina could care less about getting Harry, especially when she meets Demetrius (Denzel Washington) by literally crashing her vehicle into his. In courting Mina, Demetrius sees an opportunity to get back at his high-and-mighty ex-girlfriend, Alicia (Natalie Oliver), who dumped him to go off and pursue a singing career. But before long he's just as entranced by Mina's charms as she is with his.

There's just one small problem. Mina never tells her parents about the new man in her life, not with her father's embittered memories of being exiled by black Africans. And she may be dark-skinned for an Indian, she may even have been born in Africa, but she's not black, and there's still a strict color barrier in her little Mississippi world. So when a couple of Indians from the motel catch Mina and Demetrius in a lover's tryst, a huge scandal unfolds, and everyone from Mina's family to the smarmy white banker who lent Demetrius money to start his carpet-cleaning business has something to say about it. Demetrius's customers start canceling his services, and Mina is practically kept under lock and key.

Says one of Mina's Indian neighbors to a gossipy friend, "I'm sending my Namita to India as soon as possible. . . . They get ideas from each other, and then it spreads like a disease."

With a gentle, incisive, and even lighthearted approach, this wonderful film spotlights the lesser-known shades of racism and hypocrisy that have already spread like a disease throughout our immigrant nation. And finally, it also gives us a star-crossed lovers kind of story that doesn't make us want to slit our wrists when the end credits roll.

Mrs. Miniver

Director: William Wyler
Screenplay: Arthur Wimperis, George Froeschel, James Hilton, Claudine
West, based on the book by Jan Struther
Starring: Greer Garson, Walter Pidgeon, Teresa Wright, Dame May Whitty,
Henry Travers, Richard Ney, Henry Wilcoxon
1942, 134 min., unrated
Romance: **
Tears: ****

It's not hard to understand why Roosevelt air-dropped copies of the final stirring speech from *Mrs. Miniver* over World War II Europe or that Churchill declared the film "helped Britain more than a fleet of destroyers." It is, however, hard to understand why English character Mr. Miniver (Walter Pidgeon) hasn't even a trace of a British accent. Or for that matter, why the studio didn't see fit to hire a dialogue coach to improve the lousy accent of Richard Ney (who plays his son Vin).

But these little details will hardly even bother you, for it's Mrs. Miniver (Greer Garson) who steals the show. So captivating is this elegantly kind British lady that the timid little railroad stationmaster, Mr. Ballard (Henry Travers), decides to name his best rose after her. He also decides to enter that rose in their village's yearly garden show, a controversial move that puts the heretofore unchallenged annual winner, Lady Belden, in a high-and-mighty huff. That curmudgeonly aristocrat with a hidden heart of gold is played beautifully by Dame May Whitty.

The biggest worries in this sleepy English village are the contestants of the garden show and whether Mrs. Miniver should tell her husband she just spent a fortune on a new hat. But then one day England goes to war, and the lives of everyone are turned upside down. Mrs. Miniver soothes her children through harrowing nights hiding out in the bomb shelter, reading them stories while destruction reigns outside. She even braves a felled German pilot who wanders into her garden. She sees her son, Vin, transformed in a matter of weeks from college boy to RAF pilot. And she and Vin's new love, Carol (Teresa Wright), know that Vin may never come back.

"Then you know that every moment is precious," Carol says to Mrs. Miniver. "We mustn't waste time in fear."

This is a film about courage in the face of whatever tragedies may happen. And it's not just about the courage men must have to do battle, but rather the courage women must have to love and to keep whatever semblance of normalcy might be possible in the insanity of war. There may be an air raid any moment, but the garden show must go on. And not just because Martha Stewart would say it's a good thing, but because composing a little order and beauty with a garden is, as Phyllis Theroux said, "the closest one can come to being present at the Creation."

Muriel's Wedding

Director: P. J. Hogan
Screenplay: P. J. Hogan
Starring: Toni Collette, Rachel Griffiths, Bill Hunter, Jeanie Drynan, Daniel Lapaine, Matt Day, Gennie Nevinson Brice, Sophie Lee, Rosalind Hammond, Belinda Jarrett, Pippa Grandison
1994, 105 min., R
Heartthrob men: ★★
Romance: ★
Smart-ass women: ★★★
Tears: ★

Times have changed. We no longer feel like spinsters if we reach the age of thirty before strolling down the aisle. Some of us even wait 'til we're in our forties. Unless you've got that biological clock thing going, what's the rush? But what if we never meet Mr. Right? Will we end up looking like the "old maid" from that silly card game I used to play when I was a kid? Let's get real. Even those of us gals who scoff at publications like *Bride's* magazine probably secretly watched Princess Di get married and dreamed of being swathed in yards of white organza. Admit it, single gals, most of you want that pretty white dress, not to mention that public recognition that somebody out there wants you 'til death do you part.

Take all of those centuries of brainwashing, distill it into one character, and you've got Muriel. Of course, we'd never be as obsessed with getting married as Muriel is. We'd never, like Muriel, spend months trying on wedding dresses in every store in town when we didn't even have a steady boyfriend.

So why is Muriel so obsessed? Well, it seems that everyone in her Australian hometown of Porpoise Spit, everyone from her slimy politician of a father (Bill Hunter) to her quartet of slutty girlfriends thinks she's a loser. She's overweight, she's unemployed, she can't get a date, and the biggest cardinal sin of all: She listens to Abba. Her mom (Jeanie Drynan) is certainly no role model either; she's a weak, timid domestic slave who closes her eyes to Dad's extramarital diddling.

After her snotty girlfriends ditch her, Muriel finds salvation by stealing Dad's money and going off on an island holiday. There she runs into Rhonda (Rachel Griffiths), an old schoolmate. Rhonda's an outspoken wild woman who's determined never to return to Porpoise Spit. Most of all, she wholeheartedly accepts Muriel, who finds a new life with Rhonda in Sydney.

"Since I met you and moved to Sydney," rhapsodizes Muriel to Rhonda, "I haven't listened to one Abba song. That's because now my life's as good as an Abba song. It's as good as 'Dancing Queen.'"

Life may be good, but there's still one important detail missing—a wedding—and Muriel discovers a most bizarre way to become the high-profile bride of her dreams. But will it give her lasting happiness? Or has she failed to grasp that a wedding and a marriage aren't necessarily the same?

But we wouldn't overlook such things. We're not at all like Muriel.

Muriel's Wedding is funny, campy, and totally poignant. You'll not only love it, you'll never again think of Abba in quite the same way.

Mystic Pizza

Director: Donald Petrie
Screenplay: Amy Jones, Perry Howze & Randy Howze, and Alfred Uhry;
story by Amy Jones
Starring: Annabeth Gish, Julia Roberts, Lili Taylor, Vincent D'Onofrio, William
R. Moses, Adam Storke, Conchata Ferrell, Joanna Merlin, Porscha Rad-
cliffe
1988, 101 min., R
Heartthrob men: **
Romance: **
Smart-ass women: ***
Tears: *

Once upon a time, before Julia Roberts earned megamillions, she co-
starred in *Mystic Pizza*, a sweet, funny, and touching little movie about
three Portuguese-American pizza waitresses in Mystic, Connecticut, and
their trial-and-error forays into romantic love.

Kat (Annabeth Gish) has been accepted at Yale to study astronomy,
but it doesn't take a rocket scientist to see where she's heading with the
married father of the girl she baby-sits. Her seductive sister, Daisy
(Julia Roberts), believes her only assets are her looks, but her latest
conquest, "rich white bread" Charles Gordon Windsor (Adam Storke),
may just be way out of her depth. Their best friend, Jojo (Lili Taylor),
dreams of someday taking over Mystic Pizza, if only the kindly propri-
etress (Conchata Ferrell) will someday bequeath to her the secret of
the special spices in the sauce. Her biggest challenge right now is holding on to boyfriend Bill (Vincent D'Onofrio) after ditching him at
their wedding.

It's not that Jojo doesn't love Bill; she loves everything about him, especially the sex. But when she thinks about marriage, it conjures up images of growing old, getting fat, and drowning in a sea of dirty diapers.
Bill, however, wants to be more than just a sex toy. He wants a commitment, and he wants a wedding.

"Don't you get it, Jo?" says Bill. "I'm telling you that I love you—and
all you love is my dick. Do you know how that makes me feel?"

I say it's about time someone finally acknowledged that we women can
be just as commitment-shy and as sexually driven as men. It's about time
somebody realized that what awaits us after we get to wear the pretty
white party dress doesn't always look all that appealing. That's what I like

most about *Mystic Pizza*, that and the secret spices in the sauce. It's so good, you might just find yourself dialing up your local pizza joint for an urgent delivery.

Romantic Recipe

Except for a gallon of Ben and Jerry's or a Daniel Day-Lewis action figure, what greater delight can fill a gal's lonely night at home than a romantic movie? It's gotta be the right kind, though, the kind that inexplicably sends your boyfriend home with an urgent need to work on his transmission. That's okay, he'll only spoil your fun. You're better off watching alone or sharing this treat with your favorite gal-pal.

Ever wonder how those film people concoct those romantic delicacies? Here's how I envision their no-fault recipe:

Combine these two initially incompatible ingredients:

a spicy, saucy, or shy woman and
a mysterious, bashful, or ill-tempered stranger.

Whip both into a bubbly romantic froth.

Add one or two essentially meaningless scenes in which the heroine is wrapped in killer clothes (preferably period threads) and displayed on a platter consisting of a sumptuously appointed house or garden.

Mix in a great deal of seething, boiling emotions and generous portions of suffering before . . .

Topping off with a wildly passionate love scene that doesn't expose too much skin. However, do consider adding a quick glimpse of the hero's bottom. This always makes for a colorful garnish.

Serves one to as many as your living room will hold, and can be reheated over and over again.

Now, Voyager

Director: Irving Rapper
Screenplay: Casey Robinson, from the novel by Olivia Higgins Prouty
Starring: Bette Davis, Paul Henreid, Claude Rains, Gladys Cooper, Bonita Granville, John Lode, Ilka Chase, Lee Patrick, Mary Wickes, Janis Wilson
1942, 118 min., unrated
Great clothes: ★★★
Heartthrob men: ★★★
Romance: ★★★
Tears: ★★

After I got home the other night from a screening of *Conspiracy Theory*, I hit the jackpot while channel surfing. One of my favorite Bette Davis flicks, *Now, Voyager*, was just starting. I'd seen it several times before, but suddenly I had a flash of insight as I was watching, and bolted upright from my tuberous position on the couch. With all the lawsuits going on these days against the cigarette industry, with all the hoopla about cigarette advertising, how come nobody ever realized before that our current favorite scourge against humanity, those cancer-vending child-suborning nicotine pushers, must have been behind the making of *Now, Voyager*? If one really takes a look at this film, it's just one big infomercial for the glories of putting those seductive cylinders of death between your lips.

Take that famous scene between Bette Davis and her illicit boyfriend, Paul Henreid, the one where in lieu of consummating their lust, unsure of what the future will hold, he suavely says, "Shall we just have a cigarette on it?"

Bette watches as her man puts two cigarettes in his mouth, lights one, and hands one to her. They engage in simultaneous exhalation, their smoke mingling together in sensual delight. For in this film, smoking itself is a forbidden and therefore, a delicious act of rebellion.

The first time we see Bette Davis's character, Charlotte, all we see is her hand quickly extinguishing a forbidden smoke. Then the camera reveals someone in desperate need of a Victoria Principal makeup kit: She's drab, dowdy, pudgy, bespectacled, and saddled with eyebrows that Brooke Shields would envy. Introverted and on the edge of a breakdown from the mental abuse of her domineering mother (Gladys Cooper)—who won't allow smoking in the house—Charlotte finds refuge in the loony bin of the kindly Dr. Jackwith (Claude Rains). Although his therapeutic methods in the last third of the film are so ridiculous most shrinks probably change the channel at that point, Dr. Jackwith does give Charlotte back her self-esteem. And from the looks of it, a certificate for a Day of Beauty at Estee Lauder.

The new, glamorous Charlotte goes on a cruise where she can smoke to her heart's content (or collapse), and there she meets dreamy Jerry (Paul Henreid). They fall madly in love, but there's one hitch—he's unhappily married to a jealous, controlling woman. (For some unknown reason, in the reality of this movie, divorce doesn't seem to exist.) With Jerry, Charlotte can share everything, even a before-photo of herself in which she resembles Groucho Marx in drag. In the vulnerable Charlotte, Jerry recognizes the pain of his daughter, Tina, who, like Charlotte, was an unwanted child.

Things heat up when the transformed Charlotte returns home. Mama is determined to see Charlotte resume her submissive role and grow back her eyebrows. But Charlotte hangs on tight to both tweezers and cigarette lighter. Will she start a new life with a new beau—a nonsmoker? Or is the memory of Jerry's huffing and puffing too strong to forget?

If I had my way, the video jackets of *Now, Voyager* would be imprinted with the following:

WARNING: This film may be dangerous to the health of those who are experiencing nicotine withdrawal, especially those who are also experiencing enforced celibacy.

Persuasion

Director: Roger Michell
Screenplay: Nick Dear, based on the novel by Jane Austen
Starring: Amanda Root, Ciaran Hinds, Corin Redgrave, Sophie Thompson, Susan Fleetwood, Emma Roberts, Samuel West
1995, 104 min., PG
Heartthrob men: **
Romance: ****

"Why are all these women walking around in their nightgowns?" my friend Laura Graham naughtily whispered in my ear during a screening of Jane Austen's *Persuasion.*

Well, apparently pastel-hued empire waistlines were all the rage in early nineteenth-century England. So was marrying a man with fortune and family and connections, especially if you were a girl whose titled father pissed away the family money the second your mother died.

So now you're at the ripe old age of twenty-seven, practically an old maid, and still bemoaning the fact that your family friend/surrogate mother, Lady Russell, persuaded you eight years ago to refuse the proposal of the penniless sailor you loved with all your heart.

So what if your father's a shallow fop who treats you like a second-class citizen, your older sister, Elizabeth, treats you like a cockroach, and your married sister, Mary (the inimitable Sophie Thompson), is a bossy hypochondriac? So what if the sailor you loved is now returned from the war as the wealthy Captain Wentworth (Ciaran Hinds), and he acts like you have the plague because you long ago broke his heart? So what if your sister-in-law Louisa is shamelessly throwing herself at him and he seems to like it? Life isn't so bad, is it?

According to director Roger Michell, life is dismal indeed. The only hope for Austen's oppressed heroine, Anne Elliott, brilliantly played by the wide-eyed Amanda Root, is to find escape from her dreary existence in the arms of a man who'll truly love and appreciate her fine qualities. Lord knows, no one in her family's nest of vipers does.

Watching this quietly strong female battle her way out of impossible circumstances is the engaging focus of this film. That and Austen's satirical exposé of British class snobbery.

Can love's constancy endure eight years of separation, bitterness, and regrets? And whose love survives longer? Man's or woman's? Anne debates this quite modern question with Captain Wentworth's dear friend, Captain Harville.

"Let me just observe," says Harville, "that all histories are against you, all stories, prose, and verse. I don't think I ever opened a book in my life which did not have something to say about woman's fickleness."

"But they were all written by men," laughs Anne. "All the privilege I claim for my own sex—and it is not a very enviable one; you need not covet it—is that of loving longest when all hope is gone."

One of the things I love best about this film is that the people—particularly the women—are not Hollywood-glamorized, except for Samuel West, who plays Anne's cousin and an unexpected suitor to our heroine (inbreeding was obviously not a problem in those days). The principal women characters look like real women, somewhat plain, and definitely not wearing layers of makeup. Leading man Ciaran Hinds usually looks like he badly needs a shave. The actors look so real, in fact, that the company that put out one version of the video package saw fit to replace the real actors with pretty models on the cover. That's show biz.

Pride and Prejudice
(1995 A&E Home Video version)

Director: Simon Langton
Screenplay: Andrew Davies, based on the novel by Jane Austen
Starring: Jennifer Ehle, Colin Firth, Susannah Harker, Crispin Bonham Carter, Alison Steadman, Benjamin Whitrow, Julia Sawalha
1995, six videos, total approx. 300 min., unrated
Great clothes: ★★★★
Heartthrob men: ★★★★
Romance: ★★★★
Smart-ass women: ★★★★

How do I love this most delicious adaptation of my favorite novel by my favorite nineteenth-century author? Let me count the ways. I love all three hundred minutes of its passionate romance, caustic humor, suspenseful drama, and unparalleled excellence in truly capturing both the substance and essence of Jane Austen's *Pride and Prejudice*.

Mr. Bennet (Benjamin Whitrow), a "connoisseur of human folly," cannot legally leave his estate to any of his five daughters, and he and his shrewish hypochondriac of a wife (Alison Steadman) have long since given up hope of producing a male heir. With only a paltry sum set aside for each daughter, and the youngest three being, as Mr. Bennet proclaims, "three of the silliest girls in England," his family's only hope for the future is to find rich husbands for his two eldest: sweet-tempered Jane (Susannah Harker) and his favorite, the fiercely independent, outspoken Elizabeth (Jennifer Ehle).

Mrs. Bennet's nerves are all a-flutter when she learns that marriage material has just moved into their little corner of Hertfordshire—a Mr. Bingley (Crispin Bonham Carter) with a fortune of five thousand pounds a year.

"For a single man in possession of a good fortune," Elizabeth wryly comments, "must be in want of a wife."

The charming and openhearted Bingley quickly wins the admiration of everyone, and is soon smitten with Jane Bennet. But Bingley's snobbish, 10,000-pound-a-year best bud, Mr. Darcy, is determined to prevent his friend from entering into a most unsuitable marriage. And despite his attractive income, the "proud and disagreeable" Darcy quickly makes enemies of all the neighborhood, especially Elizabeth.

Bingley suggests Darcy dance with the very pretty Elizabeth at their first meeting at a town ball. Darcy declines, and Elizabeth overhears.

"She is tolerable, I suppose," Darcy says rudely, "but she's not handsome enough to tempt me."

Stung by this snub, Elizabeth is determined to dislike Darcy. And although he's equally determined to remain indifferent to a nearly penniless woman from an undistinguished family, he is so impressed with her intelligence, frankness, and décolletage that he quickly develops a crush.

By the way, you're not gonna believe that Colin Firth, the studly specimen who plays Darcy, is the same colorless, somewhat pudgy fellow who played Kristin Scott Thomas's hubby in *The English Patient*. I only pray this means that Colin underwent some sort of *Raging Bull* transformation for the role.

There's something else I wonder about. Before Darcy and Bingley come to Hertfordshire, they're complete strangers to everyone there. Yet knowledge of their net worth precedes their arrival. Did a town crier announce your annual income in those days?

Elizabeth and Jane already have plenty standing between them and conjugal/financial bliss, yet an amusing assortment of odious relatives step in to further muck up the works. There's the effeminate, ass-kissing clergyman, Mr. Collins, a cousin of Mr. Bennet's who is destined to inherit the Bennet estate and wishes to atone for it by marrying one of the Bennet girls. Then there's Elizabeth's sister Lydia (Julia Sawalha in a nicely done departure from her role as the mousy Saffron in the British TV comedy *Absolutely Fabulous*), an empty-headed coquette whose man-hunting machinations may lead the Bennet family to ruin. And there's also Lady Catherine de Bourgh (Barbara Leigh-Hunt), who looks and acts like the Red Queen from *Alice in Wonderland*.

Don't be surprised if you devour all six tapes in a single sitting.

Rear Window

Director: Alfred Hitchcock
Screenplay: John Michael Hayes, based on the short story by Cornell Woolrich
Starring: James Stewart, Grace Kelly, Thelma Ritter, Raymond Burr
1954, 113 min., PG
Great Clothes: ****
Romance: **
Smart-ass women: ****

Dear old Hitch may be the master of suspense, but to me, the defining moments of *Rear Window* are when Grace Kelly shows up at boyfriend Jimmy Stewart's apartment, informs him she's spending the night, and reveals the most darling, elegant little overnight bag ever seen. Inside this briefcaselike accessory is a frothy peignoir she later models, and it's better than a year's subscription to *Vogue*. This may be 1954, but Grace Kelly is definitely the quintessential modern woman—one who has unlimited funds and a great set of genes, of course.

As Lisa, Grace has everything—brains, beauty, money, and a closet full of haute couture. There's only one thing she can't fully possess, and that's her boyfriend, Jeff, played by that screen darling Jimmy Stewart. A third-world-trekking photojournalist, Jeff's not only a die-hard bachelor, he's also convinced that a socialite like Lisa could never deal with his lifestyle on the road. But she wants marriage, and tries in vain to get Jeff interested in local fashion or portrait gigs. Jeff knows he's got a good thing in Lisa, but she's almost "too perfect." After all, how many women show up at a man's apartment wearing a Paris gown and toting a lobster dinner from 21?

In Lisa's eyes, it's the least she can do for poor Jeff, who's cooped up in his stifling hot Manhattan apartment with a broken leg. His only amusement when Lisa's gone is to watch the parade of humanity in the apartment across the courtyard. And what a visual buffet it is. From the sex-crazed honeymoon couple and the pathetic Miss Lonelyhearts to the scantily clad dancer engaging in some sort of fifties version of aerobics, there's hours of entertainment.

Stella, the insurance company nurse who cares for Jeff, turns a disapproving eye on her patient's voyeurism. Played by that sarcastic gal-with-a-heart Thelma Ritter, Stella's convinced that Jeff's passive spying will only lead to trouble. Boy, is she right.

When Jeff begins to suspect that a neighbor across the way (Raymond Burr), has done in his invalid wife, Lisa gets a most astonishing and dangerous opportunity to prove to Jeff she's the woman he wants, the one who'll "go anywhere, do anything, and love it." She becomes his willing spy, one with a pair of healthy (and shapely) gams that can do the legwork needed to uncover this mystery. But is Jeff's imagination simply overactive? And is Lisa's willingness to believe him just a way of getting him to the altar?

No matter how many times you watch it, *Rear Window* is a visual, romantic, heart-stopping treat.

Rebecca

Director: Alfred Hitchcock
Screenplay: Robert E. Sherwood and Joan Harrison, based on the novel by Daphne du Maurier
Starring: Laurence Olivier, Joan Fontaine, George Sanders, Judith Anderson
1940, 132 min., unrated
Heartthrob men: ★★★
Romance: ★★★

When I took Psych 101 in college, I remember learning about random reinforcement. That's when sadistic research psychologists reward or punish unsuspecting lab animals at random intervals without rhyme or reason. Sometimes the animal will perform a task and get a tasty treat. And

other times the animal will perform the same task and get an electric shock. Sometimes relationships are like that, too.

Alfred Hitchcock's first Hollywood film, *Rebecca*, is a random reinforcement type of love story. Okay, I'll admit it's also a Cinderella story, albeit a twisted one. Any woman who's ever been enamored with dark, brooding, unpredictable men like Darcy of *Pride and Prejudice* or Mr. Rochester of *Jane Eyre* will love it. The critics certainly did. *Rebecca* was a smash hit, winning two of the eight Academy Award nominations it received, including Best Picture.

Leading lady Joan Fontaine plays a nameless, painfully shy wallflower as only that doe-eyed damsel can do. The opening sequence takes place in Monte Carlo, where she is the drably dressed paid companion to the elephantine Edythe Van Hopper, a snooty dowager who has nothing better to do with her time than boss around the hapless Joan while hobnobbing with other rich folk. Despite the fact that Joan needs a course in assertiveness training, a big shot of self-esteem, and spends most of the film looking like a lamb about to be slaughtered, it's hard not to feel some sympathy for the poor thing.

Enter the brooding, mysterious Maxim DeWinter, played by Laurence Olivier. Joan's informed by an awed Mrs. Van Hopper that Maxim is the fabulously wealthy owner of Manderley, a magnificent English estate. According to the society buzz, Maxim has never been the same since the tragic loss of his gorgeous wife, Rebecca. But while Mrs. Van Hopper languishes in bed with the flu, Joan is courted by the moody widower. One minute he's all gaiety and charm, the next he's bad tempered and distant. And like any of us gals with a taste for disapproving father figures and repetition compulsions, Joan is at once intimidated, fascinated—and hooked.

Maxim's offhand proposal of course comes as a shock to Joan, who is about to be shipped back to America with Mrs. Van Hopper.

"Either you go to America with Mrs. Van Hopper," Olivier says in a bored tone, "or you come home to Manderley with me."

"You mean you need a secretary or something?" Joan meekly inquires.

"I'm asking you to marry me, you little fool!"

Now what self-effacing gal could refuse an offer like that?

When the bride first arrives at Manderley, it hardly seems a recipe for happily ever after. Timid and terrified and still clad in her shapeless cardigans, Cinderella is way out of her depth in the cavernous mansion filled with servants and haunted by reminders of the mysterious Rebecca, whose initials seem to appear on everything from stationery to dinner napkins.

But the worst challenge Joan faces is Miss Danvers (Judith Anderson), the hostile housekeeper who was Rebecca's slavishly devoted personal maid. Danvers is fiercely jealous of the new bride who has the audacity to try to fill Mrs. DeWinter's shoes. She makes every effort to torment Joan, all done with a thin veneer of polite civility. I want to shake some assertiveness into Joan, who after all is supposed to be mistress of the house instead of an easy mark. Just how personal was Danvers's devotion to her late mistress? One can't help but wonder when Danvers cruelly displays Rebecca's handmade, inevitably monogrammed underwear to a morbidly fascinated Joan as if she were handling the relics of a saint—or an exhibit at the Frederick's of Hollywood bra museum. This, finally, inspires Joan to stand up for herself. "I am Mrs. DeWinter now," she tells an astonished Danvers.

You go, girl!

Joan realizes that everyone in Maxim's circle assumes she knows the particulars of Rebecca's life and death, but whenever she asks Maxim the most innocent question she is rewarded with angry withdrawal. The only sad conclusion she can make is that Maxim must have adored Rebecca—must still adore her. Who is Joan to think that she can replace her?

"What was Rebecca really like?" Joan shyly asks Maxim's solicitor and friend.

"I suppose she was the most beautiful creature I ever saw," he says with a dreamy look in his eyes.

Not exactly a confidence builder.

But is it true? Did Maxim really adore Rebecca? Did he marry Joan out of some momentary lonely impulse? And how does Jack Favell, the slimy cousin of Rebecca—played by the delightfully serpentine George Sanders—fit into the picture? What was Rebecca really like indeed?

The mystery unfolds with wonderful Hitchcockian twists and turns that keep you glued to your seat until the last frame of film.

In Praise of the Genteel Villain

George Sanders always played the bad guy, yet I love him. Why? Because unlike the gun-toting, bomb-exploding villains we gals are sick to death of seeing in the umpteenth sequel to the typical testosterone-fest franchise, George's bad guys always have a brain. He doesn't have to steal nuclear weapons or blow up buildings to make his point. His wit and sarcasm are the deadliest of weapons, and his cunning could hold anyone hostage. In other words, Bruce Willis wouldn't stand a chance.

A woman can respect a George Sanders villain. For one, he not only uses poly-syllabic words, he also pronounces them properly. And though not particularly good-looking, he sure knows how to seduce us with his knowledge of the finer things in life. He wines us, he dines us, and he even notices our clothes. Sure, he's only setting us up for a fall, but at least we'll die admiring this man who combines an impeccable killer instinct with such female sensibilities. In order to best him, we have to think our way past him. What a concept.

Sadly, it seems George's brand of villainy went out with black and white movies. But do check him out in *The Ghost and Mrs. Muir, Rebecca,* and at his dastardly best in *All About Eve.*

The Remains of the Day

Director: James Ivory
Screenplay: Ruth Prawer Jhabvala, based on the novel by Kazuo Ishiguro
Starring: Anthony Hopkins, Emma Thompson, James Fox, Christopher
   Reeve, Peter Vaughan, Hugh Grant, Tim Pigott-Smith, Ben Chaplin, Lena
   Headey
1993, 134 min., PG
Heartthrob men: **
Romance: ***
Smart-ass women: ***
Tears: ***

A movie about a bunch of stuffy servants nursing their repressed passions in a big fancy mansion in 1930s England might not sound like much. But take my word for it, *The Remains of the Day* is a gem that shines ever more brilliantly because of its two principals, those staples of English period pieces, Anthony Hopkins and Emma Thompson. I sure hope this film isn't any indication of how much sex the British get at home. If it is, it's no wonder their tabloids are filled with stories about high-falutin' personages like Members of Parliament and even costar Hugh Grant paying coin of the realm for all manner of extracurricular nooky.

In *The Remains of the Day*, Anthony Hopkins plays Mr. Stevens, the quintessential "gentleman's gentleman," a butler whose work for his master, Lord Darlington (James Fox), is his life. Stevens is so intent on maintaining his prized dignity before his staff as well as his master that he barely allows himself a raised eyebrow on ordinary days. Surely he'd rather die than allow such monumental events as the death of a loved one or the betrothal of the woman he loves to another man put a crease in his carefully cultivated facial expression. Perhaps his underwear is too tight, but the more likely reason for Stevens's outward demeanor is his father, who was also once a "great butler" and now in his declining years has just returned to service as Stevens's stone-faced underbutler.

In short, there's nothing on this earth that can rattle Stevens; that is, nothing except the young, pretty housekeeper Miss Kenton (Emma Thompson). She's so fetching, in fact, that he attempts to ward off her charms with rudeness. That doesn't work, however, because her assertive retaliations only serve to make her more desirable. Poor Miss Kenton: She rages; he ignores her. She cries; he says "thank you" and leaves the room. Poor Stevens: He tries to hide the fact that he's a vulnerable man; she sees right through him. She delights in teasing him, whether it's when she catches him reading a romantic novel in his private parlor, or especially when she notices him eyeing a pretty young housemaid he'd been opposed to hiring.

"Might it be that our Mr. Stevens fears distraction?" says Miss Kenton. "Can it be that our Mr. Stevens is flesh and blood after all and cannot trust himself?"

For that she is rewarded with a slightly amused smile; triumph indeed.

But despite the growing affection between them that dare not speak its name, a real relationship between housekeeper and butler is unthinkable to Stevens. That's something the more proletarian understaff occasionally do, an inconvenience to any well-ordered house that inevitably results in a need to hire replacements. Basically, it seems, if you wanted to have a career as a maid or butler, you had to see yourself as some kind of celibate nun or priest, although somehow Stevens managed to be sired by his butler father. Anyway, this is a great supporting role for Peter Vaughan, who, as Stevens's father, creates friction between Stevens and Miss Kenton. She feels the old gentleman is far too frail to carry out his duties. Of course, Stevens foolishly ignores her wise warnings.

That's not the only thing Stevens ignores. He also turns a blind eye to Lord Darlington's naive affinity for Nazis, despite horrified entreaties from Miss Kenton and his Lordship's godson (an overly pomaded Hugh Grant). Most of all, Stevens desperately tries to ignore his feelings for Miss Kenton, who, when the story opens, had left her post years before and might possibly be amenable to coming back. Will Stevens get a second chance after all these years? You'll sure hope so, for only Anthony Hopkins can make this stick-up-the-bum fellow an endearing figure.

Romy and Michele's High School Reunion

Director: David Mirkin
Screenplay: Robin Schiff
Starring: Mira Sorvino, Lisa Kudrow, Janeane Garofalo, Alan Cumming,
Julia Campbell, Vincent Ventresca, Camryn Manheim, Elaine Hendrix,
Mia Cottet, Kristin Bauer, Jacob Vargas, Justin Theroux
1997, 92 min., R
Great clothes: ★★★★
Romance: ★★

After seeing *Romy and Michele's High School Reunion*, I'll never again scoff at bleached-blond bimbos or vinyl miniskirts.

As two hot-looking, dimwitted babes, Romy (Mira Sorvino) and Michele (Lisa Kudrow) make the gals from *Clueless* look like Rhodes scholars. Yet, simply by poking fun at *Pretty Woman* in the very first scene, they instantly won my heart.

They're cute, they live to party, and they make their own clothes— thigh-high vinyl, Mylar, and spandex creations in a rainbow of colors. Inseparable best friends ever since high school in Tucson, they share a flat in Venice Beach. Life is good.

That is, until Romy has a chance encounter with Heather Mooney (Janeane Garofalo), a bitterly angry, chain-smoking former schoolmate who makes Robert De Niro in *Taxi Driver* look like a social worker. Although it's ten years since they graduated, Heather nurses a particular grudge against Michele for enthralling Heather's high school crush, a science nerd named Sandy Frank. Romy learns from Heather that their high school is about to have a ten-year reunion. And after their initial excitement at the prospect of tripping down memory lane, Romy and Michele sober at the thought of facing the authors of some very painful memories.

Then again, they're certainly a lot cuter than they were in high school, when Romy was chubby and Michele wore a back brace. In those days, the school's "A-Group" quartet of bitches, led by evil queen Christie Masters, used to make their lives a living hell. But what else have they really accomplished in the last ten years? Romy is a receptionist at a Jaguar repair shop; Michele is seriously unemployed. Neither of them went to college; both are single. Romy is dumb; Michele is even dumber. "What's the point of going," Romy points out, "if we're not going to impress people?"

There's only one solution: Lie. So—dressed in business suits (micromini, of course), driving a borrowed Jag convertible, and armed with a tale of how they invented, of all things, Post-its—Romy and Michele take their reunion by storm. That is, until Heather Mooney shows up and blows their cover.

Through high school flashbacks, skewed realities, and even a fun choreographed dance sequence, *Romy and Michele's High School Reunion* takes an outrageously funny, offbeat, and poignant look at the cruel pecking order of high school life. And, even if, like Heather says, putting a lit cigarette up your ass is preferable to the thought of revisiting those days, this film might just change your mind.

A Room with a View

Director: James Ivory
Screenplay: Ruth Prawer Jhabvala, based on the novel by E. M. Forster
Starring: Helena Bonham Carter, Daniel Day-Lewis, Julian Sands, Maggie Smith, Denholm Elliott, Simon Callow, Judi Dench, Rosemary Leach, Rupert Graves
1986, 115 min., unrated, but have your pause button poised for male frontal nudity.
Great clothes: ★★★★
Romance: ★★★★
Heartthrob men: ★★★★

Ah, romantic fantasy. The sleepy English countryside. Florence in summer. Women in long flowing dresses and parasols. Gorgeous Julian Sands nearly causing Helena Bonham Carter, the queen of period films, to swoon as he plants his burning lips on hers amidst a tall field of barley on a sun-drenched Florentine hill. It's like one of those Fabio book covers come to life. The difference is that this E. M. Forster–based story is not only deliciously romantic, but also intelligent and ironically witty. And those clothes! It's enough to make one long for a corset and a veiled hat, even in the blistering Italian summer heat.

Helena Bonham Carter is stunning as the repressed, properly English Lucy Honeychurch, whose beneath-the-surface passions are awakened by the dishy Sands, who plays the free-thinking George Emerson. (In those days, "free-thinking" meant actually daring to express your feelings openly, including poking fun at uptight English social conventions. Terribly indelicate.) I want to slap some sense into Lucy when she fearfully retreats from George and takes refuge in the safe, ever-so-stiff arms of Cecil, an effete, pompous snob played brilliantly by Daniel Day-Lewis. And Day-Lewis, whom we women know can steam up the screen when he chooses, actually convinces us in this film that he must have a stick up his butt or something, so fine an actor is he. This can't be the same guy from *Last of the Mohicans*. What a geek!

The supporting cast is outstanding, particularly Maggie Smith as Lucy's spinster pain-in-the-neck cousin, Charlotte, who never actually says what she wants but manages to manipulate everyone around her just the same. As the Reverend Mr. Beebe, Simon Callow (the stout, jolly gay fellow from *Four Weddings and a Funeral*) is wonderfully teddy-bearish, particularly when he, Sands, and Lucy's brother are discovered romping naked in a pond (indelicacy again!) by Lucy, Cecil, and her mother. Then there's Judi Dench as lady novelist Eleanor Lavish, who spouts embroidered metaphors and shockingly believes that one should be open to "physical sensation."

The story unfolds in an era of stuffy drawing rooms and stiff collars, in a time when the best way a young lady like Lucy could hope to get "stirred up," as Mr. Beebe puts it, is by playing Beethoven on the piano. Sands's George Emerson and his father, Mr. Emerson, played by Denholm Elliott, are like a breath of fresh air in this uptight environment. I love it when Mr. Emerson upstages the pompous Reverend Mr. Eager (Patrick Godfrey), who holds forth to a group of English tourists in Florence about how a particular church was "built by faith."

"Built by faith, indeed," Emerson comments loudly in Lucy's ear. "That simply means the workers weren't paid properly."

But the best scene is when Julian Sands makes his last-ditch impassioned plea to Lucy, who is stubbornly determined to marry the anally challenged Cecil. Says Sands of Cecil in a stirring speech about the concept of trophy wives:

"He's the sort who can't know anyone intimately, least of all a woman. He doesn't know what a woman is. He wants you for a possession, something to look at, like a painting or an ivory box. Something to own and to display. He doesn't want you to be real and to think and to live. He doesn't love you. But I love you. I want you to have your own thoughts and feelings, even when I hold you in my arms."

Then Lucy, the ditz, refuses to listen and orders Sands out of her home.

But when she later parrots Sands's words in the act of dumping an astonished Cecil, we actually feel sorry for the dumpee. That's how good Daniel Day-Lewis is. And Lucy still tries to evade Sands, that's how stupid she is. Will she ever come to her senses? See it and find out for yourself. I have, countless times.

Why the Names Merchant and Ivory Are Kryptonite to a Guy

by Richard Roeper

In 1995 the team of James Ivory and Ismail Merchant made a movie called *Jefferson in Paris*, with Nick Nolte as the third president of the United States. (Apparently Stallone wasn't available.) The film received a rating of PG-13 from the MPAA, with this explanation: "Mature theme, some images of violence, and a bawdy puppet show."

A bawdy puppet show? A *bawdy puppet show???* Gee, good thing they took out the sarcastic mime scene or they might've gotten an NC-17.

God, how I hate Merchant Ivory films. They're so bloody refined, so elegant, and so bloated with all those scenes of breathtaking scenery. Not to mention the stilted dialogue that only hints at what the characters are really trying to say. And it takes them two and a half hours to do this! The average Merchant Ivory film is only a bit shorter than the average major league baseball game, with the men in crisper whites. But when it's all over, nothing has happened. Nothing, I say! It's all subtext and nuance and crap like that. Oh, there's always a big message contained within the story of some repressed twit who doesn't express his love for the dainty lass across the meadow until they're both in their nineties and the automobile has been invented, but really, who cares. Every time I see a snippet of a Merchant Ivory film, I long for a Liam Neeson or a Mel Gibson to come riding through on horseback and set the whole movie on fire.

Instead, I get Anthony Hopkins as the butler.

Not that I've ever actually seen many films by these people. I've been dragged to a couple of Merchant Ivory movies on a date, and I've seen bits and pieces of their work on cable, when I didn't have control of the clicker and thus couldn't get back to *Sports Machine*. But trust me, I've seen enough to know what they're all about.

Certain actors always show up in Merchant Ivory films. Like that Emma Thompson, and that Vanessa Redgrave, and old tweedy Brits named Denholm and Simon. All these actors who talk about their "love of the thea-tuh" whenever they get interviewed.

Hugh Grant once starred in a Merchant Ivory film titled *Maurice*. He played a man named Clive who is in love with a man named, well, Maurice. Need. I. Say. More.

The only naked torso you see in these films is a naked male torso. And it's always pale and hairless. Merchant Ivory men look like skinned rats.

The supposedly hot chick in these movies is always somebody like Helena Bonham Carter. Women like to say, "Oh that Helena Bonham Carter is so beautiful." No she's not. She's a tiny woman with a big head and wiry hair and heaving bosoms, and she talks like some sort of upscale Kewpie doll. That midget woman who spiritually cleaned the house in *Poltergeist* is more attractive.

Perhaps the most famous Merchant Ivory film of all is *A Room with a View*. In that movie, Ms. Bonham Carter plays Lucy Honeychurch, while Judi Dench sparkles as "Miss Lavish," I kid you not. They have tea quite a bit in this movie. There's a kissing scene in the middle of an endless field, and one of the male characters likes to read aloud to young women.

If all movies were like that, I'd never go to the movies again.

Sabrina

Director: Billy Wilder
Screenplay: Billy Wilder, Samuel Taylor, and Ernest Lehman, from the play *Sabrina Fair* by Samuel Taylor
Starring: Humphrey Bogart, Audrey Hepburn, William Holden, Walter Hampden, John Williams, Martha Hyer, Joan Vohs
1954, 113 min., unrated
Great clothes: ★★★★
Heartthrob men: ★★
Romance: ★★★

What could the powers-that-be in Hollywood be thinking when they decided to remake *Sabrina*? Don't they realize there's only one Audrey Hepburn? If you do, by the way, want to see Julia Ormond in a role that really does her justice, check out *Smilla's Sense of Snow*. I'll grant that Greg Kinnear did a fabulous David Larrabee in the 1995 remake. But even Harrison Ford junkies like me had to feel disappointed when they saw how convincingly unstudlike Harrison is in the role of Linus Larrabee. Sure, he's supposed to be a fuddy-duddy who only gets off on the stock market. But he's Harrison Ford! He's the President of the United States! (I'm not deluded; I saw *Air Force One*.) If we can't have Audrey, have a little pity and give us girls some babe for our movie buck.

I like *Sabrina* because it's all about obsessing on a man you can't have and it's all wrapped up in a Cinderella story, a favorite gal fairy tale. Sabrina, the chauffeur's daughter on a big Long Island estate, has spent her life mooning over the good-for-nothing, designer-skirt-chasing younger son of the rich family papa works for. Sabrina watches David's every move, even spies on his amorous escapades from a tree. Today, they'd call that stalking, but on Audrey Hepburn it looks charming. Nonetheless, David Larrabee (William Holden) is too busy hunting debutantes even to notice Sabrina's alive, let alone think about getting a restraining order. But David's indifference doesn't stop her, no sir. Even two years away in Paris acquiring the essential feminine skills of cooking soufflés, hiring the right hair stylist, and dressing in chic new threads fail to dampen her ardor.

But maybe Sabrina's got the right idea. I mean, how many of you have wasted large portions of your valuable time dreaming about some worthless lout who not only uses you as a doormat—a role you gladly assume—but who also earns only minor ducats? At least Sabrina worships a man with a sizable net worth.

So anyway, when the new, improved Sabrina returns from Paris, Holden is smitten. And the rich, snobby family freaks out. So older brother Linus (played by Bogie) decides to trick Sabrina into falling in love with him so that Holden can marry into a corporate dynasty that'll send Larrabee stock soaring. If the plan works, Sabrina can then be dumped with a nice golden parachute. But they've underestimated Sabrina: She's returned home with more than just Parisian elegance; she's also brought back some real live self-confidence. And neither disapproving parents nor even David's impending marriage will shake it.

"He's still David Larrabee," warns her dad, "and you're still the chauffeur's daughter, and you're still reaching for the moon."

"No, Father," Sabrina calmly replies, "the moon's reaching for me."

I'd say that, too, if I had a five-figure Givenchy gown on my back.

So cruise stealthily past the house of the man who hasn't noticed you yet, hang up when he answers the phone, and get some more tips from *Sabrina*.

Say Anything

Director: Cameron Crowe
Screenplay: Cameron Crowe
Starring: John Cusack, Ione Skye, John Mahoney, Lili Taylor, Joan Cusack
(uncredited, for some strange reason), Aimee Brooks, Bebe Neuwirth,
Pamela Segall, Jason Gould, Loren Dean, Eric Stoltz, Chynna Phillips,
Joanna Frank, Lois Chiles (also unbilled).
1989, 100 min., PG-13
Heartthrob men: ****
Romance: ****
Tears: **

I've been trying to figure it out, and the only thing I can come up with
is that Cameron Crowe must've been trying to get on some woman's
good side when he wrote *Say Anything*. Either that or he's really one of
those rare men who knows how to think like us. How else could he have
thought up a character like Lloyd Dobler and cast him with the gal-
pleasing, eminently talented John Cusack?

An army brat who has female best friends, lives with his single-mom
big sister (real-life sister Joan Cusack), and has no life goals other than to
date his high school's lovely valedictorian, Diane Court (Ione Skye),
Lloyd Dobler is determined to prevail. Neither words of caution from gal
friends Corey (Lili Taylor) and D. C. (Aimee Brooks), nor disapproving
looks from Diane's overly protective dad (John Mahoney) will deter him
from his appointed course.

"Diane Court doesn't go out with guys like you," Corey warns. "She's a
brain."

This line does, however, betray the fact that a man wrote this script.
Sure, we want brains, ambition, and upward mobility from our men, but
what we really want above all else is their undying loyalty and adoration.
We want someone to say, as Lloyd says to Diane's father when pressed
about his future plans:

"What I really want to do with my life, what I want to do for a living,
is I want to be with your daughter. I'm good at it."

Consider this: If you end up joining the growing ranks of female primary breadwinners, wouldn't you rather come home to a Lloyd Dobler?

Although supposedly unattainable, Diane is actually an easy mark for
Lloyd's worship. She may be the smartest girl in school, but her beauty
and intellect have served to make her feel like an outsider for much of her

school career. Mismatched as they are, Lloyd's the first person who makes Diane feel like she belongs with people her own age. He'd put his coat over a puddle for her to walk upon if he could; instead he carefully steers her past some broken glass littering the sidewalk on their first date. What woman could resist such chivalry?

It's not that their relationship is devoid of challenges; far from it. Between her dad's manipulations, her impending sojourn to England on a fellowship, and possible disaster for her father's business, Diane just might be ready to call it quits.

"Don't do it, Diane!" you'll find yourself shouting at the screen. That's how much you'll get caught up in *Say Anything*, a film that celebrates first love in all its glories.

Sense and Sensibility

Director: Ang Lee
Screenplay: Emma Thompson, adapted from the novel by Jane Austen
Starring: Emma Thompson, Kate Winslet, Hugh Grant, Alan Rickman, Greg
   Wise, Gemma Jones, Imogen Stubbs, Elizabeth Spriggs
1995, 136 min., PG
Heartthrob men: ★★★★
Romance: ★★★★
Smart-ass women: ★★★
Tears: ★★★★

Ever ignore—fool that you are—the quiet, respectful soul who worships you from afar? The one whose steadfast devotion in the face of your rejection only gives you the urge to yawn? That's Colonel Brandon of *Sense and Sensibility*, played by the quintessentially sexy Alan Rickman.

Ever fall for the guy who drips passion? A man so breathtaking he could be the next James Bond—or the next Antichrist? That's John Willoughby, played by gorgeous Greg Wise.

Loosen your stays, girls, reach for your smelling salts, and rent *Sense and Sensibility*.

Set in early nineteenth-century England, *Sense and Sensibility* is a luscious period piece that centers around the romantic trials of two sisters. Although they're devoted to each other, these two gals couldn't be more dissimilar. Marianne (Kate Winslet) is all fiery passion and unbridled

emotion; Elinor (Emma Thompson) is all polite reserve and careful prudence.

Elinor's self-restraint is what pushes Marianne's buttons the most. And to Marianne's bewilderment, it appears that Elinor has fallen for an equally reserved man. That man is one Edward Ferrars (Hugh Grant), a shy fellow graced with Hugh's characteristic stutter and a posture that could do with a twentieth-century chiropractic adjustment.

"Can he really love her?" Marianne wonders. "Can the soul really be satisfied with such polite affection? To love is to burn, to be on fire, like Juliet or Guinevere or Heloise."

Marianne, of course, falls for Willoughby, a man who makes her burn in more ways than one. And she doesn't give a damn if everyone knows it.

"Why should I hide my regard?" Marianne stubbornly insists when Elinor warns her about revealing too much. And why, Marianne wonders, should Elinor hide her regard for Edward? When prodded by Marianne to reveal her true feelings, Elinor will only admit that she "likes" and "esteems" him. After all, haven't we all been taught that a man should say the "L-word" first? But Marianne will have none of those feminine strategies. Marianne, if given the opportunity, would have used *The Rules* for toilet paper.

Elinor isn't the only one with something to hide, for in *Sense and Sen-*

sibility, nothing is quite what it seems to be. And as the truth slowly unfolds, the road to romance is a treacherous one indeed.

Everything about this film is an unparalleled delight, from Ang Lee's flawless direction and Thompson's Oscar-winning script to the superb cast. So take a luxurious bath in unadulterated romance, unstoppable drama, and biting social satire. See *Sense and Sensibility*, an experience that serves up a new treasure every time you watch it.

The Austen Mystique

If Jane Austen were alive today, she'd probably be horrified watching the biggest guns in Hollywood compete in an ass-kissing contest for her favors. What is it about the stories of this sheltered, early nineteenth-century lady novelist that has today's filmgoing females salivating for more? As one who has devoured her books and seen every film adaption I can get my paws on, I have my own ideas about why dear Jane is so timely.

Today, relationships are an enigma. Consider the legion of self-help books for the lovelorn. One will tell you women are from Venus; another will prove that men don't know what to do with a penis. Others will show you how to master "the rules" of intergender deceit. And no matter whom you love, you definitely "love too much." No wonder we long for a time when gender roles were clear. Jane Austen gives us this clarity, but the best thing about her stories is watching them, not living them. I barely made it through home ec.; if my only career options were stay-at-home wife or maiden aunt I'd shoot myself.

On the other hand, some things haven't changed at all since the nineteenth century. We've all grown up dreaming of the handsome prince who will sweep us off our feet and pay off our credit cards. And we've all been reared on stories that glorify unavailable princes and unrequited love. None of us suffers fools gladly, and all of us live to mock them. Jane Austen gives us all that, too.

Most important, we all dream of happily ever after, and that's dear Jane's greatest appeal. You'll never leave the theater or close the book feeling anything less than starry-eyed.

Shadowlands

Director: Richard Attenborough
Screenplay: William Nicholson, based on his stageplay
Starring: Anthony Hopkins, Debra Winger, Edward Hardwicke, Joseph
   Mazzello, John Wood, Michael Denison, Peter Whistler
1993, 133 min., PG
Heartthrob men: ***
Romance: ****
Smart-ass women: ***
Tears: ****

"No pain, no gain," says my sadistic aerobics instructor, someone who never had a phobia of mirrors in swimsuit dressing rooms. "Pain builds character," says my well-meaning friend, someone who hasn't spent a Saturday night alone since she was fourteen. There are many platitudes about pain, but my personal favorite is the one about healing the wounded inner child, a stance usually adopted by adults who need an excuse for breaking crockery or sniping at strangers from a supermarket roof.

In *Shadowlands*, the main character, played by Anthony Hopkins, is a little more eloquent. "Pain is God's megaphone to rouse a deaf world," he proclaims. As the beloved children's author and Oxford University professor C. S. Lewis, the value of pain as teacher is what Lewis most loves to preach in the classroom and to his lecture audiences.

Despite his pretty speeches, Lewis, known as "Jack" to his friends, has built a safe, cloistered life for himself where pain cannot possibly touch him. You might not be able to relate to Jack's asexual, exclusively male academic world of Oxford in the early 1950s, but you'll instantly fall in love with him.

What's not to like? Jack adores his students, enthralls his lecture audiences, and shares a bachelor home with his older brother, Warnie (Edward Hardwicke). He also endures the good-natured ribbing of his colleagues, who wonder how a man who knows no children could be so successful writing books for them. Like children, women are another exotic species Jack knows of only from books. Fact is, the only glimpse Jack ever gets of a skirt is from the podium of his frequent speaking engagements. That is, until a literary groupie in the form of Debra Winger takes his life by storm.

As a brash, borderline obnoxious New Yawker (with an odd touch of the Midwest in her adopted accent), Debra Winger is surprisingly endearing as poet Joy Gresham. Like many of Jack's admirers, Joy starts out as a pen pal. He's amused by the letters he gets from this outlandish "Jewish Communist Christian American" specimen, but he's also intrigued. To his surprise, they become instant friends when Joy comes to England to flee a nightmare of a marriage with her adorable little boy, Douglas. Joy is unlike anyone else he's ever known. For one, she's completely outspoken, and that just isn't done in Jack's tight-assed English world. Besides, she's a woman, and a pretty darn attractive one at that. He's amused, he's distracted—and he's scared out of his wits.

Like his character in *Remains of the Day*, Jack tries desperately to ignore their mutual affection. To Jack, who remembers well the death of his mother when he was a little boy, love means loss, and loss means pain. Luckily, unlike the gal in that other film, Joy's a pushy American broad who'll have none of that British restraint. The true test comes when fate takes an unexpected twist, and Jack finds himself "suffering the torments of the damned at the prospect of losing her."

Shadowlands is basically a feast for those of us who love the child within and hate all the pop psychology platitudes. You'll love Jack, who is like a little boy frozen in time and struggling desperately to play catch-up as a man in the game of love. You'll want to pinch the cheeks of his brother, Warnie, who is initially jealous of Jack's new interest in a woman but bucks up nonetheless, even if he is a bit fussy and old maidish about it. Joy's son, Douglas (Joseph Mazzello), is completely lovable in his timid awe of the man who wrote his Narnia books. And ironically, though Joy is the only true adult of the principal cast, she's the one who inspires Jack to fulfill his childhood longings.

Have yourself a good cry. After that, you might just find yourself telling someone you love them before it's too late—even if it is the guy who reads your gas meter.

Shirley Valentine

Director: Lewis Gilbert
Screenplay: Willy Russell
Starring: Pauline Collins, Tom Conti, Gillian Kearney, Bernard Hill, Julia
  McKenzie, Alison Steadman, Joanna Lumley, Catharine Duncan, Sylvia
  Syms, Tracie Bennet, Gareth Jefferson
1989, 108 min., R
Romance: **
Smart-ass women: ***

Here, finally, is a heroine we can finally relate to: not gorgeous, a bit
stout, middle-aged, and in her own words, "beginning to sag a bit."
She's Shirley Valentine, a bored English housewife whose best friend is
the glass of wine that lessens the tedium of cooking dinner. She's also
a bit crazy, at least that's what her rigid, ill-tempered husband thinks of
a woman who routinely talks to walls and rocks—or to us in the audience.

It wasn't always like this for Shirley. She and hubby Joe used to have
laughs. Hell, they used to have sex. She used to have lots of girlfriends
with whom, way before *Seinfeld*, she could share her deepest thoughts,
like how the word *clitoris* sounds like it should be a woman's name. After
all, she points out, think of all those guys named Dick. Now that her kids
are grown and out on their own, Shirley's life is about as exciting as a cold
plate of chips and eggs.

Enter Shirley's friend Jane (Alison Steadman of *Pride and Prejudice*).
Jane's just won a two-week holiday in Greece, and invites Shirley to join
her. Shirley's always dreamed of traveling, but dreads asking Joe. So she
marshals her courage and sneaks off with Jane, who promptly dumps her
for some dude she meets on the flight.

For the first time in her life, Shirley is on her own, and Greece is paradise on earth. She doesn't really mind the solitude, especially when the
alternative is to hang with the obnoxious English tourists at her hotel
who seem to despise all things foreign, especially the food.

Her delight in authentic tastes and her wistful sadness spark the interest of Greek barkeep Costas (Tom Conti). And despite Costas's eloquent
assurances that he's not out to "make fuck" with her, Shirley samples
some of that Greek dish, too. So now that she's rediscovered "all this un-
used life," what does she do about her old one?

Inspirational, hilarious, and touching, *Shirley Valentine* is a treasure. So is the supporting cast, which includes Julia McKenzie as Shirley's better-than-you-at-everything neighbor, and Joanna Lumley (*Absolutely Fabulous*) as the picture-perfect former high school rival whom Shirley unexpectedly encounters twenty years later.

If you're a middle-aged woman who's lost hope, and if having dreams of something better makes you doubt your sanity, Shirley and a nice glass of retsina'll set you straight. Buying yourself a lovely bit of lingerie wouldn't hurt either.

Three Days of the Condor

Director: Sydney Pollack
Screenplay: Lorenzo Semple, Jr., and David Rayfiel, based on the novel *Six Days of the Condor* by James Grady
Starring: Robert Redford, Faye Dunaway, Cliff Robertson, Max von Sydow, John Houseman
1975, 118 min., R
Heartthrob men: ★★★★
Romance: ★★

Men think that all we want to see on the screen are love stories. Think again, guys. We love thrillers, too, especially ones with lots of political intrigue. The only catch is, the story's got to have a brain. So does the hero. Neanderthal martial artists and pea-brained bodybuilders just won't do for us. Having Robert Redford as that sensitive, intelligent hero doesn't hurt, either. *Three Days of the Condor* not only has Robert Redford as its hero, it has a young, pretty Robert Redford, before he became the craggy yet still studly lead in that yawn-festival *Up Close and Personal*.

Three Days of the Condor is a thinking woman's kind of thriller about a bookish, usually unarmed secret agent on the run. I'll admit it, there is also a love interest of sorts in the form of a very young and beautiful Faye Dunaway. There's major chemistry between these two, and that doesn't hurt, either.

Robert Redford plays a guy who works for the American Literary Historical Society in Manhattan, but that's just a cover name for an obscure research branch of the CIA. This odd little collection of CIA scholars reads mysteries and thrillers to see if they can suss out any international conspiracies in the making. One day, Redford leaves the office to pick up lunch for his colleagues, only to find upon his return that every single one of his coworkers has been shot to death. Frantic and terrified, he calls CIA headquarters in Washington, but quickly realizes they've marked him for death. On the run, with nowhere to turn and without a clue, he kidnaps a stranger—a lonely photographer played by Faye Dunaway—and hides out in her apartment until he can figure out what happened.

Faye's none too pleased, but she ends up doing a Patty Hearst. Who wouldn't? Her captor may sound delusional, he may tie her up, but he's sweet, gorgeous, and even appreciates the bleak loneliness of the photographs that line the walls of her apartment.

"You have good eyes," she tells Redford. "Not kind, but they don't lie, and they don't look away much. And they don't miss anything. I could use eyes like that."

And I could use a man like Redford to tie me up, too.

Redford and Dunaway are marvelous, and so is Max Von Sydow, who plays a very gentlemanly—and extremely deadly—assassin. There's also Cliff Robertson, who wears an awful toupée but does a nice job in his role as the CIA's New York head honcho. That's before the real-life financial conspiracies of a certain Hollywood producer sent him into career obscurity.

A Tree Grows in Brooklyn

Director: Elia Kazan
Screenplay: Tess Slesinger and Frank Davis, adapted from the novel by Betty Smith
Starring: Peggy Ann Garner, James Dunn, Dorothy McGuire, Joan Blondell, Lloyd Nolan, Ted Donaldson, James Gleason, Ruth Nelson, John Alexander
1945, 128 min., unrated
Romance: ★★
Tears: ★★★

If you're like me, the term *dysfunctional family* is about as new and exciting as that movie about the Brady Bunch. I mean, other than what we've learned from watching *The Waltons*, do any of us even know what a functional family is? And aren't you sick of all those TV movies and talk shows that exploit the pain and call it entertainment? How about that cable channel that calls itself "television for women"? Shouldn't it really be called "television for angry women who blame their screwed-up lives on their screwed-up families"?

If you're as tired as I am of watching films that reduce the complexities of family troubles to modern-day sound bites, take a look at Elia Kazan's heartwarming, Oscar-winning 1945 classic *A Tree Grows in Brooklyn*. The principals in this insightful look at a poor, alcohol-damaged family, especially the mom and dad figures, are too multilayered to allow for such broad strokes. They simply defy any wish you might have to condemn or champion them. With more wisdom than an AA meeting or a self-help book—and certainly more entertainment value— *A Tree Grows in Brooklyn* can enlighten single moms whose kids blame them for dad's absence, married moms who play primary breadwinner or the "bad cop" role in the family, and any of us gals who grew up with an irresponsible yet charming parent. Most important, it shows us that we are not doomed to repeat their mistakes.

Oscar-winner Peggy Ann Garner plays Francie Nolan, a dirt-poor child of the Brooklyn tenements who adores her charismatic alcoholic dad and resents her no-nonsense, practical, reality-driven mother. Francie's a smart, bookish little girl who scavenges rags and tin with brother Neely (Ted Donaldson) to earn a few much-needed pennies for the family, but what she really lives for is her escape into an imaginary world of books and stories. She enters that world through the library books she devours, but most of all through her storytelling father, whose empty promises of a better life for his family delight her heart and enrage her mother's. Dorothy McGuire, who plays Francie's long-suffering mother, Katie, is a beauty who once bought into her husband's fanciful dreams and ended up scrubbing floors to feed her perpetually hungry kids. As Francie's father, Johnny Nolan, a ne'er-do-well waiter who rarely works and generally drinks up his paychecks when he does, James Dunn also won an Oscar. No doubt he captured the hearts of the Academy as much as he captured Francie's.

The loving yet tortured relationships between Francie and her parents, and between Katie and Johnny, is the focus of this touching story. When Katie's sister tells her she's becoming hardened, Katie tries to reconnect with what she fell for in Johnny, but the burden of being the only grounded adult in the family drains her of any affection. Johnny's so charming you can't help but love him and pity him, but you also can't help but see how Katie's hand-to-mouth existence drives her away from him. And poor Francie—all she can see is her misunderstood, unappreciated dad, a man who thinks the world of her, a man who takes time to read her compositions while her too-busy mom can't be bothered, a man who from time to time gets "sick," as Katie instructs her to call his bouts of drunkenness.

From Katie's denial and Johnny's stories, Francie learns to embroider the truth herself. But when caught telling tales by her sympathetic teacher (Ruth Nelson), Francie learns about the gift embedded in her girlish imagination.

"If we tell the truth and write the lies," says her teacher, "then they aren't lies anymore—they become stories."

And from this is born Francie's dream of becoming a writer, and hopefully, not one of those who writes "television for women."

The Turning Point

Director: Herbert Ross
Screenplay: Arthur Laurents
Starring: Anne Bancroft, Shirley MacLaine, Leslie Browne, Mikhail Baryshnikov, Tom Skerritt, Martha Scott, Anthony Zerbe, Alexandra Danilova
1977, 119 min., PG
Heartthrob men: ★★★★
Romance: ★★
Smart-ass women: ★★★★
Tears: ★★

Having the opportunity to replay at will the scenes where Mikhail Baryshnikov prances around in tights was enough incentive for me to rent *The Turning Point*. He looked so good that I found myself wishing for a new fashion trend in male hosiery to sweep the nation. For example, what if that really cute guy you met last week picked you up for your first date in a short shirt and body-hugging tights that gave you a preview of coming attractions? Then again, what if that nerdy lech who works in the employees' cafeteria bussed your table wearing similar attire?

The Turning Point is a "What if" kind of movie, even though it's not about tights, just the people who wear them for a living in the ultracompetitive world of ballet. It's about Dee Dee (Shirley MacLaine), who finally reconnects with the world-famous ballet company she left twenty years before to get married and have a baby. She's spent the last two decades married to former fellow company member Wayne (Tom Skerritt), mothering three kids, teaching ballet, and wondering "What if." What if she hadn't got pregnant? What if she'd stayed with the company? Would she have been as successful as her best friend and fiercest rival, Emma (Anne Bancroft)?

Now the fruit of Dee Dee's fateful decision—her oldest daughter, Emilia—has been asked to join the ballet company of Dee Dee's youth. And Dee Dee's long-simmering jealousies begin to bubble to the surface as she sees her precious Emilia become the devoted pet of Emma. But her rival has her own "What ifs" to ponder, as it quickly becomes clear to Emma that she is too old to maintain her place as prima ballerina, the role for which she has given up everything else to attain. In fact, it seems likely that the brilliantly talented Emilia will soon take her place.

So how does Mikhail Baryshnikov fit into all of this? As Emilia's love interest, of course. But, like any man who knows he looks that good in tights, he's inevitably a womanizing scoundrel.

As Emilia's star rises, Emma's falls, and Dee Dee's resentments reach a boiling point, one of the most unflinchingly honest cat fights in cinematic history unfolds.

"You'd walk over anybody and still get a good night's sleep. That's exactly how you got where you are, Emma," says Dee Dee, drawing first blood.

More venom is traded, but Emma delivers the coup de grace.

"You got married because you knew you were second rate, and you got pregnant because Wayne was a ballet dancer, and in those days that meant queer."

Filled with breathtaking choreography and complex characters, *The Turning Point* will not only change how you look at ballet, but also at envy, competition, and the choices we all make.

Un Coeur en Hiver
(A Heart in Winter)

Director: Claude Sautet
Screenplay: Jacques Fieschi, Claude Sautet, Jérome Tonnerre, Yves Ul-
mann
Starring: Daniel Auteuil, Emmanuelle Beart, Andre Dussollier, Elisabeth
Bourgine, Brigitte Catillon, Miriam Boyer, Jean-Claude Bouillaud
1992, 105 min., unrated, in French with English subtitles
Heartthrob men: ***
Romance: ***
Tears: **

Thou shalt not covet thy boyfriend's business partner and friend—unless he's very, very good with his hands. Such is the dilemma that
Camille, the incomparably gorgeous and talented Parisian violinist
played by Emmanuelle Beart, faces in *Un Coeur en Hiver.*

So why does Camille choose to complicate her life? After all, she's already won the heart (and broken up the marriage) of her boyfriend,
Maxim, the urbane, more conventionally handsome of the duo. Maxim's
the schmoozer, the one who jets off to Geneva to buy and sell rare violins
for select clients while the reserved Stephan (Daniel Auteuil) stays behind in their little studio and repairs them. Magnanimous Maxim's the
one who fixes up a roomy love nest for his new amour while the ascetic
Stephan lives in a dinky little room off the workshop. Maxim's the one
who openly adores Camille while Stephan plays out a little scheme of advance and retreat.

But retreat is exactly what snares Camille, because advance is the only
thing this spoiled, successful, and smashingly beautiful creature has ever
known. Besides, if Camille's anything like me, she might have found it
disturbing that despite Maxim's handsome appearance, he looks like he
could be wearing an almost subliminal shade of pink lipstick. I don't
know, maybe it's a French thing that never caught on here.

Jealousies abound in this deftly directed drama, not only between
lovers, would-be lovers, and business partners, but also between Camille
and her live-in agent and friend, Regine, who's none too pleased about
being replaced as the number-one influence in Camille's life.

I've seen this film five times, and every time I see it I come up with different conclusions. Is Stephan really in love with Camille? Or is he just playing a game? Is he cold-hearted and calculating? Or is his "heart in winter" experiencing a bit of spring thaw? And is Camille really as smitten with Stephan as she believes she is? Or has she simply fallen into the seductive trap of wanting what seems to be just out of reach?

"When he's there, he's there," she tells Regine. "Then suddenly . . . it's like I don't exist."

Sound familiar, girls? It's enlightening and yes, I have to admit, perversely comforting to realize that even an angelic beauty like Camille can suffer the same kind of rejection the rest of us mortals do.

It's all in French, but it doesn't matter. You don't even need the subtitles to enjoy watching the cast throw each other subtext-rich glances while drinking espresso, applying lipstick (Camille, not Maxim), or stroking each other's instruments. So superbly masterful is this film that every gesture has meaning, every actor plays his or her part with subtle genius, and the stirring score of Ravel's Sonatas and Trio will make you run out to buy the music.

An Unmarried Woman

Director: Paul Mazursky
Screenplay: Paul Mazursky
Starring: Jill Clayburgh, Alan Bates, Michael Murphy, Pat Quinn, Kelly
    Bishop, Linda Miller, Lisa Lucas
1978, 124 min., R
Heartthrob men: ★★★
Romance: ★★★
Smart-ass women: ★★★★

How I long for the days before *feminist* became a dirty word and Camille Paglia became a best-selling author, when women weren't ashamed to say words like *consciousness raising* in public, and when exploring your female sexuality wasn't also a flirtation with death. But before I get on my soapbox, burn my Wonder Bra, and put my makeup mirror in storage, there's a film you should see for the pure fun of celebrating the joy of female bonding.

That film is *An Unmarried Woman,* an enlightening and funny exploration of the grief and loneliness of a woman in transition—and a lesson in how a woman can re-create herself through self-love.

Remember Jill Clayburgh, that darling of seventies films? She's simply wonderful as Erica Benton, a thirtysomething woman with a perfectly devoted husband and a delightfully quirky fifteen-year-old daughter, Patty (Lisa Lucas).

Jill's secure world is completely shattered when her husband, Martin (Michael Murphy), drops a bombshell on her on a public street during her lunch break from her secretarial job in a New York art gallery. Without warning, hubby starts weeping, and when Jill comfortingly asks him what's wrong, he tells her he's leaving her for another woman.

Jill is devastated, but she's no victim. She takes her strength from Sue, Elaine, and Jeannette, her three closest girlfriends who meet regularly to have dinner, watch Gal Movies, and discuss sex and men.

Now that she's single, Jill is completely unprepared for how the men in her circle start hitting on her—even her doctor. An unmarried woman is fair game, it seems—especially the newly dumped. But Jill's informal girls club rallies round her, an empathetic community that sees her through with humor, love, and unconditional support. There's nothing self-consciously political about this group of gals; they just do what comes naturally, which is to "get together once a week and complain a lot."

Jill does much more than just complain to her girlfriends. Once her shock at being left turns into anger, she patiently tries to explain her feelings to her self-centered, estranged husband. That includes reminding him that in the sixteen years they were married, they had sex at least twice a week.

"I was your hooker, Martin," she says. "I was a bright, high-priced, classy hooker, Upper-East-Side-by-way-of-Vassar hooker, but I was your hooker."

"You have a lousy shrink," he sagely replies.

Lest you think this movie is a man-hating fest, fear not. Alan Bates comes to the rescue as Sol, a sexy, highly masculine, passionate artist with whom Jill embarks on an affair.

Once-burned Jill has no intention of getting involved. "I just want to see what it feels like to make love to someone I'm not in love with," she confesses to Sol in a precoital moment.

A glutton for punishment, Sol wants to know what she's feeling after they do the deed.

"Do you want to know how I really feel?" Jill says. "As soon as the sex was over I wanted to leave."

Despite Jill's attempt to keep him as a boy toy, however, Sol is persistent, and Jill's casual affair is beginning to look a lot like a relationship. There's a great directorial choice in the scene directly following the one in which Sol tells Jill he's crazy about her. Instead of the usual clichéd dating montage, the next thing we see is Jill ice skating with her girlfriends in Rockefeller Center.

'Cause that's what this film is all about. How do you keep your center and your sense of self when you're in a relationship with a man? And does a woman's happiness depend on a man? Or on her own emotional self-sufficiency? Will Jill lose herself in this relationship? Or will she hold on to the independence and self-esteem she's struggled so hard to find?

The supporting cast is excellent, especially the girls' club. Sue (Pat Quinn) is the one who's sanguine about her husband's numerous affairs. Elaine (Kelly Bishop) is the boozy, promiscuous one. Jeannette (Linda Miller) is more concerned about her lover's parents finding out about her affair with their son than about the fact that he's only nineteen. And even Michael Tucker of L.A. Law fame shows up for a cameo with a full head of seventies hair and a mustache. That alone is worth the price of admission.

When Harry Met Sally . . .

Director: Rob Reiner
Screenplay: Nora Ephron
Starring: Billy Crystal, Meg Ryan, Carrie Fisher, Bruno Kirby
1989, 96 min., R
Heartthrob men: **
Romance: ****
Smart-ass women: ****

I've seen this delightfully hilarious and touching film no less than seventeen times and can practically recite the dialogue word for word with the actors. I can channel the characters of Harry and Sally at will, quoting them frequently in debates with my girlfriends about whether or not men and women can truly be friends. Because that's what this film is all about. Harry says, "Men and women can't be friends because the sex part always gets in the way." I love to pretend I'm Harry when teasing a particular friend of mine who has never lost her Catholic schoolgirl naïveté. I love to assure her that the new male friend she's just told me about is probably having sexual fantasies about her. She inevitably squeals in horror.

But what woman hasn't dreamed of falling in love with a guy who's not only cute and witty, but also her best buddy? That dream come true can certainly have its nightmarish moments, as played out on the roller-coaster relationship ride of Sally and Harry, who hate each other at first, then become friends, then . . . well, I wouldn't want to spoil the fun for you.

As the terminally optimistic, "high maintenance" Sally Albright, Meg Ryan is cute as a button, and while Billy Crystal's pessimistically world-weary Harry Burns isn't exactly classic hunk material, he's surprisingly attractive as a romantic interest whose principal aphrodisiac appeal is his wit. And we girls all know what a turn-on that is.

The film is filled with screenwriter Nora Ephron's unforgettable gems of male/female relationship wisdom. In the first of my two favorite scenes, we women learn a bit more than we'd like to know about how the male mind works when Harry blandly explains to Sally why it's a drag to be a single male continually bedding down new conquests.

"You have sex, and the minute you're finished, you know what goes through your mind? How long do I have to lie here and hold her before I can get up and go home? Is thirty seconds enough?"

"That's what you're thinking?" Sally asks, her baby blues widening in horror. "Is that true?"

"Sure," says Harry. "All men think that. How long do you like to be held afterwards? All night, right? See, that's the problem. Somewhere between thirty seconds and all night is your problem."

But Sally eventually manages to strike a retaliatory blow on behalf of all womankind. She accuses Harry of being "an affront to all women" because of his postcoital escape tactics. He claims he's doing nothing wrong, because he leaves his women feeling satisfied.

"How do you know?" Sally challenges. Then, annoyed at Harry's self-assured reply, she decides to enlighten him as to the all-too-common female practice of faking orgasm. But he's not buying it.

"You don't think that I could tell the difference?" Harry says incredulously.

"No," says Sally.

"Get out of here," Harry says.

So, in the middle of a crowded New York City deli, perky Meg Ryan puts down her sandwich and loudly fakes an orgasm while a no longer smug Billy Crystal observes speechlessly and restaurant patrons stare, forks frozen halfway to gaping mouths. A middle-aged female deli customer is so moved by Meg's delivery that she tells the waiter, "I'll have what she's having." (Freudian note: This choice cameo is played by director Rob Reiner's mother, Estelle.)

Just remember, guys, you may be dashing out the door, but we've just faked our orgasms!

Carrie Fisher is deliciously deadpan in her supporting role as Marie, Sally's friend who can't seem to put an end to her dead-end relationship with a married man. We're real relieved when she ends up with Jess, Harry's best male buddy, played by an uncharacteristically cuddly Bruno Kirby.

And if that weren't enough, the film is punctuated with several brief, faux-documentary scenes of adorable elderly couples who reminisce about how they first fell in love.

Yes, I can watch this film another seventeen times. No problem.

The Secret Guyness of
When Harry Met Sally . . .

Richard Roeper

I'm not surprised Laurie has seen this movie seventeen times. That's a bit obsessive, but it's only a few times more than the national average for women in America. Heck, I once dated a woman who gave me a video of this movie for Christmas. (I gave her a copy of *Hard Times,* starring Charles Bronson as a bare-knuckled fighter, and she had no interest in that, so I ended up getting *two* movies for Christmas, pretty smart huh?) Anyway, it cracks me up when women talk about how much they love this film because they don't realize that *When Harry Met Sally . . .* is really a guy movie, sappy ending notwithstanding.

Think about the life of the Billy Crystal character in this movie. We join him in college, where he's making out with his really good-looking girlfriend. He marries another babe, and when she leaves him, he responds by going to football games and hitting the batting cages with his best buddy, and having casual sex with a number of unseen but no doubt hot babes. Way to rebound! And remember, this is Billy Crystal we're talking about here. He ain't exactly Sean Connery.

Finally Billy sleeps with the fantastic Meg Ryan, but he's a guy so he immediately runs away. Naturally this makes her hate him.

But here's the great part. All Billy has to do is wait for New Year's Eve to roll around, and he can show up at a fancy party and sweep Meg off her feet. Heck, he didn't even have to pay for the night, he just ran in there all out of breath and horny!

If you think Jimmy Stewart should have been grateful in *It's a Wonderful Life,* think again about the life Billy Crystal has in this movie. He's the luckiest man in the world.

The Women

Director: George Cukor
Screenplay: Anita Loos and Jane Murfin, from the play by Clare Boothe
Starring: Norma Shearer, Joan Crawford, Rosalind Russell, Phyllis Povah,
Paulette Goddard, Joan Fontaine, Ruth Hussey, Virginia Weidler, Mary
Boland, Marjorie Main, Lucile Watson
1939, 133 min., unrated
Romance: **
Smart-ass women: ****

My favorite German word is *schadenfreude*, which means "malicious
joy or gloating." In other words, it's the elation you feel when you go to
your high school reunion and discover that the most popular girl in
school, the one who used to treat you like freshly spilled sewage, has become a dumpy hausfrau. Why do I like this word so much? I guess because
the fact that someone thought enough of that feeling to give it a name
and put it in a dictionary, even a foreign dictionary, gives it a kind of va-
lidity.

I love George Cukor's film *The Women*, because it's all about a particularly feminine brand of schadenfreude. Two of the stars of the all-women
cast, Sylvia (Rosalind Russell) and Crystal (a pre-big-eyebrow Joan Craw-

ford) vie for the title of Queen of Schadenfreude, all at the expense of dear, sweet Mary Haines (Norma Shearer). Mary's husband is shtupping Crystal, a trashy broad who hawks perfume at a fancy department store, and everyone knows—except, of course, Mary. Sylvia and Edith (Phyllis Povah) pretend to be Mary's friends, but secretly crow with feline delight over Mary's ignorance and savor delectable thoughts of just how to go about enlightening the poor thing.

Oh, this film's all about men, too—lying, cheating dogs that they are—but we never get to see a single one on screen, just a bunch of rich dames doing what any woman with unlimited funds would do—gossiping over lunch, spending big bucks on beauty maintenance at a Park Avenue salon, and going to a fashion show—the one color sequence in the entire film. I mean, what else would women possibly do with their time? In my radical feminist days I would have supervised a mass burning of every print of this movie. Today I view it as a guilty pleasure, but in my own defense I must also point out that there's plenty of sisterhood in this film.

After all, there *are* good women in *The Women* as well as clawing cats. There's Mary, who's too classy to stoop to a knock-down drag-out with her rival, too proud to forgive her hubby, and too influenced by the dictates of 1939 fashions to lose her Bozo hairdo. There's Miriam, who unapologetically defends her own right to steal husbands and in the same breath gives Mary the best piece of advice in the whole film. There's Mary's loyal friend, Nancy, who describes herself as "what nature abhors, an old maid, a frozen asset." And there's Mary's friend Peggy (Joan Fontaine), who makes up for her lack of gray matter by being well endowed in the loyalty department.

But those are merely justifications for loving this movie. Let's face it, the most deliciously campy moments are the high-level confab in the ladies' room in which Mary and her friends plan Crystal's downfall, and the hissing cat fight in which Sylvia takes on her own husband's girlfriend. The best line in the film—and there are plenty of gems—might possibly be the wise observation made by Mary's sympathetic housekeeper when she says to the maid, "You know, the first man that can think up a good explanation how he can be in love with his wife and another woman is gonna win that prize they're always givin' out in Sweden."

The clothes, hair, and prefeminist attitudes may be circa 1939, but the message never goes out of date: Stop being a victim, to hell with your pride, and most important—what goes around comes around. Just ask Sylvia.

More Gal Movies

The fifty Gal Movies reviewed in this book are only some of my favorites. If you're hungry for more opportunities to immerse yourself in high drama, romantic fantasy, haute couture, or mindless fun, there's definitely something for you on this page.

Bell, Book and Candle (1958)
Clueless (1995)
Dreamchild (1985)
Emma (1996 theatrical version)
Fairy Tale: A True Story (1997)
Four Weddings and a Funeral (1994)
The Full Monty (1997)
Living Out Loud (1998)
The Piano (1993)
Places in the Heart (1984)
The Prime of Miss Jean Brodie (1969)
Stage Door (1937)
Truly, Madly, Deeply (1992)
The Wings of the Dove (1997)
The Year of Living Dangerously (1983)

Do you have your own ideas about what a book of quintessential women's films should contain? I'd love to hear from you. Write me c/o St. Martin's Press, 175 Fifth Avenue, New York, NY 10010.

More Guy Movies

Before you call me a sissy-man for not including *your* favorite Guy Movie, back off! Only space considerations kept the following films from appearing on my list.

Bachelor Party (1984)
Blues Brothers (1980)
Casino (1995)
The Cincinnati Kid (1965)
The Dirty Dozen (1967)
Dirty Harry (1971)
Enter the Dragon (1973)
The Hustler (1961)
The Maltese Falcon (1941)
Serpico (1973)
Species (1995)
Showgirls (1995)
Taxi Driver (1976)
Total Recall (1990)
Warriors (1979)

If you've got any suggestions, write to me c/o St. Martin's Press, 175 Fifth Avenue, NY 10010.

Where to Find
the Hard-to-Find

If your local video store doesn't carry "How to Murder Your Wife" or the complete Merchant-Ivory collection, don't fret—you can rent or purchase videos from a number of services, including those listed below. (As always, proceed with caution. The authors are not affiliated with these companies, nor do we claim to have done business with all of them. We are simply listing some of the most popular and successful video-supply firms.)

Publishers' Choice Video
http://www.pubchoicevideo.com/

Reel: The Planet's Biggest Movie Store
http://www.reel.com/

Video Marketplace
http://sashimi.wwa.com/~normj/

Apex Media Video Store
http://www.apexmall.com/apexmedia/indexhome.html

Movies Unlimited
http://www.moviesunlimited.com
1-800-4-MOVIES

Videos by Mail
www.vlibrary.com
1-800-669-7157

Paul's Hobby Zone
For catalog send $4.95 to:
Dept ML
P.O. Box 650113
West Newton, MA 02165

Facets Multimedia
1517 West Fullerton Avenue
Chicago, IL 60614
773-281-9075

Mailbox Video
Send $3 for catalog to:
Mailbox Video
7650 Linden Dr.
Dept. G
W. Bloomfield, MI 48324

Video Search Service
Tel: 1-800-849-7309
Fax: 1-770-227-0873

*Internet Movie Database Search
http://us.imdb.com/

---

*While Internet Movie Database Search is not a vendor per se, it is a marvelous site containing in-depth information about thousands of movies, including virtually all of the films in this book—and it does include links to sites where you can purchase and/or rent many of these films.